Brazil, the United States, and the South American Subsystem

Brazil, the United States, and the South American Subsystem

Regional Politics and the Absent Empire

Carlos Gustavo Poggio Teixeira

LEXINGTON BOOKS
Lanham • Boulder • New York • Toronto • Plymouth, UK

Published by Lexington Books
A wholly owned subsidiary of Rowman & Littlefield
4501 Forbes Boulevard, Suite 200, Lanham, Maryland 20706
www.rowman.com

10 Thornbury Road, Plymouth PL6 7PP, United Kingdom

British Library Cataloguing in Publication Information Available

Library of Congress Cataloging-in-Publication Data

The hardback edition of this book was previously cataloged by the Library of Congress as
follows:

Teixeira, Carlos Gustavo Poggio.
Brazil, the Unites States, and the South American subsytem: regional politics and the
absent empire / Carlos Gustavo Poggio Teixeira.
 p. cm.
 Includes bibliographical references.
  1. United States—Foreign relations—Brazil. 2. Brazil—Foreign relations—United
States. 3. United States—Foreign relations—South America. 4. South America—
Foreign relations—United States.
 I. Title
 E183.8.B7 T45 2012
 327.73081—dc23   2012021157

ISBN 978-0-7391-7328-2 (cloth : alk. paper)
ISBN 978-0-7391-9277-1 (paperback)
ISBN 978-0-7391-7329-9 (electronic)

♾™ The paper used in this publication meets the minimum requirements of American
National Standard for Information Sciences—Permanence of Paper for Printed Library
Materials, ANSI/NISO Z39.48-1992.

Printed in the United States of America

Table of Contents

Abbreviations

ALADI	*Asociación Latinoamericana de Integración* (Latin American Integration Association)
CACM	Central American Common Market
CIA	Central Intelligence Agency
EAI	Enterprise for the Americas Initiative
EEC	European Economic Community
ESG	*Escola Superior de Guerra* (Superior School of War)
FTAA	Free Trade Area of the Americas
GATT	General Agreement on Tariffs and Trade
GDP	Gross Domestic Product
KGB	*Komitet gosudarstvennoy bezopasnosti* (Committee for State Security)
LAFTA	Latin American Free Trade Association
Mercosur	*Mercado Común del Sur* (Southern Common Market)
NAFTA	North American Free Trade Agreement
NATO	North Atlantic Treaty Organization

OAS	Organization of American States
RSC	Regional Security Complex
SAFTA	South American Free Trade Agreement
Unasur	*Unión de Naciones Suramericanas* (Union of South American Nations)
USSR	Union of Soviet Socialist Republics
WTO	World Trade Organization

Chapter One

Introduction

The first factor that students of US foreign policy toward Latin America immediately have to take into consideration is the obvious disparity of power between the United States and its southern neighbors. Faced with this reality, the second factor should be to avoid the temptation of translating this indisputable fact into monocausal explanations for the international relations of Latin America. While the first aspect has been diligently observed by virtually all studies of the subject, the second has met more resistance. Indeed, every important event in the history of Latin America, from peace to war, from stability to instability, for good or for bad, can be attributed to actions planned in offices in Washington under the usual framework of US-Latin American relations. As one US Ambassador once observed: "We Americans tend to be societally ethnocentric—almost narcissistic—exaggerating the influence of both our positive and our negative actions in the world."[1] This perspective is greatly helped by the fact that the customary frameworks for the study of international relations are focused on the great powers.

But reality seems to indicate that if there is a region in which it would apparently be difficult to exaggerate US influence, this would be Latin America. After all, history shows an impressive array of military interventions, both overt and covert, territory annexations, and other actions that indeed decisively changed the course of events in Latin American countries. Hence, even before the United States was described as a global empire after the end of the Second World War, it could already be characterized as a regional empire in the Western Hemisphere. For an extended period of their historical relationship, whenever a country in Latin America was perceived as contradicting US interests, Washington would repeatedly dispatch the Marines or find someone else to do the job. Nevertheless, any brief examination of these actions reveals an obvious geographic pattern concentrated north of the Panama Canal, with the vast South American region basically spared the US imperial urge. This abundance of involvement in one half of Latin America in contrast to a relative absence in the other half has been translated in an abundance of studies focusing on the former in parallel to a relative absence of studies focusing on the latter. The general result is that analyses of US policies toward "Latin America" are mostly analyses of US policies toward Mexico, Central America, and the Caribbean, with occasional references to South American countries to give an impression of homogeneity or, when the researcher chooses to focus on South American countries, the framework used is basically the same as ones used to analyze US relations with the rest of Latin America. In this latter view, the distinctiveness of South American international relations is occasionally acknowledged, but it is studied as a special case within the broader Latin American framework. In other words, these analyses interpret the different level of US involvement in South America as a mere quantitative issue.

This book aims to address this issue by first laying out a theoretical framework for understanding and investigating South America that captures and explains the distinct dynamics that have characterized the US relationship with that region in contrast to the rest of Latin America. The most evident aspect illustrating these different dynamics is the fact that, compared to its historical overinvolvement in Mexico, Central America, and the Caribbean, the United States has been a relatively absent empire in South America. This relative absence must be explained not just by looking into domestic factors in the United States, but also by detecting how particular regional dynamics help to shape the outcome of US foreign policies. Thus, the second aim of this research is to demonstrate that there is a distinct pattern of interactions within Latin America that justify treating South America as a distinct regional subsystem. In other words, South America must be distinguished from the rest of Latin America not only because of the different patterns of relations in respect to the United States, but also because there is clearly a distinctive pattern of relations within South America that is not captured by the customary concept of Latin America. The practical significance of this is that Latin America as a concept has limited applicability in the field of international relations, and its theoretical predominance often leads to errors of analysis, judgment and, ultimately, policies. In fact, this research implies that dropping the concept of Latin America altogether in favor of the notion of a South and a North American regional subsystem would lead to a significant refinement of the understanding of the international relations in the Western Hemisphere.

THE ARGUMENT OF THE BOOK

In labeling the United States as an "absent empire" in South America, this book makes a relatively bold claim. After all, the references to Latin America as the US "backyard" are abundant and the United States indeed frequently acted in the region as a true empire. Nevertheless, as mentioned above, the very notion of Latin America when used to study phenomena related to the discipline of international relations is inaccurate. A central assumption of this book is that analysts of inter-American relations would greatly benefit from a change in perspective that substitutes the culturally defined notion of Latin America for the concept of a North and a South American regional subsystem. The use of Latin America as a theoretical concept in US scholarship tends to generate two main fallacies in the study of international relations in the Western Hemisphere. Firstly, it assumes that there is somehow a level of integration—or at least a very important integrating variable—that gives the region identified as Latin America a degree of homogeneity. Secondly, and as a corollary of the first, it implicitly accepts that there is a pattern of US foreign policy towards the region that justifies treating it as a coherent unit.

This book disputes both claims. First, it demonstrates that the variables generally used to give homogeneity to Latin America, such as culture and level of development, are not evenly used to define other regions in the world, and in any case they are largely irrelevant for the purposes of international relations research. Accordingly, when only the relevant variables are used, the notion of Latin America loses its usefulness, which implies that studying the relationship between Latin America and the United States means studying the relationship between a fictional geopolitical construct and a real country. Employing the regional subsystemic approach, I argue that the relevant variables should be based on geography and patterns of interactions, and that these criteria tend to lead to the identification of a North and a South American regional subsystem. Second, and following this characterization, this research argues that a fundamental distinction should be made regarding the outcomes of US foreign policies in each of the two regional subsystems in the Western Hemisphere. This fundamental difference is captured by this book's depiction of the United States as an absent empire in South America, as opposed to being historically a very present empire in the remainder of Latin America.

Thus, the central question of this research is *what factors explain US relative absence from South America?* Although the literature has obviously noted the fact that US foreign policies toward South America have displayed distinct characteristics in relation to the rest of Latin America, the explanations given for this phenomenon have been unsatisfactory at best, especially since the central factor typically mentioned has been simply that South

America is too far away, while Mexico, Central America, and the Caribbean are too close to the United States. In addition, at the same time it acknowledges this distinction, this literature also assumes that there is no reason to see South America as a different region. This argument postulates that the United States has had the same policies towards the whole of Latin America, but because the region south of the Panama Canal is deemed as having little strategic significance, it has paid relatively little attention to South America. This is indeed a compelling argument, but although it may explain a certain lack of interest, it fails to provide explanations for the instances when the United States did pay attention to South America and yet the outcome was the same relative absence of imperial policies. Moreover, as this explanation holds that the United States has paid little attention to South America, researchers have followed suit and the result is that US relative absence from South America has been translated into a relative absence of South America in US studies on Latin America.

This book inverts the traditional argument indicated above and claims that US relative absence from South America, even in the instances when the United States demonstrated a clear interest in the region, must be understood not only in terms of South America's distance from the United States, but also in terms of its "proximity" to Brazil. The hypothesis put forward by this book is that Brazil is a status quo regional power that has affected the calculations of costs and benefits of a more significant US involvement in South America. It is shown that while Brazil historically played a role that resulted in increasing the benefits of relatively limited US involvement in the region, in more recent times it has sought to increase the costs of a more substantial US presence. As this research intends to demonstrate, this change can be understood not as a result of particular domestic circumstances in Brazil, but because of changes in the international and regional environments, with Brazilian regional strategic goal of preserving its position in the South American subsystem remaining by and large invariable throughout time. Hence, the fact that South America has been considered as a region of little strategic relevance for the United States is but part of the explanation, in which it allowed Brazil to play this role with fewer resources than would have been the case had South America been located in a more strategically important region.

THE IDEA OF LATIN AMERICA

The concept of Latin America is fairly recent in its origins and it is usually attributed as originally a French concept—where the idea of a Latin "race" was common—used since at least the late 1830s, but particularly in the 1860s to give an ideological justification for French imperialism in Mexico and to create the impression of cultural affinity in the region, of which France would be the natural "protectress" against the Anglo-Saxons in the north.[2] In a pioneering study, John Leady Phelan maintains that the first use of the expression *l'Amérique latine* was in an article entitled "*Situation de la latinité*" by L. M. Tisserand, published in January 1861.[3] Nevertheless, more recent studies demonstrate that "a number of Spanish American writers and intellectuals—many of them, it is true, resident in Paris—had used the expression 'América Latina' several years earlier."[4] Joao Feres Jr. claims that the first usage of the term was made by the Colombian poet Jose Maria Torres de Caicedo, who spent most of his life in France, in a poem called *Las Dos Americas* (The Two Americas), in 1856.[5] As the title of Caicedos's poem makes clear, not much differently from the French, these Spanish American writers employed the concept of *América Latina* to reinforce a common identity in the Americas in opposition to the "other" America in the North. In fact, Caicedo proposed a union of the "Latin American" republics against the threat of "North American" aggression, which became a particularly relevant issue after the Mexican-American War in the 1840s.

Therefore, before there was *Latin America*, there was *Amérique Latine* and *América Latina*. For these writers though, Latin America was synonymous with the Spanish American republics, and hence Brazil—which was not only Portuguese-speaking but was also a monarchy—was not included. Likewise, Brazilians also did not consider themselves as Latin American, not least because Brazil on one hand emphasized its American identity, and on the other it had a certain feeling of foreignness in relation to its Spanish-speaking neighbors; therefore it was not interested in creating a sense of separation in regards to the United States. However, with the popularization of the term in US academic circles, the idea that the nations south of the United States could be considered as part of a region called Latin America gained ground and with that Brazil was also included. As Leslie Bethell argues, it was only when "América Latina became Latin America" in the 1920s and 1930s, but most particularly after the Second World War, that Brazil became to be regarded as part of a region called Latin America.[6] Yet, only much later on, during the Cold War, would some Brazilian writers begin to identify themselves as Latin Americans, which was particularly evident among the Left seeking to reinforce the ties with the Cuban Revolution as well as the distance from the United States.

In the United States, the expression "Latin America" can be found in official documentation by the late 1890s, and before that the term used was "Spanish America" or "Hispanic America." But it was only after the First World War that "Latin America" became widely used in English. A research in the Library of Congress and the New York Public Library revealed that before 1900 there was not a single publication containing the term "Latin

America" in its title, while between 1900 and 1910 only two publications were found, between 1911 and 1920 twenty-three, between 1921 and 1930 twenty-five, with steady growth after that and burgeoning after 1960,[7] when "Latin American studies" became somewhat fashionable in the United States, owing especially to the Cuban Revolution. An interesting illustration of the problems associated with the concept of Latin America, and its struggle to be accepted as an adequate referent during its initial stages of existence, can be seen on the occasion of the foundation of the *Hispanic American Historical Review*, in 1918, which was the first journal in the United States dedicated to the study of Latin America. The editors considered naming the journal as "Latin American Historical Review," but they eventually concluded that the term was "ambiguous, misleading, and unscientific."[8] They argued that the original notion of "Hispania" included both Spain and Portugal.

As was the case when the term was employed both by French and Spanish intellectuals, in the United States the concept of Latin America was also used on one hand to create the impression of cultural affinity among the countries south of the United States, and on the other hand to create a sense of separation between the United States and its less developed "Latin" neighbors. Feres Jr. argues that the notion of Latin America, far from being a value-free geographic concept, has been used in the United States to perpetuate and justify an asymmetry between the perceptions of the American "self" in opposition to the Latin American "other."[9] For Feres Jr., "Latin America" can be understood as an "asymmetric concept, that is, a concept defined in opposition to a collective self-image and used to name a generalized other."[10]

In any case, since its inception, it seems clear that the relatively recent concept of Latin America, in its Spanish, French, and English versions, has been employed not on a geographical basis but on perceived cultural similarities and in order to establish a clear contrast in relation to the United States. Given the definitional problems associated with the concept, the fact that it is a unique case of widespread use of a term to identify a region based on cultural referents, as well as its racialist implications, it is remarkable that "Latin America" has been uncritically accepted as a scientific concept used to study the international relations of the Western Hemisphere. Like the editors of the *Hispanic American Historical Review* almost a century ago, this book also maintains that the concept of Latin America is ambiguous, misleading, and unscientific.

THE QUESTION OF EMPIRE

This book makes reference to the United States as an "empire" or as occasionally pursuing "imperial policies." Although the United States has been referred to as an empire innumerable times, the definition of what this term effectively means in this context is far from a settled issue.[11] In fact, empire is one of those terms in the social sciences that have been so overused and have occasionally acquired such emotional undertones, it has inevitably lost some of its scientific usefulness. This issue is especially controversial in the US context since it was a country born in reaction to an overseas empire and is therefore imbued with a strong anti-imperialistic rhetoric. While it is not the purpose of this book to offer a final answer to this definitional problem, it is important to make some observations regarding the broad sense in which the term is employed here, even if the term is admittedly used in a loose way.

First of all, a clear conceptual distinction must be made between empire and the notion of imperialism. Indeed, considering the way the concepts have evolved, it seems pretty reasonable to treat empire and imperialism as two distinct sets of literature. A common factor present in the studies of imperialism is an economic interpretation of history, which is insufficient to understand instances when motivations other than economic are present.[12] As Norman Etherington, who wrote one of the best accounts on the subject, remarks, "an enormous amount of confusion has been generated by using empire, colonialism, and imperialism as synonyms. Theories of imperialism were not theories of empire."[13] Some may argue that, as the concept of imperialism has historically been appropriated by the left to denounce alleged evils of capitalism, an effort to separate it from the broader concept of empire is an attempt to avoid an ideological contamination. This is not entirely wrong and even William Appleman Williams, who could hardly be considered a right-wing writer, acknowledges the problems of putting empire and imperialism in the same basket. Williams observed that "the semantic trouble began with the causal appropriation of the world *imperial*, originally associated with empire, to describe an evolving set of *different* relationships between advanced industrial societies and the rest of the world."[14] Likewise, George Liska observes that an "imperial function" is distinctive from "its deformative 'ism', aggressively expansionist imperialism."[15] Thus, it is not merely a matter of avoiding an ideological corruption, but of elucidating the fact that empire and the conventional notion of imperialism refer in fact to two different sets of relationships. This research is about empire, not imperialism.

The second important characteristic that must be emphasized regarding the use of the term empire in the present work is that it does not refer to a political entity but to *a system of relationships that may or may not be pursued as a strategy by powerful states.* In this sense, the question is not whether the United States *is* or *is not* an empire, but whether or not it has pursued imperial solutions for specific problems. In other words, power is a necessary but not sufficient condition for the establishment of imperial policies, and so the question becomes whether the reality of US power was or was not translated in imperial ways in order to pursue specific policy objectives. This perspective is similar to the one adopted by modern students of empire, such as George Liska, Geir Lundestad, Michael Doyle, Alexander Motyl, Alexander Wendt, and Daniel Friedheim.[16] All these authors define empire not as a political entity but first and foremost as a "system" or "structure" of relationships, which allows the researcher to identify which relationships between individual states display imperial characteristics and which do not. Basically, the kind of relationship that characterizes an imperial system described by these authors is one in which the anarchical aspect of the international system is challenged and elements of hierarchy come into the fore. For Doyle, who wrote one of the most relevant works that attempts to give a scientific definition to the concept, an empire is a "system of interaction" characterized by "control of both foreign and domestic policy" whereas hegemony is characterized only by the control of the first.[17] Thus, imperial control is understood as "one form of the exercise of asymmetrical influence and power" among others.[18] This distinction has also been made by Adam Watson, who distinguished between hegemony, "where a powerful state controls the external relations of its client states," and what the author calls dominion, "where it also intervenes in their domestic affairs."[19]

One useful way to differentiate an imperial relationship from other kinds of relationships, such as hegemony for example, is by relating it to the concepts of autonomy and sovereignty. While the latter relates to the classical Westphalian conception and means that the state "is subject to no other state and has full and exclusive powers within its jurisdiction,"[20] the first can be broadly understood from the perspective of international relations as the notion of freedom of action, or the opposite of dependence. Doyle remarks that while a dependent state is "a state subject to limited constraints on its economic, social, and (indirectly) political autonomy," an imperialized state is one whose "effective sovereignty" is controlled by the imperial state.[21] Similarly, a recent study on the subject of empire has defined an "imperial rule" as "a relationship in which a state assumes some degree of sovereign political control over a subordinate polity."[22] A sovereign state may enjoy more or less autonomy in the pursuit of its objectives in the international arena without necessarily affecting its condition of sovereignty. As Kenneth Waltz commented, "to say that a state is sovereign means that it decides for itself how it will cope with its internal and external problems, including whether or not to seek assistance from others and in doing so to limit its freedom by making commitments to them."[23] This limitation in freedom that

Waltz refers to can be interpreted as the autonomy aspect, which claims that the more limits are placed on its freedom, the less autonomy a state has. Because the condition of sovereignty requires a hierarchical structure in which there is no higher authority within a given territory above that of the state that controls it, whenever an imperial relationship is established, a new hierarchy is in place and the result is loss of sovereignty. For Roberto Russell and Juan Gabriel Tokatlian, who studied the question of autonomy and sovereignty specifically within the context of Latin America, the first

> was more a South American issue than a Latin American one. In northern Latin America (of which Mexico, Central America, and the Caribbean form a part), the accent was more on the question of sovereignty, given that this region has historically been the object of diverse uses of force by the United States-conquest and annexation of territories, invasion and military intervention, covert operations, and so on. South America, from Colombia to Argentina, on the other hand, had a relatively greater margin for diplomatic, commercial, and cultural maneuvering with respect to Washington. It is thus not surprising that most of the literature on the subject of autonomy has been produced in South America and, more specifically, in the Southern Cone. [24]

Therefore, when this book refers to the United States as an "absent empire" in South America, it does not imply that this country has been absent in that particular regional subsystem, which would be nonsense, but that a system of relationships between the United States and South America that could be accurately characterized as being imperial in nature has not been established. This observation is even more pertinent when one considers the kind of policies that the United States repeatedly pursued in Mexico, Central America, and the Caribbean, policies that have historically demonstrated obvious imperial characteristics, the clearest evidence for which being the fact that the United States sent troops to decisively affect domestic politics in these regions a number of times during the nineteenth and twentieth centuries in order to enforce its interests.

ORGANIZATION OF THE BOOK

This introductory chapter has made reference to the notion of "regional subsystems." This concept is not nearly as popular in international relations literature as the notion of an "international system." While the latter is the focus of much of the research in the field, the former is sparsely studied, and the result has generally been much conceptual confusion and little scientific validity. Chapter 2 addresses the advantages of the regional subsystemic approach presenting it as a useful theoretical tool to the study of international relations in terms of overcoming the traditional international-domestic dualism that has prevailed in the field, arguing that the regional level can be seen as a third level of analysis, between the domestic and the international. I define a regional subsystem as a *subset of the international system reflecting the outcome of actual patterns of interactions—including the whole spectrum between conflict and cooperation—among countries in condition of geographic proximity*. Then the chapter indicates what the regional subsystemic approach can accomplish and explores in more detail the definitional aspect by stressing its two necessary and sufficient variables: geography and patterns of interaction. In chapter 3, I apply these two variables to the case of Latin America in order to demonstrate the existence of a South American subsystem, and to subsequently emphasize the importance of Brazil within this subsystem. I draw from Robert Gilpin's work on international system change and adapt his theory to the regional subsystemic approach in order to understand what factors could potentially lead to regional subsystemic change. With this framework in mind, I am then adequately equipped to address the central claim of the book, which is that the United States has been an "absent empire" in South America. The chapter examines the usual explanations provided by the literature for this relative absence, showing that there is a latent discourse of US absence from South America that is not clearly articulated. After presenting a critique of these explanations, I offer my own point of view based on the role of Brazil affecting the structures of costs and benefits of subsystemic change for the United States. This basic explanation forms the framework for the subsequent case studies.

Chapters 4, 5, and 6 are composed of case studies selected following three main criteria. First, if a pattern of interaction was to be demonstrated, they should encompass a lengthy period of time. Indeed the chapters cover a period spanning three centuries, going from the time of the independence of Latin American states until recent years. Second, because the focus is on the regional subsystem to explain continuity rather than change, it would be useful if the case studies comprised different configurations of the international and domestic systems in order to demonstrate that regional subsystemic dynamics remained relatively constant regardless of variations in the other two level of analysis. Thus, each case study corresponds to a distinct configuration of the international system and of the corresponding US position in it: multipolar, with the United States as a regional power; bipolar, with the United States as a global power; and unipolar, with the United States as the remaining superpower. Likewise, besides comprising several different US administrations, this lengthy time period includes a wide variation of the domestic configuration in Brazil, from a newborn republic and former monarchy, to a military dictatorship, and finally to a modern democratic republic. Third, the cases selected should consider periods when the United States clearly demonstrated an interest in South America in order to detect how its policies interacted with the South American subsystem. Otherwise, just demonstrating US absence in terms of neglect would be repeating the existing arguments in the literature. Although they cover lengthy periods of time in order to present a broader and more complete perspective, each chapter focuses on a specific US policy in which South America was an important component. Therefore, chapter 4 focuses on the Monroe Doctrine in the nineteenth century, chapter 5 on the US actions in Chile during the Cold War, and chapter 6 on the US proposal for a Free Trade Area of the Americas in the post-Cold War period. The case studies show that for each period there is a corresponding Brazilian strategy affecting the structure of costs and benefits of US presence or absence. While for the first two periods Brazil sought to raise the benefits of US absence from the South American subsystem, in the latter period Brazil attempted to raise the costs of a more significant US presence. Lastly, chapter 7 presents the conclusions of the research, including some theoretical and policy implications.

NOTES

1. Nathaniel Davis, *The Last Two Years of Salvador Allende* (Ithaca: Cornell University Press, 1985), x.
2. Michel Chevalier, *Society, Manners, and Politics in the United States*, Reprints of economic classics (New York: A. M. Kelley, 1966).
3. John Leddy Phelan, "Pan-Latinism, French Intervention in Mexico (1861–7) and the Genesis of the Idea of Latin America," in *Conciencia y autenticidad históricas; escritos en homenaje a Edmundo O'Gorman, emerito, aetatis anno LX dicata*, ed. Juan Antonio Ortega y Medina (México: UNAM, 1968).
4. Leslie Bethell, "Brazil and 'Latin America,'" *Journal of Latin American Studies* 42, no. 03 (2010): 458.
5. João Feres Jr., "A History of the Concept of Latin America in the United States: Misrecognition and Social Scientific Discourse" (PhD diss., City University of New York, 2003), 68.
6. Bethell, "Brazil and 'Latin America'," 474.
7. Feres Jr., "A History of the Concept of Latin America in the United States," 363.
8. Charles E. Chapman, "The Founding of the Review," *The Hispanic American Historical Review* 1, no. 1 (1918): 17.
9. Feres Jr., " A history of the concept of Latin America in the United States."
10. Ibid., 61.
11. The examples are virtually endless, but some include, in chronological order: Robert Rutherford McCormick, *The American Empire* (Chicago: Chicago Tribune, 1952); Amaury De Riencourt, *The American Empire* (New York: Dial Press, 1968); Sidney Lens, *The Forging of the American Empire* (New York: Crowell, 1971); Jan Knippers Black, *Sentinels of Empire: The United States and Latin American Militarism* (New York: Greenwood Press, 1986); Geir Lundestad, "Empire by Invitation? The United States and Western Europe, 1945-1952," *Journal of Peace Research* 23, no. 3 (1986); Robert W. Tucker and David C. Hendrickson, *The Imperial Temptation: The New World Order and America's Purpose* (New York: Council on Foreign Relations Press, 1992); John Lewis Gaddis, *We Now Know: Rethinking Cold War History* (Oxford; New York: Clarendon Press; Oxford University Press, 1997); Walter LaFeber, *The New Empire: An Interpretation of American Expansion, 1860-1898*, 35th anniversary ed. (Ithaca, NY: Cornell University Press, 1998); A. J. Bacevich, *American Empire: The Realities and Consequences of U.S. Diplomacy* (Cambridge, MA: Harvard University Press,

2002); Michael Ignatieff, "The American Empire," *New York Times Magazine*, May 1, 2003; Niall Ferguson, *Colossus: The Price of America's Empire* (New York: Penguin Press, 2004); Chalmers A. Johnson, *Blowback: The Costs and Consequences of American Empire* (New York: Henry Holt, 2004); Greg Grandin, *Empire's Workshop: Latin America, the United States, and the Rise of the New Imperialism* (New York: Metropolitan Books, 2006); David C. Hendrickson, *Union, Nation, or Empire: The American Debate over International Relations, 1789-1941* (Lawrence: University Press of Kansas, 2009).

12. Classical studies on imperialism as used in the modern sense include the pioneering work of John Hobson and the influential piece by Vladimir Lenin: J. A. Hobson, *Imperialism; A Study* (New York: J. Pott & Company, 1902); Vladimir Ilyich Lenin, *Imperialism, the Highest Stage of Capitalism* (New York: International Publishers, 1933).

13. Norman Etherington, *Theories of Imperialism: War, Conquest, and Capital* (London; Totowa, NJ: Croom Helm; Barnes & Noble Books, 1984), 267. For other good accounts on theories of imperialism see: Richard Koebner and Helmut Dan Schmidt, *Imperialism: The Story and Significance of a Political Word, 1840-1960* (Cambridge University Press, 1964); Wolfgang J. Mommsen, *Theories of Imperialism* (New York: Random House, 1980); Earle Micajah Winslow, *The Pattern of Imperialism: A Study in the Theories of Power* (New York: Columbia Univ. Press, 1948).

14. William Appleman Williams, *Empire as a Way of Life: An Essay on the Causes and Character of America's Present Predicament, along with a Few Thoughts about an Alternative* (New York: Oxford University Press, 1980), 7.

15. George Liska, *Twilight of a Hegemony: The Late Career of Imperial America* (Dallas: University Press of America, 2003), 55.

16. Liska, *Imperial America: The International Politics of Primacy* (Baltimore, MA: Johns Hopkins Press, 1967); Liska, *Twilight of a Hegemony*; Geir Lundestad, *The United States and Western Europe since 1945: From "Empire" by Invitation to Transatlantic Drift* (Oxford, UK: Oxford University Press, 2003); Lundestad, "Empire by Invitation? The United States and Western Europe, 1945-1952."; Lundestad, *The American Empire and Other Studies of US Foreign Policy in a Comparative Perspective* (Oslo; Oxford: Norwegian University Press; Oxford University Press, 1990); Michael W. Doyle, *Empires*, Cornell studies in comparative history. (Ithaca, NY: Cornell University Press, 1986); Alexander J. Motyl, "Why Empires Reemerge: Imperial Collapse and Imperial Revival in Comparative Perspective," *Comparative Politics* 31, no. 2 (1999); Motyl, "Is Everything Empire? Is Empire Everything?," *Comparative Politics* 38, no. 2 (2006); Alexander Wendt and Daniel Friedheim, "Hierarchy under Anarchy: Informal Empire and the East German State," *International Organization* 49, no. 4 (1995).

17. Doyle, *Empires*: 12, 40.

18. Ibid., 34.

19. Adam Watson, *The Evolution of International Society: A Comparative Historical Analysis* (London ; New York: Routledge, 1992), 123.

20. Stanley Hoffmann, *Janus and Minerva: Essays in the Theory and Practice of International Politics* (Boulder: Westview Press, 1987), 172-73.

21. Doyle, *Empires*: 12-13.

22. Paul K. MacDonald, "Those Who Forget Historiography are Doomed to Republish It: Empire, Imperialism and Contemporary Debates about American Power," *Review of International Studies* 35, no. 1 (2009): 81.

23. Kenneth Neal Waltz, *Theory of International Politics* (Boston: McGraw-Hill, 1979), 96.

24. Roberto Russell and Juan Gabriel Tokatlian, "From Antagonistic Autonomy to Relational Autonomy: A Theoretical Reflection from the Southern Cone," *Latin American Politics and Society* 45, no. 1 (2003): 7.

Chapter Two

The Regional Subsystemic Approach

Virtually as soon as the system approach took hold in the field of international relations with Morton Kaplan's "System and Process in International Politics," first published in 1957, a number of international relations scholars reacted against the notion that international politics should be assumed as "total and global," and that it was imperative to consider how the fact that international politics often has a "non-global character" would impact the application of systems theory.[1] Most of those scholars were area specialists and were concerned particularly with the connection between area studies and the emerging systems approach to international relations. What derived from this incorporation of systems theory into area studies was a subsystemic approach based on regional criteria.

The literature on regional subsystems (or "subordinate systems,"[2] or "partial international systems"[3] as they have been called) gained momentum in the 1960s and 1970s, but the success of the neorealist approach in the late 1970s and its focus on the global level and the constraints imposed by the international system—which was a useful fit for the Cold War environment—eclipsed the regional approach. After the end of the bipolar configuration, however, a new wave of studies taking the region as a referent for analysis appeared. The reasons for this resurgence are commonly attributed to the fact that great powers had less incentive to intervene after the end of the Cold War, which tended to give regions more autonomy to develop with a lower degree of outside influence. Nonetheless, this literature was generally more concerned with processes of regionalization based on cooperation and the establishment of institutions and thus little room was left for the regional subsystemic approach that had been developed up until the 1970s.

THE REGIONAL SUBSYSTEMIC FOCUS

The concept of a subsystem as applied to international relations theory is straightforward: an international subsystem can be understood as "any subset" of the international system.[4] In general, a subsystem can by and large be considered as "a component of a larger system" but one "with systemic properties of its own."[5] Within this basic conception, a subsystem of the international system can actually be "any set of specific variables"[6] according to the purposes of the researcher.

In fact, the idea of a subsystem within the overall international system has been used to direct attention to different sets of variables. For example, when Kenneth Waltz refers to subsystem he means the nation-states.[7] Similarly, in his celebrated "level-of-analysis" essay, J. David Singer uses the notion of subsystem to refer to the domestic level—the choice would then be selecting between "the international system and the national sub-systems" as a referent for analysis.[8] For Morton Kaplan, subsystems can be either national actors or supranational actors such as the United Nations.[9] Thomas Robinson analyzed the "Communist System" as a subsystem of the larger international system.[10] One aspect of Niklas Luhmann's Modern Systems Theory is the notion that subsystems in the international systems are functionally differentiated. Thus, functional subsystems would include politics, law, the economy, and science.[11]

Consequently, the choice to focus on *regional* subsystems is but one choice among other possibilities for subsystemic research in international relations. The justification for this preference is based on the belief that delimiting the boundaries of international subsystems in terms of regional factors can bring significant contributions for the understanding of international politics. Perhaps the main contribution would be overcoming the conventional domestic-international dualism that has shaped the majority of the researches in international relations, thereupon opening up different possibilities for analysis by taking a step down in relation to the neorealist focus on the global system and a step up in relation to the liberal focus on the domestic system. It is not a matter of attempting to integrate both theories, but of acknowledging the existence of a third level beyond the usual two that are considered by these theories. Yet, by identifying a new locus of investigation between the nation-state and the international system, between domestic politics and international politics, the regional subsystemic approach holds the promise of bringing together foreign policy analysis and theory of international politics. It therefore seeks to transcend the notion that theory of foreign policy and theory of international politics are utterly distinct by using some of the theoretical framework provided by systemic theories of international relations in order to generate explanations for foreign policies' outcomes.[12]

Thus, a regional subsystemic approach is not "reductionist" as it does not make reference solely to unit-level attributes of particular states in order to provide explanations. This approach is in fact "systemic" but its main focus shifts from the global system to the regional system. It does not look for the domestic sources of foreign policy, but more for what one author called the "foreign sources of foreign policy."[13]

The stress on *regional* subsystems postulates an explicit assumption that geography matters in international relations.[14] This is not only "because geographic dimensions . . . are nearly always significant in discussions of political undertakings and the operational results thereof,"[15] and it thus has an impact on the aforementioned distinction between decisions and outcomes, but especially because geography shapes a number of important interactions such as "the intensity of economic exchanges and the likelihood of war."[16] This qualification is particularly relevant for the concept of subsystem used here which, as I show below, is based on interactions ranging from the whole spectrum between cooperation and conflict. Moreover, as Hans Mouritzen argued, besides anarchy, the other fundamental characteristic of the international system is the fact that "its major units are mutually non-mobile," and while the consequences of anarchy have been thoroughly explored by the international relations literature, the consequences of "non-mobility" have consistently been overlooked.[17] In fact, both theories of foreign policy as well as theories of international politics seem to neglect the importance of geography. As a result, most of the systemic theories of international relations, which were imported from other fields where the basic units are mobile, do not take into account the fact that states, contrary to firms for example, are fixed in space.[18] The major implication of this characteristic is that there is "a cleavage between unit and system" which "means that each state faces a specific and stable salient environment rather than the international system as a whole."[19] The notion of "salient environment" that is explored by Mouritzen is coterminous with the concept of regional subsystem as employed by this research.

DEFINING REGIONAL SUBSYSTEMS: GEOGRAPHY AND PATTERNS OF INTERACTION

Even though other criteria have been offered for the identification of a regional subsystem, geographic proximity and regular interactions can be considered as providing both necessary and sufficient conditions. Indeed, in a widely cited article analyzing the literature produced on regional systems up until the early seventies, William Thompson concluded that there was a "lack of uniformity" in the concept of regional subsystem and identified a total of twenty-one attributes mentioned in the literature, which he reduced to the two that were the "most consistently cited" and that were after all "already implied by the regional subsystem term": proximity and regular interaction.[20] The other nineteen characteristics attributed to regional subsystems, such as common developmental status, degree of integration, or shared ethnic, cultural, and historical bonds, were deemed neither necessary nor sufficient conditions.

Since Thompson's article was published, there have been no noteworthy challenges to the notion that proximity and patterns of interactions are the key variables to define a regional subsystem. The most significant challenge comes perhaps from David Lake and Patrick Morgan, who concentrate on the security aspect and dropped both geography and interactions as factors in order to define a "regional security complex" in terms of shared "security externalities" among its members—with all other criteria being secondary.[21] However, the more recent scholarship has generally confirmed the conceptualization of geographic proximity combined with patterns of interaction as necessary conditions. Douglas Lemke, based on Haas' earlier conception, defined a regional subsystem in terms of states' "ability to interact militarily," which he claims to combine both proximity and interaction.[22] For Barry Buzan and Ole Wæver, who developed the notion of regional security complexes, the chief criteria for defining a region must be "the actual patterns of security practices."[23] Michael Schulz et al. also stress that a regional subsystem is characterized "by the patterns of interaction," and add that they can be manifested in a variety of fields such as economic, cultural, and security.[24] Similarly, Arie Kacowicz maintains that regional subsystems "are characterized by clusters of states coexisting in geographical propinquity as interrelated units that sustain significant security, economic, and political relations."[25]

Nevertheless, as Thompson had detected, besides geography and interactions, several other criteria have been used by a number of scholars in order to identify a regional subsystem. Perhaps the most mentioned alternative, and the one that even presently seems to bring more problems to the clarity of the concept, has been the need for a collective identity and culture. Even for those authors who concentrate on the two main conditions presented hitherto, the temptation to include factors related to identity and culture has been strong. For instance, after making the case that a regional subsystem is characterized by the interrelatedness among states in a given geographic area, Louis Cantori and Steven Spiegel defined a regional subsystem as consisting of "one state, or two or more proximate and interacting states which have some common ethnic, linguistic, cultural, social, and historical bonds, and whose sense of identity is sometimes increased by the actions and attitudes of states external to the system."[26] Likewise, Kacowicz, after insisting on the geographical and patterns of interactions criteria, feels it necessary to add that an important factor is a "subjective perception of belonging to a distinctive community and having a collective identity."[27] Hans Holm and Georg Sorensen maintain that the concept of region is "multidimensional" and used Latin America as an example of "regions of identity."[28] In none of these cases is it clear how the cultural criterion is helpful for the analysis of regional subsystems, except perhaps to justify the culturally defined referent "Latin" in Latin America.

The notion of a common culture or identity, or of supposed historical affinities, is a common misconception of regional subsystems—and this is especially relevant for the case of Latin America. Since the term *Latin* America is itself culturally referenced—as opposed to being geographically referenced like every other standard regional classification in the world such as "Eastern Europe," "West Africa," or "Southeast Asia," for example, the temptation to justify treating Latin America as a regional subsystem based on cultural factors is immense. Obviously, this is true only for those who bother offering an explanation for this choice, since many analysts just assume the existence of a Latin American subsystem as a self-evident truth. Apart from the discussion of the questionable wisdom of ascribing to Latin America a "common culture, religion, language, and race,"[29] culture and identity—as well as the establishment of international organizations—only matter for regional subsystemic analysis as long as they affect patterns of interaction. As a matter of fact, again as Thompson remarked, "with emphasis on interaction, these characteristics are rendered unnecessary even though they may be frequently present and of some significance."[30]

If the culturally defined concept of Latin America is used to refer to a regional subsystem, one has to prove that it is somehow more useful, for example, to group Mexico with Brazil than to group Mexico with the United States in a regional subsystem. If culture and identity are used as the main variables, the first grouping would arguably make more sense. However, if patterns of interaction (as well as geography, for that matter) are used as the central factor, the United States and Mexico should be grouped as part of a North American subsystem. The case of Mexico is illustrative because several analyses seem to assume that including Mexico in studies that mainly focus on South America makes the notion of a supposed Latin American subsystem more credible.[31] Similarly, the inclusion of Mexico and other Latin American countries in an all-encompassing Latin American subsystem instead of in a North American subsystem is often justified on the basis of the level of development. Because the United States stands out as an industrialized developed country, the reasoning goes, it somehow does not make sense for it to be grouped with less developed Latin American states. However, like culture, a common level of development is not a criterion for the identification of a regional subsystem. In fact, as also rightfully pointed out by Thompson, "proximate and interacting actors may be rich or poor."[32]

Hence, by focusing exclusively on geography and interaction a regional subsystem is understood here as being a *subset of the international system reflecting the outcome of actual patterns of interactions—including the whole spectrum between conflict and cooperation—among countries in condition of geographic proximity.* Members of the same regional subsystem have a higher degree of interaction among themselves in relation to members outside the subsystem, and as a result their primary foreign policies concerns lie within their own regional subsystem. That means that they usually seek first and foremost to establish a position within their regional subsystem before taking into account their situation in the international system as a whole—this fact, which is commonly neglected by studies focusing on great powers, is especially consequential when it comes to analyzing the foreign policies of regional powers. Defining a regional subsystem only in terms of geographical proximity and patterns of interaction, without specifying a minimum number of states, means that there can be as many regional subsystems as there are neighboring interacting states. In fact, one could envisage a number of different regional subsystems containing only two states, and the fewer the number of states, the more coherence of the proposed subsystem. But at the same time, the larger the number of regional subsystems identified, the less parsimonious the subsystemic approach becomes. The question of drawing boundaries then is related to balancing the need for coherence with the need for parsimony in order to retain the usefulness of the regional subsystem concept as an analytical tool and a research program.

The definition proposed above has three main components that deserve careful consideration. The first is the fact that, as mentioned earlier, a regional subsystem is a subset of the international system as a whole, which means that the international system can be considered the subsystem's environment. This implicates the acknowledgment that pressures from the overall system coexist alongside subsystemic pressures, but the latter is usually more significant for the members of a regional subsystem. Second, a regional subsystem reflects *actual* patterns of interaction, including both conflict and cooperation, which implies that it can only be detected by looking at past interactions and not by measuring the potential for interaction. A regional subsystem is conceived here as being a social system and, as James Rosenau pointed out, "recurring—and therefore patterned—interaction is the distinguishing feature of a social system."[33] This means that attempts to operationalize a regional subsystem in terms of, for example, the "ability to interact militarily," is faulty in the sense that it does not reflect the actual patterns of interaction.[34] Finally, the third characteristic of the definition suggested above is the fact that a regional subsystem includes members in condition of geographic proximity. The geographic criterion is crucial regardless of the level of interconnection or interdependence of the global international system, a condition that has led some scholars to discount the importance of geography.[35] Moreover, geographic proximity is positively related to intensity and opportunities for interaction, since distance is assumed to increase costs of both trade and conflict, for example.[36]

A corollary of the concept of a regional subsystem is the notion that states in a regional subsystem have a degree of interdependence in the sense that "the activities of other members of the region (be they cooperative or antagonistic) are significant determinants of its foreign policy."[37] The caveat that the interactions can be "cooperative or antagonistic" is crucial, as the very notion of system is neutral vis-à-vis the nature of the relationship.[38] Karl Kaiser defines a subsystem in terms of pattern of interaction and adds an "awareness of interdependence among participating units" as a characteristic.[39] Similarly, Joseph Nye talks about a region as being characterized by "a limited number of states linked together by a geographical relationship and by a degree of mutual interdependence."[40] Again, it is important to remember that interdependence may involve both conflictive and cooperative aspects, friends and enemies alike. In this sense, states are considered to be interdependent "when the outcome of an interaction for each depends on the choices of the others."[41] As Wendt remarks, interdependence should be distinguished from "common fate," such as a common threat. The difference between them is that common fate does not imply interaction.[42] The interdependence aspect that characterizes the regional level is important because it determines one key assumption of the regional subsystemic approach: the notion that for a number of countries with a number of issues, the regional setting, as "a relatively self-contained network of political interactions,"[43] is more relevant than the global setting in foreign policy actions.

This reasonably parsimonious definition based solely on geography and patterns of interactions serves the purpose of international relations' research, and the field would significantly benefit if it were applied more consistently. This does not mean that there are no other ways to delimit a region depending on the purposes of the researcher. Students of geography, comparative politics, or anthropology may find it necessary to choose among a different set of variables, but if the purpose of the regional analysis is to refine our understanding of international politics and to advance theoretical propositions in this field, the regional subsystemic approach seems to be an adequate fit. For this reason, it may be useful to distinguish the term *regional subsystem* from the usual notion of *region*, with the first being the focus of investigation of international relations.[44] This distinction is not merely nominal since a region is not necessarily a regional subsystem. The perspective presented by this research, for instance, is that while the existence of Latin America as a region may be justified from the point of view of other disciplines, within the field of international relations, the view of a North and a South American subsystem is far more useful. The failure to make this distinction has led to recurrent errors of analysis, judgment, and policies.

REGIONAL SUBSYSTEMS AND REGIONALISM

When scholars turned their attention to regional dynamics with the end of the Cold War, the majority of the literature produced dealt with processes of regionalization, that is, when statesmen deliberately design strategies of regionalization through political-economic integration and formalize it in regional organizations. However, it is analytically important to make a clear differentiation between institutions and organizations. While the first refers to social practices, the latter is translated into formal structures with physical location, staff, etc. The notion of a trade regime would be an example of the former, while the World Trade Organization would be an example of the latter. Likewise, regional subsystems can be understood as institutions, while regional trade agreements are organizations, and the first may or may not coincide with the latter. This commonly overlooked distinction is important because it allows the analyst to explore the relationships between institutions and organizations. Therefore, it can be argued that empirical observable processes that characterize a given region are based on actual patterns of interactions that may or may not be eventually formalized in formal organizations. In other words, the formalization of a regional subsystem in the form of a regional organization is not an independent phenomenon, but the two generally follow previous patterns of relationships that were socially constructed. The reality of interactions precedes the building of formal organizations, which does not mean to negate the fact that the establishment of formal organizations may later affect the pattern of interactions in a given area and eventually transform a regional subsystem.[45]

As a matter of fact, one could hypothesize that a regional subsystemic perspective based on actual patterns of interactions can help to predict the relevance and effectiveness of formal regionalist schemes.[46] As David Lake observes, rather than including the establishment of institutions in the definition of regional subsystem, "it is preferable to treat the degree of institutionalization as a dimension of possible variation for further analysis."[47] Cooperation is just one extreme aspect of a spectrum of interactions in which the other end may be characterized as conflict. It is not the concern of the present study to analyze states' integration strategies or to raise normative concerns, but to make the case that the existence of regional subsystems as a social reality and as an analytical tool is an important factor to consider in the study of foreign policy. Therefore, this book assumes that, while there may be some overlapping between the literature on regionalism and the literature on regional subsystems, the two can and should be clearly distinguished.[48]

When this distinction is made, it becomes clear that while "regionalist" literature burgeoned after the end of the Cold War, the literature on regional subsystems reappeared quietly and sparsely. Probably the most significant theoretical insight among the works taking the regional subsystemic perspective to study contemporary international politics is the development of the concept of "regional security complexes" by Barry Buzan and the so-called "Copenhagen School." Buzan adapted much of the early literature on regional subsystems in order to apply it specifically to the context of security. He criticized, for instance, Cantori and Spiegel for attempting "to tackle regions across the whole agenda of international relations" which would be "too complex and cumbersome to establish a generally followed understanding of region." Thus, by focusing on security, Buzan seeks to "provide a narrower and more manageable approach." The problem with this argument is that, while claiming to offer a "narrower" approach, the concept of security itself employed by Buzan and the Copenhagen School in general, is considerably broader, covering military, political, economic, societal, and environmental security. Buzan characterizes a regional security complex, or RSC, as being "defined by durable patterns of amity and enmity taking the form of subglobal, geographically coherent patterns of security interdependence"[49] and that has a "mediating effect . . . on relations between the great powers and the local states."[50] Consequently, even though geographical proximity is considered to be an important factor, the author remarks that RSCs "are socially constructed in the sense that they are contingent on the *security practice* of the actors."[51] The fact that RSCs are "socially constructed" evidences its "constructivists roots," given the fact that regional subsystems are "dependent on the actions and interpretations of actors, not just a mechanical reflection of the distribution of power."[52] Hence, as regions are then defined both by geographic factors as well as "by the actual patterns of security practices,"[53] it becomes clear that the regional subsystemic perspective used by Buzan is similar to the one that is used here.

Perhaps one of the major reasons that the regional subsystemic literature has not enjoyed the importance it deserves in the field of international relations is the irregularity in defining what a regional subsystem is. When it is equated with integration, it loses significance as it is absorbed by the overwhelmingly larger literature on regionalism. When variables other than geography and pattern of interactions are included, it loses definitional consistency, thus becoming of little use for theoretical purposes. If one uses cultural variables to define a regional subsystem in one area, but uses a different set of variables for another, the result is typically conceptual confusion and the subsequent loss of scientific utility.[54] This book hopes to help to clarify the concept of regional subsystem in order to allow for its application in current international relations research.

NOTES

1. Leonard Binder, "The Middle East as a Subordinate International System," *World Politics* 10, no. 3 (1958): 409.

2. For example: ibid; Larry W. Bowman, "The Subordinate State System of Southern Africa," *International Studies Quarterly* 12, no. 3 (1968); Michael Brecher, "International Relations and Asian Studies: The Subordinate State System of Southern Asia," *World Politics* 15, no. 2 (1963); I. William Zartman, "Africa as a Subordinate State System in International Relations," *International Organization* 21, no. 3 (1967). Additionally, Peter Berton used the term "submacro" to refer to regional subsystems, while Michael Wallace talked about "cluster of nations." Peter Berton, "International Subsystems—A Submacro Approach to International Studies," *International Studies Quarterly* 13, no. 4 (1969); Michael D. Wallace, "Clusters of Nations in the Global System, 1865-1964: Some Preliminary Evidence," *International Studies Quarterly* 19, no. 1 (1975).

3. For example: Stanley Hoffmann, "Discord in Community: The North Atlantic Area as a Partial International System," *International Organization* 17, no. 3 (1963); Karl Kaiser, "The Interaction Regional Subsystems: Some Preliminary Notes on Recurrent Patterns and the Role of Superpowers," *World Politics* 21, no. 1 (1968).

4. Michael Haas, "International Subsystems: Stability and Polarity," *The American Political Science Review* 64, no. 1 (1970): 100.

5. William R. Thompson, "The Regional Subsystem: A Conceptual Explication and a Propositional Inventory," *International Studies Quarterly* 17, no. 1 (1973): 97.

6. Morton A. Kaplan, *System and Process in International Politics*, ed. Andrew Lakoff and Stephen J. Collier, ECPR Classics (Colchester, UK: European Consortium for Political Research Press, 2005), 20.

7. Waltz, *Theory of International Politics*: 62-63.

8. J. David Singer, "The Level-of-Analysis Problem in International Relations," *World Politics* 14, no. 1 (1961): 78.

9. Kaplan, *System and Process in International Politics*.

10. Thomas W. Robinson, "Systems Theory and the Communist System," *International Studies Quarterly* 13, no. 4 (1969).

11. Mathias Albert and Lena Hilkermeier, *Observing International Relations: Niklas Luhmann and World Politics* (London ; New York: Routledge, 2004).

12. For a classic defense of the distinction between the two see Kenneth N. Waltz, "International politics is not foreign policy," *Security Studies* 6, no. 1 (1996). He also stresses this point in Waltz, *Theory of International Politics*.

13. Kjell Goldmann, "The Foreign Sources of Foreign Policy: Causes, Conditions, or Inputs?," *European Journal of Political Research* 4 (1976).

14. Some authors have made reference to "the power of place." John A. Agnew and James S. Duncan, *The Power of Place: Bringing Together Geographical and Sociological Imaginations* (Boston: Unwin Hyman, 1989); Harm J. De Blij, *The Power of Place: Geography, Destiny, and Globalization's Rough Landscape* (Oxford ; New York: Oxford University Press, 2009).

15. Harold Hance Sprout and Margaret Tuttle Sprout, *The Ecological Perspective on Human Affairs, with Special Reference to International Politics* (Princeton, NJ: Princeton University Press, 1965), 12.

16. Peter J. Katzenstein, *A World of Regions: Asia and Europe in the American Imperium*, Cornell studies in political economy (Ithaca, NY: Cornell University Press, 2005), 12.

17. Hans Mouritzen, *Theory and Reality of International Politics* (Brookfield, VT: Ashgate, 1998), 5.

18. The analogy between international relations theory and microeconomics and thus between states and firms is famously made by Waltz in Waltz, *Theory of International Politics*.

19. Mouritzen, *Theory and Reality of International Politics*: 1, 8.

20. Thompson, "The Regional Subsystem: A Conceptual Explication and a Propositional Inventory," 96.

21. David A. Lake, Patrick M. Morgan, and University of California Institute on Global Conflict and Cooperation., eds., *Regional Orders: Building Security in a New World* (University Park, PA: Pennsylvania State University Press, 1997).

22. Douglas Lemke, *Regions of War and Peace* (Cambridge, UK: Cambridge University Press, 2002), 69; Haas, "International Subsystems: Stability and Polarity," 1970.

23. Barry Buzan and Ole Wæver, *Regions and Powers: The Structure of International Security* (Cambridge, UK: Cambridge University Press, 2003), 41.

24. Michael Schulz, Fredrik Söderbaum, and Joakim Öjendal, eds., *Regionalization in a Globalizing World: A Comparative Perspective on Forms, Actors, and Processes* (London ; New York: Zed Books, 2001), 251.

25. Arie Marcelo Kacowicz, *Zones of Peace in the Third World: South America and West Africa in Comparative Perspective* (Albany, NY: State University of New York Press, 1998), 8.

26. Lynn H. Miller, "Regional Organizations and Subordinate Systems," in *The International Politics of Regions*, ed. Louis J. Cantori and Steven L. Spiegel (Englewood Cliffs, NJ: Prentice-Hall, 1970), 6-7.

27. Kacowicz, *Zones of Peace in the Third World,* 8.

28. Hans Henrik Holm and Georg Sørensen, eds., *Whose World Order?: Uneven Globalization and the End of the Cold War* (Boulder: Westview Press, 1995), 2.

29. Weston H. Agor and Andres Suarez, "The Emerging Latin American Political Subsystem," *Proceedings of the Academy of Political Science* 30, no. 4 (1972): 153.

30. Thompson, "The Regional Subsystem: A Conceptual Explication and a Propositional Inventory," 99.

31. A good example is Carlos Alberto Astiz, ed. *Latin American International Politics: Ambitions, Capabilities, and the National Interest of Mexico, Brazil, and Argentina* (Notre Dame, IN: University of Notre Dame Press, 1969). The section on Mexico's foreign policy obviously concentrates on its relation with the United States and it barely mentions Mexico's relations with other Latin American countries. When it does, it is mostly Cuba, such as the discussions about expelling Cuba from the Organization of American States.

32. Thompson, "The Regional Subsystem: A Conceptual Explication and a Propositional Inventory," 101.

33. James N. Rosenau, "The Functioning of International Systems," *Background* 7, no. 3 (1963): 112.

34. This criterion is offered by Lemke, *Regions of War and Peace*. The author gives an objective measurable definition of regional subsystems based on the distance that can be covered by day between a "home country's locus of power to the nearest point of its dyadic partner" in miles per day and its share of regional power. Then he calculates "what each state's adjusted power [to consider distance] is at other state's national capitals." If it's less than 50 percent of the local state's power share, then it's not militarily reachable, thus it is not considered as part of a region.

35. For example, by 1969 one author had stated that the geographic criterion used to identify regional subsystems "may no longer be sufficient in the face of a vastly expanding technology in electronic communications." Instead, the criterion he used was based on "news flows analysis": John H. Sigler, "News Flow in the North African International Subsystem," *International Studies Quarterly* 13, no. 4 (1969): 382.

36. As John Vasquez observes, "contiguity is the single largest factor promoting interactions." John A. Vasquez, "Why Do Neighbors Fight? Proximity, Interaction, or Territoriality," *Journal of Peace Research* 32, no. 3 (1995): 280. Well known theoretical perspectives in which the variable distance is central to determine opportunities for interactions are the "gravity model" developed by Jan Tinbergen, in the case of trade, and the "loss of strength gradient" developed by Kenneth Boulding, in the case of military power: Jan Tinbergen, *Shaping the World Economy: Suggestions for an International Economic Policy* (New York: Twentieth Century Fund, 1962); Kenneth E. Boulding, *Conflict and Defense: A General Theory* (New York: Harper, 1962). For a more recent examination on how distance affects conflict and cooperation see: Yuan-Ching Chang, Solomon W. Polachek, and John Robst, "Conflict and Trade: The Relationship Between Geographic Distance and International Interactions," *Journal of Socio-Economics* 33, no. 4 (2004).

37. Miller, "Regional Organizations and Subordinate Systems," 1.

38. This is a key difference between the literature on regional subsystems and the literature on regionalism/regional integration as will be seen below.

39. Kaiser, "The Interaction Regional Subsystems: Some Preliminary Notes on Recurrent Patterns and the Role of Superpowers," 87.

40. Joseph S. Nye, *Pan-Africanism and East African Integration* (Cambridge, MA: Harvard University Press, 1965), vii.

41. Alexander Wendt, *Social Theory of International Politics* (Cambridge, UK: Cambridge University Press, 1999), 344.

42. Ibid., 353.

43. Haas, "International Subsystems: Stability and Polarity," 1970.

44. Even though both terms have often been employed interchangeably by scholars of international politics, as for example in Cantori and Spiegel, *The International Politics of Regions.*

45. The idea that regional institutions shape patterns of interaction is a central claim in the literature on regional integration. See for example Edward D. Mansfield and Helen V. Milner, eds., *The Political Economy of Regionalism*, New Directions in World Politics (New York: Columbia University Press, 1997).

46. Kupchan makes a similar argument, but in contrast to the argument made here, his notion of region is more focused on identity and cooperation than on actual patterns of interactions. For Kupchan, "conceiving of a certain group of states as a region can be a necessary precondition for inducing them to behave as if they belong to that region and thus enabling them to share in the associated benefits. Structure shapes agency . . . Ideational change precedes, and does not follow from, changes of behavior. A region is conceived of, then it comes to exist" Charles Kupchan, "Regionalizing Europe's Security: The Case for a New Mittleleuropa," in *The Political Economy of Regionalism*, ed. Edward D. Mansfield and Helen V. Milner (New York: Columbia University Press, 1997), 211.

47. Lake and Morgan, *Regional Orders: Building Security in a New World*, 47.

48. The literature on processes of regionalization based on cooperation and the establishment of formal institutions is considerably large. By 1956, for example, one researcher observed that this literature had "already become voluminous" and offered thirty pages of selected bibliography on the subject: Norman J. Padelford, "A Selected Bibliography on Regionalism and Regional Arrangements," *International Organization* 10, no. 4 (1956). With the end of the Cold War, the literature on regionalism burgeoned, at the same time that the literature on regional subsystems subsided, and in many cases they were treated as synonymous. See, for example, Louise L'Estrange Fawcett and Andrew Hurrell, *Regionalism in World Politics: Regional Organization and International Order* (New York: Oxford University Press, 1995); Andrew Hurrell, "Explaining the Resurgence of Regionalism in World Politics," *Review of International Studies* 21, no. 4 (1995); Mansfield and Milner, *The Political Economy of Regionalism*; Etel Solingen, *Regional Orders at Century's Dawn: Global and Domestic Influences on Grand Strategy* (Princeton, NJ: Princeton University Press, 1998); Björn Hettne, András Inotai, and Osvaldo Sunkel, *Globalism and the New Regionalism* (New York: St. Martin's Press, 1999); Schulz, Söderbaum, and Öjendal, *Regionalization in a Globalizing World: A Comparative Perspective on Forms, Actors, and Processes*; Mary Farrell, Björn Hettne, and Luk van Langenhove, eds., *Global Politics of Regionalism: Theory and Practice* (London: Pluto Press, 2005).

49. Buzan and Wæver, *Regions and Powers*: 45.

50. Ibid., 191.

51. Ibid., 48.

52. Ibid., 40.

53. Ibid., 41-191.

54. For example, Cantori and Spiegel argue that "primarily political boundaries divide East and West Europe; social and political boundaries divide Latin America and North America; geographic boundaries help to identify the Middle East and divide North Africa from the rest of

Africa." The authors do not explain why a different set of criteria is used for different regions. Louis J. Cantori and Steven L. Spiegel, *The International Politics of Regions* (Englewood Cliffs, NJ: Prentice-Hall, 1970), 6.

Chapter Three

The South American Subsystem

As explained in the previous chapter, geographic proximity and patterns of interaction constitute the necessary and sufficient variables for the identification of a regional subsystem. In the Western Hemisphere, the division between a North and a South American continent is part of the "standard seven-part continental scheme employed in the United States," which would immediately provide evidence that the geographic criterion for the establishment of a regional subsystem is fulfilled. But dividing and labeling the globe into continents implies a great deal of arbitrariness, and in much of Latin America, for example, North and South America are grouped as one "American" continent, which was indeed the view prevalent among geographers until the nineteenth century. In any case, even though there is a degree of arbitrariness in any geographic division, from the point of view of a pure spatial analysis, when one looks at "the massive triangles of North and South America, tenuously linked by the Panamanian isthmus,"[1] it becomes clear that if one intends to divide the Americas in two parts, common sense would advise the line to be drawn at the Panamanian isthmus rather than at the Rio Grande. In fact, in a study of South American geopolitics, Philip Kelly described North America and South America as "two largely disconnected American continents" which are "widened by great distances, sometimes harsh climates and topographies."[2] Ronald Steel notices that "New York is closer to Paris than it is to Lima; closer to Athens than to Buenos Aires. Seattle is nearer to Tokyo than it is to Santiago. Geographically, most of South America might as well be in another hemisphere, which indeed it is."[3] In sum, this brief geographical digression is just to make obvious that if the only criterion used to divide the Americas was geographic proximity, the notion of Latin America would probably not subsist.

What this discussion is meant to make clear is that the concept of Latin America is not based on spatial geographical considerations—even though it is often used as a geographical concept—but on presumed cultural similarities. It is not the purpose of this book to challenge the assumption of cultural homogeneity in Latin America, but rather to present a critique of the use of cultural variables as the primary factor for regional classification. If culture is assumed to be the central variable for the identification of regions for the purposes of international relations analysis, several—if not all—other conventional regions of the world would have to be reclassified. Additionally, a case would have to be made as to what cultural aspects matter the most for the purposes of identification of regional subsystems. If it is assumed to be, for example, religion and language, then it makes as much sense to disassociate the United States from Mexico as it makes disassociating France from England, Egypt from Israel, and India from Pakistan and locating them in different regional subsystems. Nevertheless, very few international relations scholars would make the case that it is practically and analytically useful to do so. In fact, the implicit reason why it would not be helpful to do so is exactly because France and England, Egypt and Israel, and India and Pakistan are proximate and interacting states and this is what really matters when analyzing their international relations.

On the other hand, some would say that even though it is proper to conclude that Latin America does not fit the geographic criterion, it might very well suit the criterion of patterns of interaction. Before evaluating this claim, it is necessary to clarify the idea of patterns of interaction. In its broader sense, interaction is understood as being the result of reciprocal responses of action and reaction.[4] In international relations, forms of interaction may include, for example, diplomatic, political, social, economic, cultural, and personal interactions.[5] Likewise, the instruments of interaction can be diplomatic, psychological, cultural, economic, or military. These interactions can range in a spectrum from conflictual to cooperative. Conflictual interactions include events such as war, intervention, blockade, clandestine actions, embargoes, covert intelligence activities, etc. Cooperative interactions consist of, for example, trade, capital investment, aid, military grant, arms transfers, personnel exchanges, etc.[6] These different interactions "may exhibit regularities, or patterns, in space and through time, both in the foreign policies of particular states and in political relations of two or three or many states."[7] Therefore, by examining the spectrum of interactions through space and time in a given area of the world, certain regularities may be uncovered and general patterns can be identified. Some states will exhibit a higher degree of interactions with particular states in comparison with others. More often than not, neighboring states will tend to exhibit a relatively high degree of interaction, which is why geography matters. This relatively high degree of interaction is likely to create all sorts of interdependencies among states.

States are considered to be interdependent "when the outcome of an interaction for each depends on the choices of the others."[8] For example, states have security interdependence when they are linked "together sufficiently closely that their securities cannot be considered separate from each other."[9] In contrast, the lower the degree or intensity of interaction, the lower the interdependence, the extreme case being indifference. A regional subsystem is then characterized by a higher degree of interaction—and thus of interdependence—among the states in the subsystem relative to states outside the subsystem. Detecting these patterns of interaction across space and time helps the analyst to draw the boundaries of different regional subsystems.

For example, Haas and Lemke concentrate on the military aspect, Buzan and Wæver on security patterns, and Wallace on international organizations membership.[10] This book does not intend to dwell upon interaction in order to unravel this operationalization issue because its main concern is not the analysis of the South American subsystem per se, but how it interacts with and affects the outcomes of US foreign policy. In any case, a few remarks must be made in order to make the case for this book's assumption of the existence of a South American subsystem in terms of patterns of interaction. Along with these remarks, I will make a suggestion on how to operationalize the notion of patterns of interaction.

The first prerequisite for operationalizing patterns of interactions is that it should be made in such a way as to cover at least one aspect of each end of the interaction spectrum, which means including variables that account for both conflict and cooperation. Moreover, it would be useful to include different forms and instruments of interaction, such as economic, military, and political. It would also be noteworthy if the data required were easily available in order to make this operationalization effort attainable. Taking into consideration these qualifications, three variables could be used in order to evaluate patterns of interactions: wars and/or armed conflicts, trade, and regional organizations. Although far from reflecting all possibilities of interaction among states, these three variables characterize three important kinds of interstate interaction within the range between conflict and cooperation. Wars and armed conflicts represent conflictual interactions, while trade and regional organizations correspond to cooperative interactions. Moreover, these three variables cover military, economic, and political instruments and forms of interaction. Finally, data collection for these variables is readily available.

By using the approach suggested above, we can at least indicate evidence that there are two different patterns in Latin America which justify treating it as two distinct regional subsystems. A number of authors have made mention of wars in Latin America to justify patterns of interaction at the conflictual end of the interaction spectrum. Cantori and Spiegel, for example, argue that what they identify as the Latin American subsystem was at that time charac-

terized by a low level of conflict, but they except the Chaco War between
Paraguay and Bolivia, as well as "a variety of disputes which include Peru
vs. Ecuador, Chile vs. Peru and Bolivia, Argentina vs. Chile, and Argentina
vs. Brazil."[11] The fact that all exceptions mentioned by the authors are in
South America seems to have escaped their analysis. Atkins mentions a
number of "inter-Latin American" disputes and conflicts to express conflictual patterns of interaction and makes reference to the Chaco War, conflicts
between Peru and Ecuador, Colombia and Peru, Ecuador and Peru, and Argentina and Chile. It is true that, contrary to Cantori and Spiegel, he at least
mentions other conflicts outside South America, such as disputes between
Haiti and Dominican Republic in the thirties and the war between El Salvador and Honduras in the sixties, as well as a variety of "Central American
conflicts" during the eighties.[12] Similarly, Robert Burr talks about "intra-
Latin American rivalries" adding that "above all, the Latin American nations
are concerned with rivalries among themselves." He mentions rivalries between Argentina and Brazil, Paraguay and Uruguay, Chile, Peru, and Bolivia, Peru and Ecuador, Dominican Republic and Haiti, Guatemala and other
Central American countries, and Mexico and Guatemala.[13] What becomes
obvious from this picture is that what is termed by these authors as "inter-
Latin American" conflicts are not exactly inter-Latin American, but inter-
South American, inter-Caribbean, or inter-Central American. This is because
there is no way to provide evidence that there is a pattern of conflict in Latin
America; instead, the patterns of conflict have followed the subsystemic
division proposed here. The obvious reason for this pattern is that in most of
these conflicts—particularly in South America—there was some kind of territorial dispute involved. This is an unquestionable example of geographical
proximity affecting patterns of interaction and of the fact that geography is
the main factor contributing to the durability of regional subsystems.

Patterns of conflict are especially important because they determine one
key systemic characteristic: because a system is defined by the interaction
among the units, a change in one unit tends to cause changes in others. This
means, for example, that an arms race caused by higher defense spending in
one state of the subsystem that is not a global power tends to be confined
within the regional subsystem. If Honduras suddenly decided to acquire new
weapons to modernize its army, it is conceivable that Bolivia or Argentina
would not be as concerned as El Salvador or Nicaragua, for example. As a
matter of fact, in 2007, there were reports about an arms race in South
America that did not spill over to other places in Latin America. At the same
time Venezuela started acquiring military equipment from Russia, Brazil
announced an increase in defense spending.[14] When Chile started upgrading
its armed forces, Bolivia, Peru, and Argentina reacted.[15] This example shows
clearly that, as Robert Pastor noticed, the "principal geopolitical concerns" of
the countries in the South American subsystem "are with each other. Many

have fought each other; some have lost territory to another."[16] In fact, one scholar examined the works of sixteen South American writers in the field of geopolitics and concluded that one common theme among them was that "their geopolitics pertain to South American regional and subregional affairs."[17] This makes evident the interdependence aspect that is characteristic of a regional subsystem.

But demonstrating the absence of any serious conflict that is truly "inter-Latin American" is a relatively straightforward and uncomplicated task that, once examined with more careful attention, becomes self-evident. Nevertheless, patterns of trade could reveal a different picture. A comprehensive investigation of the patterns of trade would require looking at every individual country and assessing the percentage of exports and imports with every other country in the hemisphere across a reasonably long period of time. Although this investigation is beyond the scope of the present book, evidence suggested by other studies seems to indicate that if this task were to be completed, it would reinforce the notion of two different subsystems in the Americas and these would not be Latin America and North America, but South America and North America. For example, in his classificatory effort in the 1970s to identify regions, Russet, when using only the criterion of economic interdependence based on trade, concluded for the existence of a South American and a North/Central American region. Indeed, he observed that the major discrepancy in the western hemisphere was on trade "where the hemisphere was split into two components, a North and Central American aggregate, and one for South America."[18] Because Russet's book was published in 1975, the data he used went only until the 1970s. Later, Gordon Mace and Louis Belanger examined trade patterns in the western hemisphere using data from 1975 to 1994. Using a variety of statistical tools, the authors concluded that the "pattern clearly reveals the relative weakness of the Southern Cone's relationship with North America, as well as its remarkable lack of economic ties with Central America and the Caribbean." Additionally, when looking at the four last years of their data, they detected a pattern showing that "the Southern Cone is developing a distinct regional trading structure" and that the "Southern Cone's integration into the region as a whole is relatively weak."[19] Similarly, Jeffrey Schott, when analyzing trade patterns in the Americas, observed that "[t]he trade profiles of Western Hemisphere countries differ markedly from one side of the equator to the other," with the countries in the northern half of the hemisphere generally far more dependent on the United States.[20] Mace and Belanger's conclusion is particularly relevant for the purposes of this research and deserves to be quoted in full. They see

a growing concentration of commercial relations around two main centers: In
the northern part of the hemisphere, Canada, Mexico, and the countries of
Central America and the Caribbean are coalescing around the United States,
which acts as the central magnet. A similar situation is developing in South
America around the Brazil-Argentina axis.[21]

For the authors, the future of any hemispheric integration scheme will be
determined by how these two centers interact.

Beyond conflictual relations and trade patterns, the separation between
the South American subsystem and the North American subsystem can also
be demonstrated in political terms. Traditional analyses of the emergence of
the so called Inter-American System that culminated with the creation of the
Organization of American States (OAS) begin by distinguishing two phases:
before and after 1889.[22] The reason is that only after 1889, with the First
Pan-American Conference, the conferences summoned were truly inter-
American in the sense of including most Latin American countries and the
United States. Before that year, there were four Hispano-American confer-
ences—thus with limited participation and not including both the United
States and Brazil—with few concrete results: in 1826, 1847, 1856, and 1864.
The usual historiography informs that these first conferences helped to estab-
lish the "fundamental rules of national behavior destined later to become
basic features of inter-American cooperation," thus giving the impression
that the Inter-American system was the result of the absorption by the United
States of patterns of interaction that had been previously established among
Latin American states.[23] However, closer examination again indicates the
existence of two regional subsystems from the political interaction point of
view, even at that early stage. For example, by focusing on the Hispano-
American conferences, these analyses overlook that, in 1888, one year before
the First Pan-American Conference, Argentina and Uruguay summoned a
"South American Congress of International Private Law" in Montevideo
which was attended also by Brazil, Bolivia, Peru, Paraguay, and Chile. Commenting on the fact that the conference included only South American states,
the Foreign Minister of Argentina justified it on the basis of "their close
bonds of political and commercial interests and even of neighborliness. The
other states of North and Central America either would not come or would
come late, and perhaps one of them would assume a disturbing role of supre-
macy."[24] This short sentence expressed the two main components of the
South American subsystem—distinct patterns of interaction given especially
their "neighborliness," and a certain wariness regarding the potential influence of the United States in the region.

Like most analyses on the emergence of the Inter-American System,
those who concentrate on the establishment of regional institutions to demonstrate the level of political interaction in Latin America often overlook the

existence of a double pattern. Cantori and Spiegel claim that "Latin American relations are characterized by cooperation of the alliance variety, as is evidenced in LAFTA and the Central American Common Market."[25] Again, what the authors present as evidence of a Latin American subsystem actually confirms the notion of two different subsystems, the first organization basically a very limited South American scheme of integration that included Mexico, while the second was exclusively Central American. To reinforce the notion of Latin American political cohesiveness, the authors add that Latin American leaders had "met with President Johnson at Punta del Este, Uruguay, in April 1967 and declared their intention to create a region-wide Common Market by 1985."[26] While this meeting indeed took place, when one goes beyond a declaration of intentions and examines what actually happened afterwards, one will again detect that regional subsystemic pressures seem to have contributed to keep South America a separate subsystem. Following the meeting with President Johnson, Central American states issued a separate invitation to the United States for a "Central American Summit Conference," and what actually happened in 1985 was the initial push for the creation of a Southern Common Market, when Brazil and Argentina signed a cooperation agreement that would eventually develop into the Mercosur. Indeed, as Atkins observed, the "actual practice of Latin American integration favored the subregional approaches." The author mentions several integration schemes from the 1950s to the 1990s, all basically organized around two areas: "Circum-Caribbean" and "South American."[27] It is curious, though, to notice that Atkins refers to NAFTA—the North American Free Trade Area—as a "hemispheric" arrangement, even though it is clearly a North American arrangement.[28] However, as some authors have remarked, NAFTA in North America and Mercosur in South America can actually be seen as "competing models" of integration in the hemisphere.[29]

Therefore, evidence indicates that in all three variables considered here to measure interaction among states, it is possible to detect two different patterns of interaction in the region referred to as Latin America. From this point of view, it makes little sense to think about a Latin American subsystem, since Latin America, as a Brazilian scholar has recently put it, is "separated not only by the Panama Canal, but it is actually divided by divergent interests, economic links, and conflicting geopolitical factors."[30] On the other hand, by any criterion of actual interactions, Mexico, for example, "would appear to be entirely North American."[31] The same would also be true for Central American and Caribbean states. Nevertheless, by focusing on other variables, a significant portion of scholarship has given little attention to the actual patterns of interaction in the Americas. It is true that when studies focusing on regions resurfaced after the Cold War, the analytical disadvantages of treating Latin America as a coherent unit of analysis became more evident. Even though there seems to currently be a more widespread acceptance that South America comprises a distinct subsystem, its implications have to be considered more deeply than has been the case thus far. Acknowledging that there are analytical and empirical grounds to treat South America as a distinct regional subsystem in its own right opens up unique possibilities for research that are usually neglected by the customary approaches to studying the international politics of Latin America.

BRAZIL AND THE SOUTH AMERICAN SUBSYSTEM

Comprising about half of South America's territory, GDP, and population, sharing borders with every South American country except Ecuador and Chile, and having the second largest economy of the Americas, Brazil stands out as the backbone of the South American regional subsystem and is the key country for explaining it. Because of its size, population, and economy, Brazil is the country with the greatest capability of affecting patterns of interaction in the region. It also is the country that connects the "hard core" of South America—the Southern Cone—with the northern part of the continent, thus giving a certain level of coherence to the subsystem. Brazil connects the La Plata, the Andes, and the Amazon region, and it could hardly be ignored by any South American country. This combination of factors means that "Brazil's looming, at times threatening, presence seems to imprint strongly on the foreign policy of the other republics" in South America.[32] As Buzan and Wæver argue, even though the differences between the southern and the northern parts of South America could be "striking enough to justify seeing them as distinct subcomplexes, Brazil remains the linchpin that holds the South American" regional subsystem together.[33]

This is why it is justified to include the northern countries of South America in the regional subsystem, particularly after the 1970s when Brazil began to be more concerned about developing and populating its northern part. A clear example of Brazil's "looming" presence imprinting on the foreign policy of northern South American states was the fact that, by the early 1970s, when Brazil's military government had laid down the plans to develop the Amazon region, the Venezuelan president visited six countries in South America and suggested a Spanish-American alliance against "Brazilian expansionism" at the same time he initiated efforts to develop Venezuela's southern region as a response.[34] Likewise, the 1969 Andean Pact, signed by Bolivia, Chile, Ecuador, and Colombia, and joined by Venezuela in 1973, was motivated in part by a desire "to counter growing Brazilian power" in the region.[35] In 1976, Brazil proposed a treaty of cooperation with the members of the Andean pact as an effort "to reduce fears of Brazilian imperialism,"[36] which were "particularly [evident in] Peru and Venezuela."[37] The

Amazon Pact was finally signed in 1978 after Venezuelans and Peruvians were reassured of the inexistence of "Brazil's expansionist intentions."[38] In fact, as John Martz argues, Venezuela has historically been interested in Central America and the Caribbean, especially because of economic interests, but "territorial integrity and national security necessarily lie at the core of foreign policy interests," thus the importance of neighboring South American countries of Brazil, Guyana, and Colombia in the formulation of its foreign policy.[39] Obviously, the opposite is also true. For example, in its annual report of 1956, the Brazilian army noted that "the impetuous development of Venezuela requires special attention" adding that the possibility that Venezuela would become a military power should "demand closer vigilance."[40]

The focus on Brazil for the purposes of studying the South American regional subsystem is also justified for theoretical reasons. If, as Waltz claims, the traditional systemic approach to international relations should be "necessarily based on the great powers,"[41] it follows that the regional subsystemic approach should likewise be based on the regional powers. According to Robert Gilpin, the international system's focus on the major powers is justified because the system generally tends to reflect the interests of the most powerful actors, which have "determined the patterns of international interactions and established the rules of the system."[42] In a passage that could be better applied to the regional subsystemic than to the international systemic approach that he makes the case for, Gilpin argued that "[t]he boundaries of the system are defined by the area over which great powers seek to exert control and influence . . . geographic boundaries do matter, in that they affect which other actors and considerations a state must take into account in the formulation of its foreign policy."[43] This same theoretical position generally used to analyze the international system can be applied to regional subsystems. Donald Hellman also stressed that point when he asserted that the regional subsystem should be seen not only in terms of patterns of conflict and cooperation but also "in terms of the actions and capabilities of the major regional powers."[44]

Hence, it is unlikely that any analysis of the South American regional subsystem that neglects the role of Brazil will be entirely successful. The history of South America also shows that Argentina and Chile could play the role of regional leaders. However, contrary to Brazil, these countries are limited by their geographic position, which tends to confine their concerns to a more restricted area. Recognizing the role of Brazil as the key to understanding the South American subsystem does not imply considering Brazil as a regional hegemon with power to dictate the course of the subsystem as it pleases. In fact, as David Myers observed, for reasons of domestic and regional considerations, "Brazil is far from being a regional hegemon."[45] But Brazil is and has consistently been a regional power, and even if only because of its size, population, and geographic circumstance, this is a fact to be taken into consideration by the other states' foreign policies. Likewise, Brazil's foreign policy choices and behavior are definitely important to determine the dynamics of the subsystem. "A stable Brazil tends to stabilize the continent," writes Kelly, and any radical transformation of Brazil, such as breaking up into smaller independent countries, would radically transform the South American subsystem.[46] Correspondingly, had Brazil, like the Spanish-American republics, had its territory fragmented when obtaining its independence from Portugal, the history of the South American subsystem would most likely be considerably different.

A central characteristic of the South American regional subsystem is that not only must the other states of South America necessarily take Brazil into consideration in matters of conflict and cooperation, but also, as will be explored later, Brazil has historically considered South America as its privileged area of influence. This assumption by Brazilian policymakers is one key factor determining the boundaries of the subsystem. If the boundaries of the international system, as Gilpin argues, can essentially be "defined by the area over which great powers seek to exert control and influence,"[47] the same should be true for the boundaries of a regional subsystem, which could be then defined by the area over which regional powers seek to exert influence. According to Moniz Bandeira, it is the "geopolitical" notion of South America that has effectively guided the foreign policy of Brazil, and not the "ethnic" concept of Latin America, which "is not consistent with its actual economic, political, and geopolitical interests."[48] For this reason, a former Brazilian foreign minister mentioned "the South American component" as a central aspect of Brazil's "international identity."[49] Thus, if US policymakers have occasionally seen the whole of Latin America as its sphere of influence, their Brazilian counterparts have seen consistently throughout history the hemisphere's two halves in a different way—a South American half, where Brazil would strive to exert influence, and a North American half that constituted the sphere of influence of the United States in which Brazil would thus abstain from being seriously involved. By the same token, Brazil would attempt to limit US influence in South America.

SUBSYSTEMIC CHANGE AND STABILITY

Focusing on the most important powers in the system is also vital to detect and understand potential processes of systemic change. In his prominent endeavor to study political change in international politics, Gilpin distinguished between three types of international change: system change, systemic change, and interaction change. While the first entails a change in the nature of the most important actors that compose the system—for example, from nation-states to empires or multinationals—the second is a change within the system in which the focus is the relative changes of power culminating with "the replacement of a declining dominant power by a rising dominant power."[50] The third type of international change described by Gilpin involves modifications in the patterns of interaction and may presage systemic changes. In fact, Gilpin comments that both systemic and interaction changes involve changes in "the rules and rights embodied in the system."[51] We can adapt this framework originally created for the study of international systems to the study of regional subsystems. According to Gilpin's approach, the central factor to understand the destabilization of the system and systemic change is the rise of new powers and the consequent redistribution of relative power in the overall system. What is central in his argument is the idea that the power of the members of the international system changes at different rates, and thus this "differential growth in power of the various states" is the most important factor in explaining systemic change.[52] This theory can also be applied at the regional level, but while Gilpin considers the international system as whole and thus must find the sources of power redistribution exclusively within the system, the regional subsystem approach allows for a second source of power redistribution which comes from outside the subsystem.

In the case of the South American subsystem, the main candidate for changing the regional distribution of power from the outside is the United States, which seems to be the only actor that could incorporate the South American subsystem in an all-encompassing American system. If the United States acted in South America the same way it has done in the rest of Latin America, the concept of a South American regional system would indeed lose much of its analytical muscle as the North American country would absorb most of their regional interactions. There is little doubt that the United States has possessed the capabilities to change the subsystemic status quo in South America and to effectively affect the distribution of power in the subsystem through direct action either in the form of military intervention or some action of the kind that Cantori and Spiegel called "politically significant involvement," which "is expressed by the possession of a colony; economic or military aid producing an alteration in the balance of power in the region; formal alliance, troop commitment, or any agreement which causes the external power to act in ways which resemble the types of actions that would ordinarily be taken by a country indigenous to the region."[53]

For Gilpin, the international system tends toward stability as long as no state judges that it is profitable to change it.[54] Adapting Gilpin's framework to the study of the regional subsystem, if US policy makers at some point concluded that the benefits of transforming the South American subsystem's status quo would outweigh the costs, they could have attempted to do so through significant political involvement. The argument of this book is that Brazil has affected this calculation by either increasing the costs or reducing the benefits of subsystemic change for the United States. Therefore, the stability of the South American subsystem must be explained not only in reference to geography, but also through the interaction between the United States and Brazil, which has contributed to maintaining the United States as an "absent empire" in South America in contrast to other regions of Latin America. From this follows that the present, past, and at least the near future of the South American subsystem depends largely on the relationship between the United States and Brazil. In other words, the structure of the South American subsystem affects the outcomes of US foreign policies but does not determine them, and, depending on how the interactions between the United States and Brazil develop, this structure can be changed, whether because the United States may be willing to pay the costs of change or because Brazil may be unwilling to affect US calculations.

An important assumption of this book is that, as a regional subsystem develops, regionally influential states value their position in the subsystem and thus they have an incentive to maintain the integrity of the subsystem by reducing opportunities for outside penetration, which could at the limit promote subsystemic change if the regional distribution of power was substantially affected. Because their main focus is usually regional rather than global, regional powers tend to concentrate their attention primarily on their own regional subsystems. Accordingly, at the same time these states adopt strategies to maintain their influence within the subsystem, they work either to limit influence from outside or to shape that influence in accordance with their interests. The capacity of regional powers to restrict outside penetration is obviously limited by the power relationship between them and the external powers, but they can be successful if they create conditions that reduce the incentive or the opportunity for outside penetration, thus affecting the structure of costs and benefits of subsystemic change. Correspondingly, they may also be unable or incompetent to affect the structure of costs and benefits, in which case outside penetration can lead to subsystemic change. Weaker states within the subsystem may also bargain with outside powers to improve their own positions but they generally have little to gain by completely ignoring the pressures of more powerful neighboring states.

Because of its privileged geographic situation in South America, Brazil has been a "quintessential status quo power,"[55] which means it has had a lot to gain by maintaining the stability of the subsystem. The argument proposed here is that Brazil, which has historically displayed "a strong vested interest in regional stability,"[56] has successfully manipulated the structure of costs and benefits of subsystemic change for the United States in two main ways. First, it has reduced the benefits of subsystemic change by acting as a "sub-hegemonic state"[57] or a "hegemonic stabilizer"[58] at the regional level, thus preempting the role that could potentially be played by the United States, and consequently reducing the opportunities and incentives for US interference. Because, like Brazil, the United States has also been a status quo power when it comes to Latin America in general and to South America in particular, there has been "a congruence of US-Brazilian interest in stability in the region,"[59] in spite of occasional divergence of interests. Thus, while standard explanations for the relative stability of South America would argue that "American hegemony mutes a real conflict,"[60] this research takes a different approach. As one observer put it in the late seventies,

> Not U.S. intercession, but Brazilian power diplomacy seems most responsible to date for preventing the outbreak of violence in the region. If this is true, there may exist some basis for beginning to think of South American relations in terms of a regional balance of power (in which Brazil plays the role of balancer) rather than in the more conventional framework of North American hegemony.[61]

Therefore, Brazil has played in South America—although essentially through other means—a similar role as the United States has played in other parts of Latin America, which explains in part why the US military interventions on behalf of a "search for stability" could be regionally restricted to the north of Panama. On the other hand, Brazil has attempted to increase the costs of subsystemic change by increasing the incentives for other states in participating in the subsystem and at the same time avoiding openly playing the "subhegemonic" role. This is both a conscious decision by Brazilian policymakers as well as a reflection of Brazil's limited means to be a hegemonic power. Both strategies—decreasing the benefits and increasing the costs of subsystemic change—have often been used simultaneously to affect the profitability of change, but the first was more evident during the Cold War, while the second became preeminent after the 1980s. The cases selected for study in the next chapters will better explore these arguments.

Therefore, the patterns of interaction aspect of the South American subsystem is characterized both by distinct patterns of cooperation and conflict within the subsystem as well as by a relative US absence in comparison to the rest of Latin America. Both of these factors are interrelated and contribute to keeping South America as a separate regional subsystem. While the first has already been emphasized, this research will focus on the latter. The main goal is to demonstrate that the resulting interaction between the United States and the South American regional subsystem has not led to a subsystemic change in South America, which would mean its outright incorporation into either a Latin American or an American subsystem. In other words, this book aims to explain the remarkable degree of stability of the South American subsystem and to make the case for the analytical strength of treating South America as a separate regional subsystem in order to assess, and possibly predict, the outcomes of given US foreign policies initiatives toward the region.

EXPLAINING ABSENCE

Evidently many authors have noticed the relative US absence from South America in comparison to the rest of Latin America. These authors focus generally on the most manifest aspect of this difference—the lack of direct unilateral US military intervention south of Panama. Two basic sets of explanations are usually provided to account for this difference—South America is too far away or it has little strategic significance, and South American states are more stable than other countries in Latin America. Typically, the combination of these two factors—proximity and political instability—is used to explain the abundance of US military involvement in Central America and the Caribbean in contrast to South America. For example, Pastor argues that Central America's and Caribbean's "proximity, vulnerability, and instability" are the three characteristics that "make the region of special concern to the United States."[62] For Harold Molineu there are "obvious security interests" that arise "out of the region nearness."[63] Ronald Steel asserts that, while the Caribbean is of immediate interest, some nations in South America "are twice as far from the United States as Europe" and therefore they could be considered "irrelevant" for the security of the United States.[64] David Myers sees South America as less subjected to US influence in general because of the "greater difficulty of projecting North American military, diplomatic and economic power into an arena that is larger, more populous and geographically remote."[65] The notion of "geographic proximity" as "the most important factor" in explaining US involvement in Central America and the Caribbean is also present in more recent studies.[66] David Healy and Thomas Leonard single out the "search for stability" as the main characteristic of US actions in Central America and the Caribbean.[67] Likewise, for Molineu "the constant seeking of stability for its own sake may be the common denominator in understanding the definition of U.S. interests in Latin America."[68] Louis Perez Jr. remarks that American officials saw US presence in the Caribbean as necessary to bring "political stability and fiscal responsibility."[69]

From the perspective presented by the present research, there are three main aspects of these approaches that deserve particular consideration. The first is that, by focusing on how geographical proximity affects interactions between the United States and the two different subsystems in Latin America, the approaches implicitly acknowledge the existence of a North American subsystem distinct from a South American subsystem. However, because this is just implicit, the research is unable to explore the consequences of this separation and to go beyond an overemphasis on Central America and the Caribbean. In fact, it seems apparent that the overwhelming majority of the works on "United States-Latin America relations" are works on the relations of the United States with Mexico, Central America, and the Caribbean, with occasional references to one or other South American state just to give the impression of covering the whole region. Because South America is considered too far away, too irrelevant, or relatively stable, it does not deserve any deeper analytical treatment by specialists in US foreign policy. In other words, studying a region where the United States has been an absent empire is far less interesting than looking at the instances where the imperial urge has been very present. Thus, the result of US relative absence from South America results in an absence of South America in the study of US foreign policy.

The second aspect that deserves consideration is closely related to the first. As mentioned, geographic proximity and instability are often mentioned as the main reasons for why the United States has been less involved in South America in comparison to the rest of Latin America, but with the overemphasis on the "unstable" Central American and Caribbean states, little attention is given to the supposed stability of South American states. While geographic distance is self-explanatory, the sources of stability or instability are not an unchangeable and permanent fact of nature and must therefore be explained. In addition, while geographic distance is definitively a sound explanation for the lack of involvement in South America until around the first two decades of the twentieth century—when the United States lacked actual power projection in the region and had to compete with a strong European presence there—it becomes less compelling after the United States became a global power. After all, geographic distance did not restrain the United States from occasionally employing imperial policies in different parts of the globe.

Finally, the third aspect of the explanations mentioned above is that, at best, they can explain a supposed lack of US *interest* towards South America. Nevertheless, the explanatory power of those approaches is unequipped to account for the instances when the United States demonstrated a clear interest in South America and yet the actual outcome was relative absence. Lacking an adequate theoretical approach to explain these cases, authors frequently attempt to fit their interpretations within the usual "United States-Latin America" framework, where dissimilar events in what are actually two distinct regional subsystems are seen as equivalent. This is clearly evident and especially relevant in one case in which the United States undoubtedly demonstrated an interest in South American events and that turned out to be definitely the most mentioned event by any scholar trying to demonstrate a supposed coherent pattern of US intervention in Latin America as a whole—

the 1973 Chilean military coup. By making reference to the Chilean case along with a number of US interventions in Central America and Caribbean, those who propose to analyze US foreign policy towards Latin America feel satisfied and relieved that they were able to find a case to demonstrate a consistent pattern for the whole region, and therefore are free to concentrate on aspects considered more important.

Therefore, the cases studied in the next three chapters will attempt to address these three aspects from the regional subsystemic perspective in order to tackle their shortcomings. First, by providing a framework for the study of the international relations of South America, this research aims to bring attention to an important region of the hemisphere that is commonly neglected by the majority of the studies on United States-Latin America relations for the fact that the United States has not been as active in South America as it has historically been in other regions of Latin America. In other words, by providing explanations for the relative US absence from South America, this research seeks to overcome the relative absence of South America in US studies on Latin America. This is especially relevant given the rising interest in Brazil as an important power in the evolving configuration of the international system.[70] Second, by considering reasons beyond the mere geographic remoteness and lack of interest, this research intends to provide alternative explanations for US absence, as well as to address the question of apparent "stability" of South America as compared to the other regions of Latin America. And lastly, by focusing on particular case studies when the US policy makers demonstrated a clear interest in South America, this book intends to offer explanations for the actual outcome of US initiatives. In his pioneering study on regional subsystems Binder compared extraregional power to rays of light that were "refracted" when projected into regional subsystems.[71] In the same way, the goal of this research is to help to understand how US power is "refracted" when projected into the South American subsystem.

Perhaps the major casualty brought about by the regional subsystemic perspective as applied to South America is the usual framework of US "hegemony" in Latin America as multipurpose explanation for the international politics of the Western Hemisphere. In terms of interpretation, this approach equates, for instance, the 1954 Guatemalan coup with the 1973 Chilean coup as equivalent events, both being examples of countries that "were unable to break away from U.S. dominance."[72] In terms of analysis, the US hegemony approach would predict, for example, that the regional integration model set by NAFTA would inevitably be extended to all Latin America "because of U.S. power."[73] The traditional focus on the United States is reminiscent of the conventional global systemic approach to international relations. Nevertheless, outside the boundaries of the North American subsystem—that is, in regional subsystems where the United States is an external power, and not an integral member—a disproportionate focus on US actions often leads to neglecting the dynamics of the regional subsystemic game that is being played simultaneously. Obviously, in some circumstances the distinction between the United States (or any other great power, for that matter) as an external power or as an integral member is blurred—the United States in Western Europe in the 1950s, for example, comes to mind. Yet, even in those extreme situations, regional subsystemic pressures are at play, and geography makes sure that states will remain concerned about their neighbors and attempt to manipulate external powers for their own advantage in order to achieve a better position in the regional chessboard.

For the reasons aforementioned, the role of Brazil as a regional power will be emphasized in order to explain the interaction between the United States and the South American regional subsystem. This does not mean to negate the role of the United States, or to assume that Brazil has "more power" or "more influence" than the United States in South America, or that somehow there is a balance of power between Brazil and the United States in that subsystem. What it does mean, is that the supposed hegemonial role of the United States in South America has not been exercised as it could have been because of the particular dynamics of the South American subsystem in which Brazil has played a central role by manipulating the cost-benefit structure of subsystemic change. If the United States has acted occasionally as an empire in other regions of Latin America, in South America it has been an absent one, even though it has had the required capabilities to be a present one. Geographic distance obviously plays an important role, but it is far from being a sufficient explanation—the regional subsystemic perspective is thus required in order to allow us to detect alternative reasons.

As mentioned in the previous chapter, the fact that regional subsystems are subsets of the broader international system means that they cannot be studied in complete isolation. A complete analysis of regional subsystems can only claim to be satisfactory if it includes references to the international system that constitutes the environment of the regional subsystems. For this reason the next chapters are arranged in accordance with different configurations of the international system. The first period, which goes from the time of the independence of the American states until the first decades of the twentieth century, is considered by many analysts as being multipolar, but this multipolarity was essentially restricted to the European context. In the Western Hemisphere the United States was the major power and its foreign policy had basically a regionalist orientation, of which the Monroe Doctrine is the clearest example. The second period under study is the Cold War, when an actual international system came about, together with a bipolar configuration of power. During this period, the United States adopted a global orientation in its foreign policy, focused mainly on the European continent, at the same time it reached the peak of its influence in Latin America.

The Cold War is a particularly relevant period for the purposes of this study because the United States had then clearly both the incentive and the capability to become a "present empire" in South America. Finally, the last period under consideration goes from the end of the Cold War until the present days, when the disappearance of the Soviet Union left the United States as the "lonely superpower."[74] For each of these configurations of the international system, a corresponding role for Brazil in the South American subsystem is identified. The first period could be characterized as the "unwritten alliance" with the United States; the second could be termed as the "regional imperialist" phase; and in the third period, the role of Brazil could be described as the "leader of a South American bloc." The juxtaposition of these three factors— the configuration of the international system, the role of the United States, and the role of Brazil—will be the basic framework to analyze the three periods under study. It is the expectation of this research that this framework is a better alternative to understand US foreign policy towards South America than the ones offered by the existing literature.

NOTES

1. Martin W. Lewis and Kären Wigen, *The Myth of Continents: A Critique of Metageography* (Berkeley: University of California Press, 1997), 2-3.
2. Philip Kelly, *Checkerboards & Shatterbelts: The Geopolitics of South America* (Austin: University of Texas Press, 1997), 161.
3. Ronald Steel, *Pax Americana* (New York: Viking Press, 1970), 186.
4. Sprout and Sprout, *The Ecological Perspective on Human Affairs, with Special Reference to International Politics*: 24.
5. Michael Brecher, *The Foreign Policy System of Israel: Setting, Images, Process* (New Haven, CT: Yale University Press, 1972), 51.
6. G. Pope Atkins, *Latin America and the Caribbean in the International System*, 4th ed. (Boulder, CO: Westview Press, 1999), 16-17.
7. Sprout and Sprout, *The Ecological Perspective on Human Affairs, with Special Reference to International Politics*: 24.
8. Wendt, *Social Theory of International Politics*: 344.
9. Buzan and Wæver, *Regions and Powers*: 43.
10. Haas, "International Subsystems: Stability and Polarity"; Lemke, *Regions of War and Peace*; Buzan and Wæver, *Regions and Powers*; Wallace, "Clusters of Nations in the Global System, 1865-1964: Some Preliminary Evidence," International Studies Quarterly vol. 19, no. 1 (1975).
11. Cantori and Spiegel, *The International Politics of Regions*: 61.
12. Atkins, *Latin America and the Caribbean in the International System*: 325-43.
13. Robert N. Burr, "International Interests of Latin American Nations," in *The International Politics of Regions*, ed. Louis J. Cantori and Steven L. Spiegel (Englewood Cliffs, NJ: Prentice-Hall, 1970), 101.
14. Andrew Downie, "A South American Arms Race?," *Time*, December 21, 2007.

15. Alex Sanchez, "Chile's Aggressive Military Arms Purchases Are Ruffling the Region, Alarming in Particular Bolivia, Peru and Argentina," *Council on Hemispheric Affairs*, August 7, 2007. http://www.coha.org/chile%E2%80%99s-aggressive-military-arm-purchases-is-ruffling-the-region-alarming-in-particular-bolivia-peru-and-argentina/ (accessed September 17, 2010).

16. Robert A. Pastor, *Whirlpool: U.S. Foreign Policy toward Latin America and the Caribbean* (Princeton NJ: Princeton University Press, 1992), 24.

17. Kelly, *Checkerboards & Shatterbelts: The Geopolitics of South America*: 84. For an extensive examination of geopolitical thought in South America see: Howard Taylor Pittman, "Geopolitics in the ABC countries: A Comparison" (PhD diss., American University, 1981).

18. Bruce M. Russett, *International Regions and the International System: A Study in Political Ecology* (Westport, CT: Greenwood Press, 1975), 175.

19. Gordon Mace and Louis Bélanger, eds., *The Americas in Transition: The Contours of Regionalism* (Boulder, CT: Lynne Rienner Publishers, 1999), 50-51.

20. Jeffrey J. Schott, *Prospects for Free Trade in the Americas* (Washington, DC: Institute for International Economics, 2001), 92.

21. Mace and Bélanger, *The Americas in Transition*: 244.

22. For example J. Lloyd Mecham, *The United States and Inter-American Security, 1889-1960* (Austin: University of Texas Press, 1961) and Gordon Connell-Smith, *The Inter-American System* (London, New York: Royal Institute of International Affairs, 1966).

23. Mecham, *The United States and Inter-American Security, 1889-1960*: 46.

24. Thomas Francis McGann, *Argentina, the United States, and the Inter-American System, 1880-1914* (Cambridge: Harvard University Press, 1957), 78.

25. Cantori and Spiegel, *The International Politics of Regions*: 61.

26. Miller, "Regional Organizations and Subordinate Systems," 70.

27. Atkins, *Latin America and the Caribbean in the International System*: 179-93.

28. Ibid., 203. Other authors share the same view, which seemed to be prevalent in the 1990s before the failure of the FTAA became clear. Perhaps this is because of the implicit assumption that Latin America is indivisible, which means that any arrangement between the United States and any Latin American country is logically "hemispheric." Andrew Hurrell, for example, sees NAFTA as an example of "hemispheric regionalism." What the author calls "Latin American regionalism" is actually the development of Mercosur in South America. Andrew Hurrell, "Regionalism in the Americas," in *Regionalism in World Politics: Regional Organization and International Order*, ed. Louise L'Estrange Fawcett and Andrew Hurrell (New York: Oxford University Press, 1995).

29. Ivan Bernier and Martin Roy, "NAFTA and Mercosur: Two Competing Models?," in *The Americas in Transition: The Contours of Regionalism*, ed. Gordon Mace and Louis Bélanger (Boulder, CO: Lynne Rienner Publishers, 1999); Katzenstein, *A World of Regions*: 231. This issue will be further explored in chapter 6.

30. Moniz Bandeira, "O Brasil como Potência Regional e a Importância Estratégica da América do Sul na sua Política Exterior," *Revista Espaço Acadêmico*, no. 91 (2008): 18.

31. Robert O. Keohane, "Between Vision and Reality: Variables in Latin American Foreign Policy," in *Latin America in the New International System*, ed. Joseph S. Tulchin and Ralph H. Espach (Boulder, CO: Lynne Rienner Publishers, 2001), 207.

32. Kelly, *Checkerboards & Shatterbelts*: 48.

33. Buzan and Wæver, *Regions and Powers*: 332.

34. Robert D. Bond, "Venezuela, Brazil, and the Amazon Basin " in *Latin American Foreign Policies: Global and Regional Dimensions*, ed. Elizabeth G. Ferris and Jennie K. Lincoln (Boulder, CO: Westview Press, 1981), 154; John D. Martz, "Venezuelan Foreign Policy toward Latin America," in *Contemporary Venezuela and its Role in International Affairs*, ed. Robert D. Bond (New York: New York University Press, 1977), 162-63.

35. Elizabeth G. Ferris, "The Andean Pact and the Amazon Treaty: Reflections of Changing Latin American Relations," *Journal of Interamerican Studies and World Affairs* 23, no. 2 (1981): 147.

36. Bond, "Venezuela, Brazil, and the Amazon Basin " 159-60.

37. Riordan Roett, "Brazil Ascendant: International Relations and Geopolitics in the Late 20th Century," *Journal of International Affairs* 29, no. 2 (1975): 151.

38. Ferris, "The Andean Pact and the Amazon Treaty: Reflections of Changing Latin American Relations," 155.

39. Martz, "Venezuelan Foreign Policy toward Latin America," 188.

40. Diniz Esteves, *Documentos Históricos do Estado-Maior do Exército* (Brasília: Edição do Estado-Maior do Exército, 1996), 334.

41. Waltz, *Theory of International Politics*: 73.

42. Robert Gilpin, *War and Change in World Politics* (Cambridge, UK: Cambridge University Press, 1981), 42-43.

43. Ibid., 38.

44. Donald C. Hellmann, "The Emergence of an East Asian International Subsystem," *International Studies Quarterly* 13, no. 4 (1969): 422.

45. David J. Myers, ed. *Regional Hegemons: Threat Perception and Strategic Response* (Boulder: Westview Press, 1991), 226.

46. Kelly, *Checkerboards & Shatterbelts*: 53.

47. Gilpin, *War and Change in World Politics*: 38.

48. Bandeira, "O Brasil como Potência Regional e a Importância Estratégica da América do Sul na sua Política Exterior," 3.

49. Celso Lafer, "Brazilian International Identity and Foreign Policy: Past, Present, and Future," *Daedalus* 129, no. 2 (2000): 218.

50. Gilpin, *War and Change in World Politics*: 43.

51. Ibid., 42-43.

52. Ibid., 13.

53. Cantori and Spiegel, *The International Politics of Regions*: 26.

54. Gilpin, *War and Change in World Politics*: 50-51.

55. Kacowicz, *Zones of Peace in the Third World*: 90.

56. Buzan and Wæver, *Regions and Powers*: 314.

57. Michael J. Francis and Timothy J. Power, "South America," in *Handbook of Political Science Research on Latin America: Trends from the 1960s to the 1990s*, ed. David W. Dent (New York: Greenwood Press, 1990).

58. Buzan and Wæver, *Regions and Powers*: 313.

59. Stephen M. Gorman, "Present Threats to Peace in South America: The Territorial Dimensions of Conflict," *Inter-American Economic Affairs* 33, no. 1 (1979): 70.

60. Cantori and Spiegel, *The International Politics of Regions*: 59-60. See also Guy E. Poitras, *The Ordeal of Hegemony: The United States and Latin America* (Boulder: Westview Press, 1990).

61. Gorman, "Present Threats to Peace in South America," 53.

62. Pastor, *Whirlpool*: 23.

63. Harold Molineu, *U.S. Policy toward Latin America: From Regionalism to Globalism*, 2nd ed. (Boulder: Westview Press, 1990), 10.

64. Steel, *Pax Americana*: 195.

65. Myers, *Regional Hegemons*: 244.

66. Todd R. Greentree, *Crossroads of Intervention: Insurgency and Counterinsurgency Lessons from Central America* (Westport, CT: Praeger Security International, 2008), 22. Likewise, Crandall has explained this difference in involvement by the fact that "Central America and the Caribbean are much closer" than South America, while O'Brien notices that "most of the nations of South America were large and lay at a considerable distance from the borders of the United States." Russell Crandall, *Gunboat Democracy: U.S. Interventions in the Dominican Republic, Grenada, and Panama* (Lanham [Md.]: Rowman & Littlefield Publishers, 2006), 11; Thomas F. O'Brien, *Making the Americas: The United States and Latin America from the Age of Revolutions to the Era of Globalization* (Albuquerque: University of New Mexico Press, 2007), 106.

67. David Healy, *Drive to Hegemony: The United States in the Caribbean, 1898-1917* (Madison, WI: University of Wisconsin Press, 1988); Thomas M. Leonard, *Central America and the United States: The Search for Stability* (Athens: University of Georgia Press, 1991).

68. Molineu, *U.S. Policy toward Latin America*: 10.

69. Louis A. Perez, Jr., "Intervention, Hegemony, and Dependency: The United States in the Circum-Caribbean, 1898-1980," *The Pacific Historical Review* 51, no. 2 (1982): 171.

70. Especially since the concept of "BRIC"—referring to Brazil, Russia, India, and China— was introduced in 2001 by Jim O'Neil: Jim O'Neill, "Building Better Global Economic BRICs," in *Global Economics Paper No: 66* (London: Goldman Sachs, 2001).

71. Binder, "The Middle East as a Subordinate International System," 415.

72. David R. Mares, "Middle Powers under Regional Hegemony: To Challenge or Acquiesce in Hegemonic Enforcement," *International Studies Quarterly* 32, no. 4 (1988): 454.

73. Katzenstein, *A World of Regions*: 223.

74. Samuel P. Huntington, "The Lonely Superpower," *Foreign Affairs* 78, no. 2 (1999).

Chapter Four

The Monroe Doctrine and the Early Development of a South American Subsystem

On December 2, 1823, when the independence of the American states was recently completed, the Monroe administration issued a message to Congress that would later become probably the most resilient doctrine of its history: the Monroe Doctrine. Aiming especially at the European states that then constituted the Holy Alliance—composed of Russia, Prussia, Austria, and France—which entertained plans to help Spain regain their lost colonies in America, President Monroe declared that "the American continents, by the free and independent condition which they have assumed and maintain, are henceforth not to be considered as subjects for future colonization by any European powers" and that if they attempted to do so, this would be interpreted "as the manifestation of an unfriendly disposition toward the United States."[1] The Monroe Doctrine was thus a unilateral declaration by the United States instituting a separation between Europe and the Americas through the commitment to actively oppose any new European colonization attempts in the Western Hemisphere.

Nevertheless, the doctrine itself was not born in 1823. In fact, Monroe's message to Congress only became an actual doctrine after the principles enunciated in 1823 were articulated, interpreted, and turned into a guide for policy by subsequent administrations. Only by examining how this process unfolded can one make generalizations about the scope of the Monroe Doctrine. It has been a common and apparently obvious assumption that the Monroe Doctrine had a truly hemispheric character, one that was evident both at the time of the message of 1823 and afterwards. The Doctrine has been successively interpreted as "the overarching hemispheric policy of the

49

United States,"[2] meaning that "the whole of the American continent has been straightforwardly designated as a sphere of United States interest."[3] This interpretation remains very much in vogue in more recent studies.[4] Likewise, the most important offshoot of the doctrine, the Roosevelt Corollary, has also been interpreted within the same framework. According to this interpretation, the Roosevelt Corollary to the Monroe Doctrine meant that the United States claimed the right "to intervene in intra-American conflicts in South and Central America in order to maintain economic stability and democracy,"[5] that the United States would take "corrective actions whenever Latin Americans reneged on international debts,"[6] thus acting as the "sole policeman of the Western Hemisphere."[7]

This chapter examines the evolution of the Monroe Doctrine beyond its original promulgation in 1823 in order to demonstrate that the development of the interactions among the countries in the hemisphere made it progressively clear that, rather than being a policy directed to be homogeneously applied in all Latin America, the Monroe Doctrine and its offshoots—such as the Roosevelt Corollary—were explicitly Caribbean. In South America, the doctrine acquired a rather different character. I argue that both distance and the relative stability of key South American countries allowed for this development of an embryonic South American subsystem organized around Argentina, Brazil, and Chile. I show that Brazil in particular considered itself as a guarantor of the Monroe Doctrine in South America and thus it pursued an "unwritten alliance" with the United States, meaning that each country would take care of its respective regional subsystem. Although this was not entirely reciprocated, the understood alliance was relatively convenient for the United States as Brazil was a friendly country and because it would allow the United States to concentrate its actions in the Caribbean. I show that Roosevelt in particular clearly understood the geographical scope of the Monroe Doctrine and of his corollary. Finally, I claim that as Chile's power declined and Argentina adopted a foreign policy with a strong anti-US orientation, Brazil's position became even more relevant.

ACTION AND REACTION: DEFINING THE SCOPE OF THE MONROE DOCTRINE

Those who concentrate on the Monroe Doctrine only as it was promulgated in 1823 may conclude that no differentiation should be made in regards to its geographical application in the Americas. After all, at no point in Monroe's message was this differentiation made. Nevertheless, the Monroe Doctrine should be studied not as an isolated episode but as a historical development, which means taking into consideration a broader historical perspective in terms of how it developed through time. In other words, what should be determined is how the process of interaction among the American states shaped the actual outcome of US policies following the 1823 declaration.

Because there was no previous significant interaction among the independent countries in the Western Hemisphere, the enunciation of the Monroe Doctrine, given its presumed hemispheric reach, can be considered as equivalent to a "first social act" creating "expectations on both sides about each other's future behavior" thus setting in motion a process of action and reaction that would lead to the creation of "intersubjective meanings,"[8] which would eventually determine important aspects of the patterns of relationship in the Western Hemisphere. In fact, the first reactions when Monroe's message reached the Latin American states seem to have varied from indifference to enthusiasm. The indifference aspect is explained by the fact that many governments in Latin America were still more connected to Europe than to the other countries in the Americas and tended to look to Great Britain more than to the infant United States as a source for protection. Yet, the possibility of being able to rely on a second power in their own hemisphere to ward off the European powers could not be completely ignored by the newly independent Latin American states. Alejandro Alvarez notices that four countries took special interest in the doctrine: Argentina, Brazil, Colombia, and Mexico.[9] Dexter Perkins adds that also in Chile "the message was better received than in any other part of Spanish America."[10] All of these countries, recently independent and fearful of possible attempts of reconquest by Spain or Portugal, became interested in finding out more about US intentions and indeed they "asked point-blank what means the United States intended to use for their protection."[11] The Empire of Brazil was the first country in South America to take notice of the Doctrine and within two months requested a defensive-offensive alliance with the United States. A similar call for an alliance was made by Mexico and by Simon Bolivar's Colombia. A few years after Monroe's message to the US Congress, the Argentinean government called for the application of the Doctrine in a conflict against Brazil because, according to the Argentinean president at the time, of the "obvious connection between Europe and Brazil, more especially of Portugal."[12] The US response was basically the same in all cases. To the Colombian government, Secretary of State Adams replied that "the fear of intervention by the Holy Alliance in the countries of the New World had practically disappeared," and therefore there was no need for a formal alliance.[13] In the case of Brazil, the United States government was cool towards the request for an alliance and "excused itself, believing this compact unnecessary," and later on the two countries signed a more limited commercial treaty.[14] The Argentinean government was informed by Secretary of State Clay in 1828 that the request for intervention against Brazil was unfounded, and that "the United States did not consider itself obliged to intervene in defense of the Monroe Doctrine at every request of interested parties."[15] To leave no doubts about his views, Clay added that "[e]ven if Portugal and Brazil had remained united, and the war had been carried out by their joint arms, against the Argentine Republic, that would have been far from presenting the case which the message contemplated."[16] Similarly, to the Mexican president, Clay explained that the Monroe Doctrine did not mean that the United States had contracted any kind of legal obligation to maintain it.[17] But in contrast to the South American countries, Mexico would soon learn that the Monroe Doctrine was silent about the United States' own ambitions.

Obviously, given the fact that during the most part of the nineteenth century the European powers were more capable than the United States to project power in South America, it could hardly be conceivable that US statesmen would be willing to take any significant action in a region that was far from their borders. By the 1840s, Secretary of State Daniel Webster felt it necessary to make clear that the Monroe Doctrine "did not commit us, at all events, to take up arms at any indication of hostile feeling by the powers of Europe toward South America," adding that it would be a "very different case" if any European power "landed on the shores of the Gulf of Mexico, and commenced a war in our immediate neighborhood."[18] While in the 1860s the United States was so concerned about the French presence in Mexico as to plan to use all means necessary to force their withdrawal, when Chile went into conflict with Spain at about the same time, Secretary of State William H. Seward offered no more than "the moral support of a sincere, liberal, and, as we think it will appear, a useful friendship."[19] In summary, the actual actions of the United States made clear that, as the Monroe Doctrine acquired the contours of a policy rather than a declaration of intentions, a clear separation between the North and the South American part of the American continent was beginning to take shape.

During this process of action and reaction between the United States and the Latin American governments, the actual scope of the Monroe Doctrine became progressively more delineated. In a message to Congress in 1845, US President James Polk had already "formally confirmed the geographical limitations of the Doctrine"[20] when he declared that it would

> apply with greatly increased force should any European power attempt to establish any new colony in North America . . . The reassertion of this principle, especially in reference to North America, is at this day but the promulgation of a policy which no European power should cherish the disposition to resist. . . . It should be distinctly announced to the world as our settled policy that no future European colony or dominion shall with our consent be planted or established in any part of the North American continent."[21]

This explicit declaration by President Polk demonstrated categorically that the Monroe Doctrine was in actuality a Caribbean rather than a hemispheric doctrine. The repeated allusions to "North America" in lieu of hemispheric references continued to be made throughout the latter half of the nineteenth century. In making the case for the annexation of Santo Domingo as "an adherence to the Monroe Doctrine," President Grant stated in 1871 that he believed that "we should not permit any independent government within the limits of North America to pass from a condition of independence to one of ownership or protection under a European power."[22]

Perhaps the only exception to this overall concentration "within the limits of North America" was during Venezuela's boundary dispute with the British colony of Guyana, but in this case it appears that the personal characteristics of Secretary of State Richard Olney played a significant factor. The Venezuelan government had been disputing the Guyana boundary with Britain since the 1880s, but until 1895, when Olney succeeded Walter Gresham as Secretary of State, the United States "pursued a most cautious and circumspect course."[23] It was only after Olney became Secretary of State that the United States decided to take a firm stand on the issue by forcing Great Britain to accept US arbitration, and making reference to the Monroe Doctrine as "the accepted public law of this country."[24] In what appears to be an effort to extend the geographical scope of the doctrine as it had been tacitly defined until then, he added that the American states "South as well as North, by geographical proximity, by natural sympathy, by similarity of governmental constitutions, are friends and allies, commercially and politically, of the United States."[25] This was not only a matter of friendship, the Secretary of State observed, but also the reality of the growing American power. As Olney famously put it: "Today the United States is practically sovereign on this continent, and its fiat is law upon the subjects to which it confines its interposition."[26] It must be recalled that Monroe's original message referred explicitly to new European colonies and not existing ones, which means that Olney's application of the Monroe Doctrine as a justification for US intervention in a boundary dispute was a singular interpretation that led the British government to respond, in astonishment, that even though admitting that "the Monroe Doctrine in itself is sound," the "disputed frontier with Venezuela has nothing to do with any of the questions dealt with by President Monroe. It is not a question of the colonization by a European Power of any portion of America." The note, written by Prime Minister Lord Salisbury, concluded that Olney's interpretation of the Monroe Doctrine was a "strange development."[27] Albert Hart, whose book provided the aforementioned quotes, commented that "[n]o previous President or Secretary of State had ever taken such a broad and sweeping ground" and that Olney's interpretation was "little related to the doctrine of 1823."[28] In fact, the Venezuela-Guiana boundary dispute seems an isolated case within an overall pattern,

but while Hart concentrates on the question of the application of the Monroe
Doctrine to an issue apparently unrelated to the original declaration, for the
purposes of this book, the relevant aspect is the fact that the Venezuelan case
was perhaps the only instance when the Doctrine was explicitly invoked to
justify US actions south of Panama. Indeed, Secretary Olney himself declared in the following year, when the Cuban insurrections occupied the
minds of American statesmen, that the United States was in fact "interested
in any struggle anywhere for freer political institutions, but," he added, "necessarily and in special measure in a struggle that is raging almost in sight of
our shores."[29] Once again, the actual practices forced the confinement of the
geographical application of the doctrine.

Evidently, as the true scope of the Monroe Doctrine became clear for
Latin Americans, reactions differed radically from the almost unanimous
support received right after it was first promulgated. In particular, the United
States' expansion into Mexican territory after 1848 made clear to Mexico and
to the nearby Central American and Caribbean countries, that "the Monroe
Doctrine was never a guarantee against ambitious designs of the United
States itself."[30] When a "policy of hegemony" came to be considered as a
"natural complement of the Monroe Doctrine" by US statesmen, it is not a
surprise that some countries, Mexico in particular, began to develop "a great
aversion to the Doctrine, for they look upon it ordinarily no longer under the
aspect which it had in 1823 but under the new aspect which has been given to
it."[31] During the Spanish-American War in 1898, when the United States
took at once Guam, Puerto Rico, and the Philippines, this notion was greatly
reinforced. Predictably, by the beginning of the twentieth century, a Mexican
president stated publicly his opposition to the Monroe Doctrine, because,
from his point of view, it "attacks the sovereignty and independence of
Mexico and would set up and establish a tutelage over all the nations of
America."[32] The growth in US power and the relative decline of Europe
changed the initial view that a number of Latin American states initially had
of the Monroe Doctrine as a guarantee against intervention. The question
which now dominated several of the Pan American Conferences was how to
deal with the major power in their own hemisphere. As Gordon Connell-
Smith remarks, "a system which was promoted to prevent extra-continental
intervention became at once concerned with the question of intervention by
the promoting power."[33] After the Spanish-American War and a number of
interventions in Central America and the Caribbean throughout the first
decades of the twentieth century, it would become evident that the notion of a
homogeneous US "Latin American" policy was in fact far more restricted in
its geographical scope.[34] Having defeated a decadent European empire at the
turn of the century, and still living in a world of empires, the United States
flirted with imperial solutions for itself.[35] Nevertheless, the scope of this
American "empire" rarely reached the countries south of Panama. As will be

seen below, because of their different experiences with US power, the South American countries by and large developed a very different outlook than the one developed by the rest of Latin America, which can be clearly illustrated by the cases of Mexico and Brazil.

THE EARLY DEVELOPMENTS OF A SOUTH AMERICAN SUBSYSTEM

The strategic importance of the Caribbean area in comparison to South America is just one dimension of the explanation for the US lack of involvement further south in these first years of interaction among the independent American states. The other dimension must be found in the simultaneous development of a "continental South American system of power politics" around the core formed by Argentina, Brazil, and Chile.[36] Geographic distance allowed this system to develop during the nineteenth century, before the United States was actually capable of effectively projecting power in the Southern Cone of South America. Therefore, when the United States eventually acquired the capabilities for transforming the Monroe Doctrine into an authentic hemispheric doctrine beyond its Caribbean scope, it had to deal with a regional subsystem that had already been reasonably advanced in a way that was considerably different than in the rest of Latin America.

In contrast to other former Spanish colonies, Argentina and Chile managed to develop early in their independence relatively stable governments. Despite some moments of political precariousness—especially in the case of Argentina—neither of these two countries experienced the kind of political upheaval that prevailed in Mexico, for example, in which several different governments took turns between 1821 and 1848. Brazil was a different case, which, contrary to Spanish America, had not been fragmented into parts and experienced no great political ruptures when it achieved independence from Portugal. Suffice it to say that the first ruler of independent Brazil, Dom Pedro I, the Portuguese Prince, ruled as Emperor of Brazil for nine years. The second ruler, Emperor Dom Pedro II, was Dom Pedro I's son and ruled for forty-eight straight years until Brazil became a republic in 1889—again with no bloodshed. Contrary to what his long reign may suggest, far from being a typical Latin American caudillo, Dom Pedro II was an erudite and liberal statesman who allowed freedom of press and speech, and invested heavily in education.[37] Because of a functioning and active parliament, "with solid and competitive parties,"[38] one author even characterized the Brazilian Empire as "a crowned democracy."[39] After meeting Dom Pedro II, British Prime Minister William Gladstone referred to him as "a model to all sovereigns of the world."[40] When Dom Pedro II died, the *New York Times* wrote an extremely flattering obituary—which was a relatively unusual deference for any Latin American leader in the late nineteenth century—making reference to Gladstone's remarks, adding that Dom Pedro II was "one of the most enlightened monarchs of the century . . . a liberal patron of letters, arts, and sciences," and commenting that "Dom Pedro made Brazil as free as a monarchy can become."[41] The following day, the US newspaper referred to him as a "genial philosopher" and—what is really surprising in light of Monroe's original idea of separation between the European and the American systems of government—questioned the wisdom of establishing a republic in Brazil, saying that "it is doubtful whether a republic meets the requirements of Brazil so well as a monarchy."[42] In fact, the popularity that the Brazilian emperor enjoyed was so substantial that the most renowned statesman of the early years of the Brazilian Republic was the Baron of Rio Branco, a diplomat during the Empire and son of another prominent statesman during Dom Pedro II's reign. Rio Branco was the Brazilian Minister of Foreign Affairs under four different administrations, from 1902 to 1910. Therefore, along with Brazil's sheer size, this relative continuity of policies and stability, with no significant breaks or political upheavals, provided the country with the basis for its consolidation as a regional power in South America.

As one author observes, by the beginning of the twentieth century, Argentina, Chile, and Brazil "represented at the time literally the only group of historically mature, constitutionally stable, traditionally peaceful, and physically secure sovereign states to be found anywhere in the world."[43] This unique condition allowed for development of a regional subsystem early on in the international life of those states. Because of the existence of three countries in geographical propinquity with the potential for playing the role of regional powers as well as the relative absence of the United States during the first years of their independence, states in South America were less concerned about the overwhelming power of the North American country than about themselves, which was clearly the opposite situation in relation to the countries in the northern half of the hemisphere. Robert Burr describes the development of a system of power politics in South America throughout the nineteenth century, first with two relatively separate regions—the Plata and the Andean region—which eventually joined in a single "continental" system by the 1860s.[44] Therefore, South American statesmen, at least since the second half of the nineteenth century, "tended to think is terms of a continent-wide balance-of-power system,"[45] and used to make constant references to a "South American equilibrium."[46] As Burr argues, by the end of the nineteenth century, "the idea of a balance of power had become an accepted part of the international life of South America."[47] Nevertheless, the notion of a separation between South and North America was manifest in the minds of South American statesmen at least as early as 1840. For example, when internal problems in Mexico indicated that an attempt to summon a conference among American states that year was about to fail, the Chilean government suggested that "it would perhaps be well for the South American plenipotentiaries to meet together . . . without awaiting the arrival . . . of their Mexican and Central American colleagues," adding categorically that "[t]he republics of South America and the Brazilian Empire form a compact system whose ties with Mexico and Central America are comparatively weak."[48]

While their distance from the United States put the South American countries outside the actual scope of the Monroe Doctrine and made them less preoccupied about the possibility of US intervention, as the relative strength and stability of Argentina, Brazil, and Chile became clear by the end of the nineteenth century, policy makers in the United States began to entertain new possibilities for the application of the Monroe Doctrine and the maintenance of stability in the Americas. Although this is barely mentioned in the literature, it would become a key feature of the separation between the North and the South American regional subsystems in these formative years—the United States would take direct responsibility for its area of immediate strategic interest in North America, while it would seek to involve the stronger South American countries in the affairs of the South American continent. Indeed, this prospect was already mentioned by the end of the nineteenth century when President Grant considered intervening in the dispute between Chile and Peru. Leaving aside the unilateral phraseology commonly used when dealing with Mexico, Central America and the Caribbean, the US President mentioned the possibility of intervention by stating that the United States "would hold itself free to appeal to the other Republics of this continent to join in an effort to avert consequences which cannot be confined to Chili [sic] and Peru."[49] Nevertheless, the notion of a possible entente between the United States and some South American countries took shape by the time the most famous extension of the Monroe Doctrine was promulgated—the "Roosevelt Corollary," which was officially announced in 1904. Indeed, Theodore Roosevelt, who famously brandished the "big stick" to maintain order in the Caribbean area, is perhaps the first US president to explicitly consider the advantages of shared responsibilities for the enforcement of the Monroe Doctrine in the southern half of the hemisphere.

THE ROOSEVELT COROLLARY

In a chapter of his autobiography entitled "The Monroe Doctrine and the Panama Canal," Roosevelt starts out by acknowledging that the Spanish-American War left the United States "with peculiar relations to the Philippines, Cuba, Porto Rico, and with immensely added interest in Central America and the Caribbean Sea,"[50] therefore clearly establishing the boundaries of the US sphere of influence at the time, as many of his predecessors had done. A few lines later, he makes clear the differentiation in the Western Hemisphere between that area and South America, when he adds:

> The great and prosperous civilized commonwealths such as the Argentine, Brazil, and Chile, in the southern half of South America have advanced so far that they no longer stand in any position of tutelage toward the United States. They occupy toward us precisely the position that Canada occupies. Their friendship is the friendship of equals for equals. My view was that as regards these nations there was no more necessity for asserting the Monroe Doctrine than there was to assert it for Canada. [51]

Roosevelt concludes that if some European nation attempted to occupy one of these countries, the United States would provide assistance, but "the initiative would come from the Nation itself, and the United States would merely act as a friend whose help was invoked." Evidently, as he immediately recognizes, the situation would be "widely different" in the case of "the states in the neighborhood of the Caribbean Sea." [52]

Roosevelt's reasoning for the often overlooked double standard for the enforcement of his famous corollary to the Monroe Doctrine seems to be based on two pillars. The first is strategic-military. Already by 1901, the General Board of the Navy had produced a report that clearly stated:

> Whether the principle of the Monroe Doctrine, so far as it is the policy of this Government, covers all South America, including Patagonia and the Argentine, is not for the consideration of the General Board, but only the fact that the principles of strategy and the defects in our geographical position make it impracticable successfully to maintain naval control by armed force beyond the Amazon, unless present conditions are radically changed. [53]

This view was shared by the prominent strategist Captain Alfred Mahan, who believed "that United States security concerns ended at the Amazon River, making it unnecessary to apply the Monroe Doctrine south of it." [54]

To this strategic-military aspect Roosevelt added a second pillar, based on the notion of state capacity, that is, the states requiring US intervention would be the ones that proved incapable "to do their duties to outsiders or to enforce their rights against outsiders." [55] In his original message to Congress which gave birth to the Roosevelt Corollary, Roosevelt famously mentioned that "wrongdoing or impotence" would be the causes for US intervention in the hemisphere, adding that if the countries in the Caribbean area had the same "progress in stable and just civilization . . . which so many of the republics in both Americas are constantly and brilliantly showing, all questions of interference by this Nation with their affairs would be at an end."[56] Later, Roosevelt explicitly singled out "Brazil, the Argentine, Chile," which, he said,

> have achieved positions of such assured . . . progress, of such political stability and power and economic prosperity . . . it is safe to say that there is no further need for the United States to concern itself about asserting the Monroe Doctrine so far as these powers are concerned.[57]

On another occasion, Roosevelt remarked that

> There are certain republics to the south of us which have already reached such a point of stability, order, and prosperity, that they themselves, though as yet hardly consciously, are among the guarantors of this Doctrine . . . If all the republics to the south of us will only grow as those to which I allude have already grown, all need for us to be the special champions of the Doctrine will disappear, for no stable and growing American Republic wishes to see some great non-American military power acquire territory in its neighborhood.[58]

This notion that the more stable South American republics could be the guarantors of the Monroe Doctrine led one scholar to comment that Roosevelt viewed some countries like Argentina and Brazil "as junior partners that would help enforce the Corollary."[59] Another author stated that "[i]n a burst of enthusiasm," Roosevelt "is reported to have told Chile that, had Santo Domingo been in the Pacific, he would have called her to police the island."[60] When he was already out of office, Roosevelt confirmed this view of Argentina, Brazil, and Chile as partners that could enforce the corollary, in a letter to his son, when he wrote that

> it would be mere folly, the silliest kind of silliness, to ask Mexico [fallen into revolution], Venezuela, Honduras, Nicaragua, to guarantee the Monroe Doctrine with us. It is eminently proper to ask Brazil, the Argentine and Chile to do it . . . but to ask the other countries I have named to guarantee it would be about like asking the Apaches and Utes to guarantee it.[61]

What the above quotations intend to make evident is that, if Theodore Roosevelt is often associated with the pursuit of a US "empire," his views about how South America would fit in his scheme should serve to reinforce the notion that in the Western Hemisphere this imperial urge was geographically limited.[62]

Part of this growing recognition in the United States that Latin America should be disaggregated based on different levels of state capacity seems to be the work of Roosevelt's Secretary of State Elihu Root, who was the first sitting Secretary of State to visit South America (or any foreign country for that matter), where he was warmly received. Like his predecessors, Root is

quoted as acknowledging that "as one passes to the south and the distance
from the Caribbean increases, the necessity of maintaining the rule of Monroe becomes less immediate and apparent."[63] Like Roosevelt, Root believed
that this was so not only because of geographic distance, but because of the
different level of organization that he attributed to key South American
states. In one instance, Root claimed that he wanted to help Central America
to go "along the road that Brazil and the Argentine and Chile and Peru and a
number of other South American countries have travelled—up out of the
discord and turmoil of continual revolution into a general public sense of
justice and determination to maintain order."[64] These statements by both
Roosevelt and Root plainly contradict some observations regarding the
Roosevelt Corollary at that time (and since) that pointed to the fact that US
statesmen "seem to be blind to actual conditions in the largest and most
important parts of Latin America, such as Brazil, Argentina, and Chile."[65]
This kind of interpretation tends to assume that the Monroe Doctrine and the
Roosevelt Corollary applied homogenously to Latin America, when it clearly
did not.

BRAZIL AND THE "UNWRITTEN ALLIANCE"

As Schoultz remarks, the "disaggregation" of Latin America in two regions
was not only supported by the United States, but by South American countries as well.[66] However, there is more to this support than Schoultz's observation that the South American countries were indeed willing to "let the
United States dominate the Caribbean region."[67] As mentioned earlier, a
system of power politics had developed in South America that had little
relation to North America, so that South American countries were less concerned about Mexico, Central America, and the Caribbean than they were
about their own regional subsystem, whose core was then composed of Argentina, Brazil, and Chile. If proximity from the United States led nearby
countries to generally fear US power, geographic distance and regional power politics provided South American states with a different perspective.
Contrary to the general assumption, their policy towards the United States
was generally "subordinate" to their "South American policy," which means
that they tended to look to the United States mostly in terms of their own
regional situation.[68] The same was true for smaller South American countries, which were generally more concerned about their own neighbors. For
example, Arthur Whitaker shows that prominent Uruguayan statesman Luis
Alberto de Herrera saw US friendship as "exceptionally important to Uruguay because (and he recorded this comforting thought twice in three pages)
a mere hint from 'that great power' would be enough to 'call our neighbors to

order' and 'restrain Argentina's pretensions in the Plata estuary.'"[69] For Herrera, who was the Uruguayan envoy to the United States in the early 1900s, the United States "would continue to expand, but not south of Panama, and it would not intervene in South America 'in this century,' for 'no urgent interest calls the Colossus here.'" He therefore concluded that the Monroe Doctrine "is no threat to us."[70] Around the same period, an Argentinean author observed that "in the two opportunities that called for" the application of the Monroe Doctrine in the case of Argentina, the United States did not act: during the imbroglio with Great Britain involving the Falkland Islands, and during the Anglo-French blockade of Buenos Aires.[71] Hence, he deduced that South America was "out of reach of Monroeism" and could develop itself as an independent center of international politics.[72] As a matter of fact, one author remarked that by the early twentieth century there was in Argentina an "awareness of the fact that [Roosevelt] had distinguished between Central and South America," and when he visited Buenos Aires as an ex-president in 1913 "he received ovations wherever he went" and reinforced once again that "the Monroe Doctrine is not intended to apply to Argentina," implying that Argentina had the means to protect itself.[73]

No country in South America had a more favorable view of the Monroe Doctrine and of US policies at the time than Brazil, which, after Root's visit to the country on the occasion of the third Pan American Conference, changed the name of the building where the sessions were held to "Monroe Palace." Indeed, the interpretation of the Monroe Doctrine given by Brazil was very similar to the notion expressed by Theodore Roosevelt himself. One possible reason for this is that, contrary to Mexico, which had good reasons to be suspicious of US power, for Brazil, US interventions in the North American half of the Western Hemisphere not only did not threaten its national interests but apparently it "raised the matter of whether Brazil might be able to manifest greater influence, greater hegemony, on its borders as well."[74] This notion that Brazil would acknowledge the hegemony of the United States in North America while hoping that the United States would respect Brazilian pretensions of having its own sphere of influence in South America was the basis of what E. Bradford Burns famously called the "unwritten alliance" between the two countries.[75] Brazil, which had been the "only Latin American nation sympathetic to the United States during the Spanish-American War," gave its own "multilateral interpretation" of the Monroe Doctrine as a "responsibility of the hemisphere."[76] Thus, whereas other Latin American countries stressed the unilateralist aspect of the Monroe Doctrine, Brazil emphasized its "collectivist nature" instead.[77]

As such, the new Republic of Brazil saw the Roosevelt Corollary with very clear eyes. One example can be found in the following sentence: "If those countries do not know how to govern themselves, if they do not possess those elements necessary to avoid continual revolutions and civil wars that follow one another ceaselessly, they do not have a right to exist and ought to give up their place to a stronger, better organized, more progressive, and more virile nation."[78] What sounds like a statement coming from the mouth of Theodore Roosevelt himself is actually an excerpt of an interview from Rio Branco, the renowned Brazilian Foreign Minister, to an Argentinean journalist. In fact, in stark opposition to the majority of Latin American countries, Brazil was generally much less critical of US policies in Central America and the Caribbean. While this position can be "partly explained by the fact that Brazil had little political or economic contact with the area,"[79] it also reflected the Brazilian view of South America and North America as two distinct systems that operated with different logics. For example, when the United States intervened in Cuba in 1902, Brazil was largely sympathetic but when the United States seemed to support Bolivia in a dispute with Brazil in the same year, the Brazilian government reacted by ordering the closure of the Amazon River to foreign shipping, which irritated the United States.[80] Similarly, when Panama seceded from Colombia in 1903 with US backing, Brazilian official reactions "were generally favorable," and the public opinion was "indifferent."[81] In contrast, Rio Branco "reacted energetically" when the United States attempted to favor Peru in a territorial dispute with Brazil[82] and threatened to break diplomatic relations with the United States when the Taft administration, in consonance with the "Dollar Diplomacy" that was then underway, issued an ultimatum to Chile to pay reparations in an issue involving a private US company.[83] Commenting on the US interference in the case of the territorial dispute with Peru in a telegram to Joaquim Nabuco, the Brazilian ambassador in Washington, Rio Branco remarked that "I understand to be our right to operate in this part of the continent without asking for permission or to give explanations to this [US] government, as for the several proofs of our friendship we have the right to expect that they do not get involved to help our opponents on matters in which we are engaged."[84]

Moniz Bandeira interprets Rio Branco's notion of a special relationship with the United States as a view of "the transformation of the continent in a sort of condominium, where Brazil would have a free hand to exert its hegemony in South America" and therefore would "preserve its independence of action" in that regional subsystem, even if that occasionally meant confronting the United States.[85] For Joseph Smith, Rio Branco used a "strategy combining firmness with friendliness" in the cases of border disputes with its neighbors in order to keep the United States out of South American affairs.[86]

In the United States, for the most part, the view that Brazil could be responsible for enforcing the Monroe Doctrine in the southern part of the hemisphere seemed to find "a climate of opinion favorable to its claim of moral hegemony over South America."[87] One article in the newspaper *The Washington Star* about Root's tour to South America asserted that the purpose of the US government was "to arrange an informal—but none the less strong—alliance with Brazil, and to relegate to her the policy of the Monroe Doctrine in South America."[88] Two years later, the *New York Times* commented that "The two republics [United States and Brazil] are working out on the Northern and Southern Continents of America aims of substantially the same nature, by institutions and methods closely allied in principle."[89]

Another aspect of Rio Branco's strategy within the framework of an unwritten alliance with the United States was the organization of the South American space along with the other two regional powers, Chile and Argentina. If US statesmen treated the North American and the South American regional subsystems differently, this attitude was reciprocated by the South American leaders, particularly in Brazil. Like Roosevelt and Root, Rio Branco considered that Brazil, Argentina, and Chile had no reasons to be concerned about the Roosevelt Corollary, adding that "the Latin American republics that feel threatened by the US international police" should simply decide to "choose honest and provident governments."[90] Thus, in order to do its part in South America, Rio Branco conceived a pact that became known as the ABC, which would give Argentina, Brazil, and Chile the responsibility for guaranteeing the maintenance of peace and order in the southern half of the Americas. For Burns, the purpose of the ABC pact was to establish a "moral policing by the large South American republics" with a purpose similar to Roosevelt's in North America, that is, "the maintenance of stable and responsible governments."[91] One Brazilian scholar, who examined primary Brazilian sources during the initial formulation of the ABC treaty, concluded that Rio Branco's central objective was to establish a "shared hegemony" in South America among the signatories.[92] Nevertheless, traditional regional rivalries hindered the formalization of the ABC treaty as conceived by Rio Branco in 1909. A few years later, however, on May 25, 1915, Argentina, Brazil, and Chile finally signed a formal treaty with a more limited scope than the original Rio Branco's conception and the aim of facilitating the solution of controversies among the three South American countries. The treaty was initially received with concern by the Wilson administration, which thought it could "compete with the Pan American pact."[93] Although it was never ratified by the governments, the ABC Treaty represented an important diplomatic effort and consolidated the view of the three countries as the key to US policies in the Southern part of the hemisphere.

FROM ABC TO B

As for the relation between the ABC countries and the United States, some noteworthy changes occurred in the first decades of the twentieth century, which contributed to giving Brazil a central role in US foreign policy to-

wards South America. The first change was the decline of the relative power
of Chile, which had been one of the most powerful countries in the hemisphere. Two factors contributed to this decline: first, there were internal
disorders that eventually led to a civil war in 1891[94] and the growth of
relative power by the other two South American powers, Brazil and Argentina, which now struggled for continental predominance. The second change
that affected the relations between the United States and the three countries
that composed the core of the South American regional subsystem was the
foreign policy that was eventually followed by Argentina during and after the
First World War. Like Chile and Mexico, Argentina was neutral during the
conflict, but, after the war, the Argentinean government adopted a posture
that at times was frontally opposed to the United States. In fact, during the
war, the Argentinean attitude was "regarded as a fully conscious challenge to
United States leadership in the hemisphere."[95] This posture was generally
kept throughout the Second World War as well, and Argentina was one of the
few countries refusing to make an open commitment to the war effort, which
helped to undermine US attempts to implement the "Good Neighbor Policy"
in that part of the hemisphere. When Argentina later joined the Allies in
breaking relations with Germany and Japan—with the war already practically over—its actions justified more in terms of sympathies towards Great
Britain than because of any belief in hemispheric solidarity. In fact, the
"Argentina problem" was a constant preoccupation for US policy makers
when dealing with South America around the period of World War II.[96] In
his memoirs, Secretary of State Cordell Hull went as far as to call Argentina
a "bad neighbor."[97] This Argentinean approach to foreign policy would only
change in the late eighties, when "Argentina developed a bond with the
United States unlike it had ever had before."[98]

In a stark contrast, Brazil's policy was decidedly friendly and conciliatory
towards the United States. Rio Branco's conception of an unwritten alliance
with the United States—even if at times it was not reciprocated by the North
American country—was kept with impressive dependability. For example,
by the time of the sixth Pan American Conference in Havana in 1928, Brazil
sided with the United States against the criticism that the latter country was
receiving because of the constant interventions in the Caribbean.[99] Most
importantly, Brazil was the only Latin American country with effective participation in both world wars. During the First World War, it was the only
country in the hemisphere to cooperate militarily with the United States, and
in the Second World War it even contributed with an infantry division that
engaged in combat on the Italian front, again the only Latin American country to do so. One explanation for this Brazilian position, which was evident
since the years of Rio Branco, was that US friendship was seen as guaranteeing Brazilian security in face of potential hostility from its Spanish-speaking
neighbors. Therefore, whereas Argentina had, since the First World War,

"flirted with Pan Hispanic alternatives" of integration, Brazil remained steadily supportive of US hemispheric approach, thus becoming the "pivot" of US policies in South America.[100]

For the purposes of this book, the important thing to observe in regards both to the Argentinean and Brazilian foreign policies was that they represented two different approaches with similar ends—to achieve a privileged position in their own regional subsystem. In this sense, the two countries' relationships with the United States should be looked at beyond the mere bilateral framework, but especially within the context of their own regional subsystemic preoccupations. For example, when Argentinean officials—concerned about the military collaboration between the United States and Brazil—approached the United States during the Second World War, the Argentinean foreign minister asked his US counterpart if the United States would make a "gesture of genuine friendship" by sending armaments to Argentina in order "to restore Argentina to the position of equilibrium to which it is entitled with respect to other South American republics."[101] Because of Argentina's lack of collaboration in the war, this request was promptly rejected by the United States, but it again serves to show that the main concern of Argentina was its relation to other South American countries. Conversely, Brazil's collaboration with the United States was intimately related to its regional ambitions to become the major power in South America, which in fact happened with US help when Brazil received economic and military assistance during World War II, finally surpassing Argentina as the leading military power in the region after the war. Thus, Brazil's unwritten alliance with the United States helped to advance Brazilian foreign policy goals such as "the neutralization of Argentine designs of regional leadership."[102] Indeed, Brazil saw the support of US foreign policies in regions other than South America as the better strategy to guarantee the Brazilian position in its own regional subsystem. For example, when one of the most prominent Brazilian diplomats, Oswaldo Aranha, was ambassador in Washington, he commented to Under Secretary of State Summer Welles in 1935 that "nothing explains our support to the United States in its Central American and world issues, without a reciprocal attitude of support to Brazil in South America."[103]

CHAPTER CONCLUSION

The examination of the early interactions among the independent American states offers a good opportunity to detect the development of patterns of relationships between the United States and the different parts of Latin America that were functions both of geography and of the particular charac-

teristics of some South American states. These factors reciprocally reinforced each other, as both distance and internal characteristics allowed South
America to develop a system of power politics that was often just marginally
connected with the United States and which evidently was not the case for
Mexico, Central America, and the Caribbean. Nevertheless, in order to make
these patterns more evident, it is necessary to reinterpret the policy that was
definitely the most significant US initiative towards Latin America during
these early stages—the Monroe Doctrine. While the original declaration of
1823 did not make any differentiation between the two halves of the Americas, the actual practices after 1823 increasingly made evident the Caribbean
scope of the Monroe Doctrine. In fact, two of the most interventionist US
presidents of the twentieth century in Latin America, Theodore Roosevelt
and Woodrow Wilson, explicitly made a differentiation between South
America and the rest of Latin America. They were able to make this differentiation because South America could be organized around a core of states—
the ABC countries—that were relatively stable and therefore could be
counted on to stabilize their own neighborhood. This meant that the Roosevelt Corollary, commonly seen as a prime example of US unilateral and
imperial disposition in Latin America, actually had a multilateral component
that is often neglected by the literature.

No other country in South America was more enthusiastic about the
multilateral facet of the Roosevelt Corollary than Brazil. For the largest
South American country, Roosevelt's approach to the Monroe Doctrine was
a confirmation of Brazil's view of South America as its area of influence,
which was the basis for the Brazilian policy of an "unwritten alliance" with
the United States. This policy meant that while Brazil would support US
designs in the North American subsystem, composed by Mexico, Central
America, and the Caribbean, it would expect the United States to support
Brazilian aspirations in South America. This became increasingly evident as
Brazil was often the lonely Latin American supporter of US actions in the
North American subsystem, beginning with the Spanish-American War,
while it reacted strongly against a number of US attempts to meddle in affairs
that affected Brazilian interests in South America. The fact that Brazil was
the main supporter of the multilateral view of the Monroe Doctrine became
progressively more significant as Chile decreased in power by the end of the
nineteenth century and Argentina adopted a foreign policy that was often
confrontational towards the United States by the early decades of the twentieth century.

Both Argentinean and Brazilian foreign policies basically sought to establish predominance in South America, but while Argentina believed it could
achieve this by keeping the distance from the United States in order to show
autonomy and lead the Spanish-speaking countries, Brazil had a different
perspective in which it saw the approximation with the United States as an

important factor for its pretensions in South America. In other words, while one sought leadership through distancing from the United States, the other sought it through approximation. One author remarks that, in the end, both Brazil and Argentina had "the same independent policy" towards the United States, with the difference being "that Brazil publicly and privately at every turn assured the United States of its solidarity, whereas Argentina seemed to take pride in open confrontations with Washington."[104]

By reducing the benefits for the United States to change the subsystemic configuration in South America—or increasing the benefits for the maintenance of the status quo—the US-Brazilian unofficial entente contributed to hold the United States generally at arm's length in the southern part of the hemisphere. This relative absence meant that the foreign policies of South American states were primarily concerned with their own neighbors, and the relationship with the United States was subordinate to their regional subsystemic considerations. This assumption was and has been valid ever since, and it should be taken into consideration when analyzing both the foreign policy of the United States towards South America as well as the foreign policies of South American countries. Nevertheless, when the Cold War transformed the United States in a global superpower with concerns beyond the Western Hemisphere, it also greatly increased the incentives for the United States to become more actively involved in South America in order to stop the advance of Communism. Brazil would have to review the earlier "unwritten alliance" strategy in order to affect the new structures of costs and benefits for US intervention.

NOTES

1. Dexter Perkins, *The Monroe Doctrine, 1867-1907* (Gloucester, MA: P. Smith, 1966), 3.
2. Jan Knippers Black, *United States Penetration of Brazil* (Philadelphia: University of Pennsylvania Press, 1977), 8.
3. William Bloom, *Personal Identity, National Identity, and International Relations* (Cambridge UK: Cambridge University Press, 1990), 92.
4. See, for example: M. A. Heiss, "The Evolution of the Imperial Idea and U.S. National Identity," *Diplomatic History* 26, no. 4 (2002); Martin Sicker, *The Geopolitics of Security in the Americas: Hemispheric Denial from Monroe to Clinton* (Westport, CT: Praeger, 2002); Sidney Lens, *The Forging of the American Empire: From the Revolution to Vietnam, a History of U.S. Imperialism* (London; Sterling, VA: Pluto Press; Haymarket Books, 2003); Jay Sexton, *The Monroe Doctrine: Empire and Nation in Nineteenth-Century America* (New York: Hill and Wang, 2010).
5. Gretchen Murphy, *Hemispheric Imaginings: The Monroe Doctrine and Narratives of U.S. Empire*, New Americanists (Durham: Duke University Press, 2005), 6.
6. Mark T. Gilderhus, "The Monroe Doctrine: Meanings and Implications," *Presidential Studies Quarterly* 36, no. 1 (2006): 10.
7. Serge Ricard, "The Roosevelt Corollary," *Presidential Studies Quarterly* 36, no. 1 (2006): 17.

8.   Alexander Wendt, "Anarchy is what States Make of it: The Social Construction of Power Politics," *International Organization* 46, no. 2 (1992): 405.

9.   Alejandro Alvarez, *The Monroe Doctrine, its Importance in the International Life of the States of the New World* (New York: Oxford University Press, 1924), 10.

10.   Perkins, *The Monroe Doctrine, 1867-1907*: 160.

11.   Albert Bushnell Hart, *The Monroe Doctrine: An Interpretation* (Boston: Little, Brown, and Company, 1916), 92.

12.   Watt Stewart, "Argentina and the Monroe Doctrine, 1824-1828," *The Hispanic American Historical Review* 10, no. 1 (1930): 29; Alvarez, *The Monroe Doctrine*: 11; David Y. Thomas, *One Hundred Years of the Monroe Doctrine, 1823-1923* (New York: Macmillan, 1923), 45.

13.   Alvarez, *The Monroe Doctrine*: 10.

14.   Ibid.

15.   Ibid., 11.

16.   Stewart, "Argentina and the Monroe Doctrine, 1824-1828," 31.

17.   Alvarez, *The Monroe Doctrine*: 11.

18.   Hart, *The Monroe Doctrine*: 92.

19.   Ibid., 153.

20.   Lester D. Langley, *The Banana Wars: United States Intervention in the Caribbean, 1898-1934*, rev. ed. (Lexington, KY: University Press of Kentucky, 1985), 21.

21.   Hart, *The Monroe Doctrine*: 114.

22.   Ibid.

23.   George B. Young, "Intervention Under the Monroe Doctrine: The Olney Corollary," *Political Science Quarterly* 57, no. 2 (1942): 248.

24.   Hart, *The Monroe Doctrine*: 195.

25.   Ibid., 196. One critic commented that, by mentioning "geographical proximity," Olney "overlooked the fact that the largest cities in South America are geographically nearer to Spain and Portugal than to New York and New England": Hiram Bingham, *The Monroe Doctrine: An Obsolete Shibboleth* (New Haven: Yale University Press, 1913), 18.

26.   Hart, *The Monroe Doctrine*: 196.

27.   Ibid., 200.

28.   Ibid., 203.

29.   Ibid., 208.

30.   Ibid., 72.

31.   Alvarez, *The Monroe Doctrine*: 19-20.

32.   Thomas, *One Hundred Years of the Monroe Doctrine, 1823-1923*: 395.

33.   Connell-Smith, *The Inter-American System*: 10.

34.   Martin Sicker counts thirty-four US interventions in Central American and the Caribbean between 1890 and 1928. Sicker, *The Geopolitics of Security in the Americas*. In contrast, as G. Pope Atkins observes, the United States "never landed its troops in the Southern Cone." Atkins, *Latin America and the Caribbean in the International System*: 143.

35.   See, for example: Ernest R. May, *Imperial Democracy : The Emergence of America as a Great Power* (Chicago: Imprint Publications, 1991); Richard E. Welch, *Imperialists vs. Anti-Imperialists: The Debate over Expansionism in the 1890's* (Itasca, Ill: F. E. Peacock Publishers, 1972); David Healy, *US Expansionism: The Imperialist Urge in the 1890s* (Madison, WI: University of Wisconsin Press, 1970).

36.   Robert N. Burr, *By Reason or Force: Chile and the Balancing of Power in South America, 1830-1905* (Berkeley, CA: University of California Press, 1967), 3.

37.   See: Lilia Moritz Schwarcz, *As Barbas do Imperador: D. Pedro II, um Monarca nos Trópicos* (São Paulo, Brazil: Companhia das Letras, 1998).

38.   José Murilo de Carvalho, *A Monarquia Brasileira* (Rio de Janeiro: Ao Livro Tecnico, 1993), 65.

39.   Manuel de Oliveira Lima, *O Movimento da Independencia (1821-1822)*, 6. ed. (Rio de Janeiro: Topbooks, 1997), 451.

40.   Aluízio Napoleão, *Rio-Branco e as Relações entre o Brasil e os Estados Unidos* (Rio de Janeiro: Ministério das Relações Exteriores, 1947), 65.

41. *New York Times*, "Brazil's Old Ruler Dead," December 5, 1891.
42. ———, "Dom Pedro and Brazil," December 6, 1891.
43. Glen St John Barclay, *Struggle for a Continent: The Diplomatic History of South America, 1917-1945* (London: Sidgwick and Jackson, 1971), 27.
44. Robert N. Burr, "The Balance of Power in Nineteenth-Century South America: An Exploratory Essay," *The Hispanic American Historical Review* 35, no. 1 (1955); ———, *The Stillborn Panama Congress: Power Politics and Chilean-Colombian Relations During the War of the Pacific* (Berkeley, CA: University of California Press, 1962); ———, *By Reason or Force*.
45. ———, *The Stillborn Panama Congress*: 113.
46. Ibid., 17, 29.
47. ———, "The Balance of Power in Nineteenth-Century South America: An Exploratory Essay," 59.
48. ———, *By Reason or Force*: 62-63.
49. Hart, *The Monroe Doctrine*: 180.
50. Theodore Roosevelt, *An Autobiography* (New York: Charles Scribner's Sons, 1913), 502.
51. Ibid., 503.
52. Ibid.
53. Langley, *The Banana Wars*: 20.
54. Healy, *Drive to Hegemony*: 144.
55. Roosevelt, *An Autobiography*: 503.
56. Theodore Roosevelt and Alfred Henry Lewis, *A Compilation of the Messages and Speeches of Theodore Roosevelt, 1901-1905*, vol. 2 (New York: Bureau of National Literature and Art, 1906), 857-58.
57. Healy, *Drive to Hegemony*: 144.
58. Hart, *The Monroe Doctrine*: 322.
59. Marc D. Weidenmier and Kris James Mitchener, *Empire, Public Goods, and the Roosevelt Corollary* (Cambridge, Mass: National Bureau of Economic Research, 2004), 11.
60. Thomas, *One Hundred Years of the Monroe Doctrine, 1823-1923*: 376.
61. Lars Schoultz, *Beneath the United States: A History of U.S. policy toward Latin America* (Cambridge, MA: Harvard University Press, 1998), 204.
62. For recent views associating Theodore Roosevelt with the notion of a U.S. "empire" see James Bradley, *The Imperial Cruise: A Secret History of Empire and War* (New York, NY: Little, Brown and Co., 2009); Evan Thomas, *The War Lovers: Roosevelt, Lodge, Hearst, and the Rush to Empire, 1898* (New York: Little, Brown and Co., 2010).
63. Hart, *The Monroe doctrine*: 237.
64. Schoultz, *Beneath the United States*: 197.
65. Bingham, *The Monroe Doctrine: An Obsolete Shibboleth*: 55. As the title suggests, this pamphlet, published in 1914, presents a strong criticism of the Monroe Doctrine during the Roosevelt years. However, the author concentrates mainly on South American countries in order to demonstrate the inadequacy of the policy. At some point, Bingham suggests that a better policy for the United States would be joining forces with Argentina, Brazil, and Chile "in protecting the weaker parts of America against any imaginable aggressions by the European or Asiatic nations," (p. 96) which in fact seemed to dovetail Roosevelt's actual approach, as presented here.
66. Schoultz, *Beneath the United States*: 194.
67. Ibid.
68. Burr, *By Reason or Force*: 261.
69. Arthur Preston Whitaker, *The United States and the Southern Cone: Argentina, Chile, and Uruguay* (Cambridge, MA: Harvard University Press, 1976), 364.
70. Ibid.
71. Carlos Alfredo Becú, *El "A. B. C." y su Concepto Politico y Juridico* (Buenos Aires: Libreria "La Facultad" de J. Roldán, 1915), 14.
72. Ibid., 18.

73. McGann, *Argentina, the United States, and the Inter-American System, 1880-1914*: 303-04.

74. Frederick C. Turner, "Regional Hegemony and the Case of Brazil," *International Journal* 46, no. 3 (1991): 498.

75. E. Bradford Burns, *The Unwritten Alliance: Rio-Branco and Brazilian-American Relations* (New York: Columbia University Press, 1966).

76. Ibid., 61, 147.

77. Frederic William Ganzert, "The Baron do Rio-Branco, Joaquim Nabuco, and the Growth of Brazilian-American Friendship, 1900-1910," *The Hispanic American Historical Review* 22, no. 3 (1942): 446.

78. Burns, *The Unwritten Alliance*: 152.

79. Joseph Smith, *Unequal Giants: Diplomatic Relations between the United States and Brazil, 1889-1930*, Pitt Latin American series (Pittsburgh, PA: University of Pittsburgh Press, 1991), 97.

80. ———, *Brazil and the United States: Convergence and Divergence, The United States and the Americas* (Athens: University of Georgia Press, 2010), 52.

81. Burns, *The Unwritten Alliance*: 87.

82. Bandeira, "O Brasil como Potência Regional e a Importância Estratégica da América do Sul na sua Política Exterior," 6.

83. ———, *Brasil, Argentina e Estados Unidos—Conflito e Integração na América do Sul: da Tríplice Aliança ao Mercosul, 1870-2001* (Rio de Janeiro: Revan, 2003), 111.

84. ———, *Presença dos Estados Unidos no Brasil: Dois Séculos de História*, Coleção Retratos do Brasil v. 87 (Rio de Janeiro: Civilização Brasileira, 1973), 177.

85. Ibid., 169-70.

86. Smith, *Unequal Giants*: 41.

87. Burns, *The Unwritten Alliance*: 174.

88. Ibid., 163.

89. *New York Times*, "Brazilian Friendliness," January 16, 1908.

90. Bandeira, *Presença dos Estados Unidos no Brasil*: 169.

91. Burns, *The Unwritten Alliance*: 153.

92. Guilherme Frazão Conduru, "O Subsistema Americano, Rio Branco e o ABC," *Revista Brasileira de Política Internacional* 41(1998): 79.

93. Mark T. Gilderhus, *Pan American Visions: Woodrow Wilson in the Western Hemisphere, 1913-1921* (Tucson: University of Arizona Press, 1986), 55.

94. In this same year the relations between the United States and Chile deteriorated because an incident involving U.S. sailors on shore leave from the warship USS Baltimore being attacked by a mob of Chileans in the port of Valparaiso, in the event known as the "Baltimore Crisis." The US government strongly demanded an apology, which was later given by the new Chilean government.

95. Barclay, *Struggle for a Continent*: 15.

96. John Child, *Unequal Alliance: The Inter-American Military System, 1938-1979* (Boulder, CO: Westview Press, 1980), 81.

97. Cordell Hull and Andrew Henry Thomas Berding, *The Memoirs of Cordell Hull*, vol. 2 (New York: Macmillan Co., 1948), 1377.

98. Deborah L. Norden and Roberto Russell, *The United States and Argentina: Changing Relations in a Changing World*, Contemporary Inter-American Relations (New York: Routledge, 2002), 1.

99. Regarding the constant criticism that the United States received from South American countries because of its activities in the Caribbean the Assistant Secretary in charge of Latin America, Francis White, commented with Secretary of State Henry Stimson in 1930 that " as soon as South America realizes that our Central American policy is not a South American one, it will cease to care what we do in Central America. True, Central America may object, but I think they simply have got to lump it." Schoultz, *Beneath the United States: A History of U.S. Policy toward Latin America*: 289. Once again, this demonstrates how U.S. officials clearly separated South America from the rest of Latin America.

100. Gilderhus, *Pan American Visions*: 81.

101. Barclay, *Struggle for a Continent*: 166.

102.   W. Michael Weis, "Pan American Shift: Oswaldo Aranha and the Demise of the Brazilian-American Alliance," in *Beyond the Ideal: Pan Americanism in Inter-American Affairs*, ed. David Sheinin (Westport, CT: Greenwood Press, 2000), 135.

103.   Moniz Bandeira, *Relações Brasil-EUA no Contexto da Globalização*, 2. ed., vol. 2 (São Paulo: Senac, 1997), 34.

104.   Stanley E. Hilton, *Brazil and the Great Powers, 1930-1939: The Politics of Trade Rivalry*, Latin American monographs no. 38 (Austin: University of Texas Press, 1975), 227.

Chapter Five

The United States and the South American Subsystem During the Cold War: The Case of Chile

With the end of the Second World War and the reconfiguration of the international system, the United States would take on new priorities in its foreign policy and turn its eyes mostly toward Europe, which meant that its policies in the hemisphere tended to be generally relegated to a second plan. As Whitaker remarks, after the forties, the main substance of the "Western Hemisphere Idea" with its emphasis on the separation between the American and the European continents, was basically lost since, from the point of view of US policy makers, the world was now divided between communists and non-communists and Western Europe became a natural ally.[1] The kind of interests the United States had when it was a regional power would thus be reframed to fit the new international environment in which it occupied a key position as a global power.

The ideological aspect of the Cold War bipolar system was particularly important in US relations with Latin Americans countries, which meant that the central goal of US foreign policy during the Cold War—to contain the spread of communism—would strongly characterize the hemispheric approach of the United States. Even though the United States had essentially the same policy towards the whole of Latin America, the argument put forward by this book is that the regional subsystemic perspective allows the analyst to uncover distinct regional dynamics of a policy that was global in character. The objective of this chapter is to show that despite having now both the capabilities and the interest to shape new patterns of relationships in the hemisphere that would lead to a regional system change, regional subsystemic dynamics contributed to keep the stability of the South American subsystem. In other words, even during the Cold War, a case can be made that if the United States could be characterized as a global empire, in the South American subsystem it remained a relatively absent one, which evidently does not mean that it was not a relevant player.[2]

Obviously, within the North American subsystem, the United States was anything but absent, despite often-heard claims of episodes of "neglect."[3] US troops invaded the Dominican Republic in 1965, Grenada in 1983, and Panama in 1989, and although it did not send troops, the United States was actively involved in overt and covert operations to topple governments—including equipping and training armed groups—in Guatemala in 1958, in Cuba in 1961, and in Nicaragua in the 1980s. These interventions—all of them north of the Panama Canal—were carried out under different administrations, when both Republican and Democrat presidents occupied the White House. In fact, the period of the Cold War provides perhaps the clearest evidence of the existence of two different regional subsystems in the Americas, but typical analyses based on the notion of Latin America as a homogeneous entity in international politics coupled with a perspective that neglects regional subsystemic pressures often overlook this reality. To help to make their case, these analysts commonly present as evidence of a pattern of relationships throughout Latin America the case of the military coup that overthrew the Salvador Allende government in Chile, in 1973.

This chapter puts the military coup in Chile in a broader perspective by demonstrating that both before as well as after the election of Allende, the Brazilian military government was at least as concerned as the United States about the possibility of governments perceived as associated with communism coming to power in South America. The chapter begins by looking into the examples of Bolivia and Uruguay, both of which precede the overthrow of Allende, and concludes by examining the case of Suriname, which happened about a decade after. In all these instances, the Brazilian military government actively sought to influence the political outcome, and at least once this meant developing plans for overt military intervention. In discussing these cases, this section seeks to demonstrate the existence of a pattern of interaction in which the Chilean case is an additional example.

The bulk of the chapter is focused on the US participation in the overthrow of the Chilean government in 1973 in order to demonstrate that both the Johnson and the Nixon administrations were greatly concerned about the Chilean situation, and yet they stopped short of pursuing truly imperial policies that would have had a better chance to decisively affect the outcome of events. The chapter shows that the bulk of US actions was concentrated before Allende was elected in 1970 and were aimed toward preventing him from taking office. Allende's eventual ascension to the presidency in Chile is thus a clear illustration of the limitations of the kind of policies the United States pursued. Additionally, this chapter asserts that while there is no clear evidence of US direct involvement in the coup that eventually overthrew Allende, there are a number of indications pointing towards a Brazilian connection, which is little explored by the literature because of the lack of available documentation, especially when compared to the abundance of documents from the US side. It is demonstrated that Brazil's military regime's involvement in Chile can be largely understood as an extension of its overall policy in South America, both before and after 1973, which permitted the United States to limit its involvement in the region. In other words, Brazil's interventionist disposition, which could be termed as a sort of "regional imperialism," increased the benefits of subsystemic stability for the United States. The chapter claims that Brazil's position was not subordinated to US policies, but rather that its interests coincided with those of the United States. To reinforce this point, the role of the United States in the 1964 military coup in Brazil is put in perspective.

BUILDING A NARRATIVE

The case of the military coup that overthrew the Salvador Allende government in Chile fits perfectly the common narrative of an American (or Latin American) regional subsystem in which US hegemony is exercised rather homogeneously in what is, after all, typically considered to be its "backyard." For example, in his otherwise insightful work on regions, Peter Katzenstein argues that, contrary to Asia and Europe, there are no regional powers in the American continent because the "overwhelming presence of the United States dwarfs all other states and has prevented the emergence of states both supportive of American purpose and power and central to the region's political affairs."[4] The "region" that Katzenstein has in mind is a coherent entity composed of Latin America plus Canada, both uniformly subjected to US power, since they would be "close to the center of the American imperium."[5] In the case of Latin America, this overwhelming US presence would yield a particular kind of regionalism based on "informal rule, patron-client relations, coercive diplomacy, and military interventions."[6] As evidence of this pattern of relationship, Katzenstein mentions US interventions in Central America together with the "deep U.S. involvement in the overthrow of the Salvador Allende government in Chile" as being both equally strong examples of "the behavior of a traditional imperial power."[7] Similarly, David Mares mentions that, contrary to Cuba, "Guatemala (1954) and Chile (1973) were unable to break away from U.S. dominance."[8] Likewise, Cole Blasier puts US activities in Chile together with Guatemala, Cuba, and the Dominican Republic under the same category of US "interference" in Latin America.[9] This narrative still remains strong. A recent book on United

States relations with Latin America argues that the United States "has shaped Latin American history, intervening at key moments (Guatemala 1954; Chile 1973; Nicaragua 1979; El Salvador 1979-82)."[10]

The examples above suggest that, by bundling together US actions toward Chile with interventions elsewhere in Latin America, an impression of cohesiveness is created. The problem with this approach is that it not only neglects fundamental differences between the US participation in the overthrow of Salvador Allende in Chile and, for example, the overthrown of Jacobo Arbenz in Guatemala, but also overlooks the important role played by external forces other than the United States in the South American case. One reason for these analytical simplifications may be the use of approaches that are excessively US-centered, coupled with the lack of a theoretical framework able to offer explanations beyond the domestic-system/international-system dichotomy. This book maintains that the regional subsystemic perspective can fill this gap and provide a distinctive narrative for the Chilean case in particular, and for South America in general. This alternative narrative would relativize the role of the United States by stressing regional subsystemic pressures.

Obviously, in the Cold War environment of the time, successive US administrations were concerned about the situation in Chile, Brazil, and elsewhere in South America where forces that were perceived as being sympathetic to communism could gain influence. This concern was indeed translated into policies that actively sought to prevent these forces from coming to power, or to negatively affect them subsequently. To expect the United States to stay on the sidelines during the Cold War whenever there was a perception of increased Soviet influence in Latin America would be unrealistic. However, putting unilateral armed interventions in Central America and the Caribbean under the same category of the kind of actions the United States undertook in South America is confounding an imperial policy with a great power policy. The objectives of the United States were the same in all Latin America, as they were in the rest of the world during the Cold War: to contain the spread of communism. Nevertheless, it can be argued that the outcome of these policies varied according to the particular configuration of distinct regional subsystems. In the North American subsystem, both during and before the Cold War, the United States often acted as an empire, sending its own troops or training and equipping mercenary armies in order to pursue its objectives. In the South American subsystem the same measures were not taken—not necessarily because the US could not or did not want to, but mainly because, as will be shown below, it did not need to. Treating Latin America as a coherent regional subsystem where US influence is exercised homogenously blurs this distinction and oversimplifies the analysis with detrimental consequences for policy makers and academics alike.

THE BRAZILIAN MILITARY COUP AND US INFLUENCE

Because the role of the Brazilian military government is central for the argument developed in this chapter, it is necessary first to address the extent of US influence in the Brazilian case. As in the case of Chile, the correlation between the US foreign policy establishment's wishes and the actual unfolding of events is often interpreted as evidence of a causal relationship. For example, Jan Black saw US influence as a "significant contributing factor" to the 1964 military coup in Brazil[11] and interpreted this and the subsequent coups in South America as evidence of the "the consolidation of U.S. hegemony, or dominance, over the furthermost reaches of the South American continent."[12] In a study of US interventions after World War II, William Blum contends that in the case of the military coup in Brazil, the "American Embassy had been intimately involved."[13] In his well-known *CIA Diary*, former CIA officer Phillip Agee wrote from Uruguay in an entry one day after the Brazilian coup that the overthrow of the civilian regime was "without doubt largely due to careful planning and consistent propaganda campaigns dating at least back to the 1962 election operation," when the US government financed opposition candidates in Brazil.[14] Agee reaches this post-factum conclusion even though there is barely any mention of CIA activities in Brazil earlier in his diary, the first entry of which goes back to 1956. Therefore, as in the case of Chile, the political outcome in Brazil in 1964 is also commonly mentioned as evidence of a uniform dominance of the United States over Latin America, even though there seems to be an acknowledgment that the extend of US involvement in the Brazilian case was far less significant than in the Chilean coup of 1973.

Basically, two kinds of evidence are frequently presented to make the case for US influence on the Brazilian military takeover of 1964. The first and most recent, which was uncovered several years after the coup, is the fact that the United States government had prepared a "contingency plan" to intervene in Brazil and support the plotters in the case of a prolonged civil war. The second relates to the period before the coup, when the United States on one hand supported opposition candidates and anti-communist forces, and on the other made efforts to indoctrinate the Brazilian military. As for the first evidence, the support is usually offered through quotes from US officials and the so called "Operation Brother Sam," which consisted of a plan for providing equipment and especially petroleum to the coup plotters. In fact, official documents declassified in 2004 show President Lyndon Johnson saying over the phone that "we ought to take every step that we can, be prepared to do everything that we need" to support the overthrow of Brazil's civilian government. These documents also show that arrangements were made for the shipment of weapons, ammunition, and oil to Brazil.[15] Although then US ambassador to Brazil Lincoln Gordon later remarked that the coup plotters "knew nothing whatever about the 'Brother Sam' task force," other analysts dispute this information. [16] One recent study on the "Operation Brother Sam" by the Brazilian historian Carlos Fico, who examined a number of official US and Brazilian declassified documents, maintains that Brazilians were, in fact, aware of the operation. [17] Indeed, one of the most active coup plotters stated in an interview that he had actually asked the US military attaché Vernon Walters if the United States could supply petroleum in case the coup led to a prolonged fight, which in turn would have led to the "Operation Brother Sam." [18] It should be noted that this passage is the only reference made to US participation in the long interview he gave to the book editors. In fact, it is hard to find any mention of decisive US participation or influence in the memoirs published by the Brazilian officers who participated in the coup.

In any case, the best conclusion that can be reached by analyzing the currently available documentation is that it demonstrates an "interventionist disposition" of the United States. [19] Johnson's statement on being "prepared to do everything we need to do" was made on March 31, 1964, and Brazil already had a military government on the next day without a civil war or significant disorder. Likewise, preparations for "Operation Brother Sam" began in late March and, as Gordon points out, "was still ten days' sailing time away when Goulart abandoned the presidency." [20] The fact of the matter is that all US planning proved unnecessary, as the coup went forth without any help from the United States. Indeed, it is clear that "Brazil's military leaders resolved to act, with or without Washington's approbation." [21] As Phyllis Parker remarked, [a]ll planned U.S. support was of a marginal nature" and the United States was not involved in the coup "because there was no need to be." [22] When the Johnson administration decided it should help the coup to come about, it was already too late. Although occasionally underplaying the extent of US knowledge about the coup, the evidence to date seems to corroborate Ambassador Gordon's confirmation: "that we welcomed the overthrown of Goulart is well known. But there was no American participation in his removal by military force." [23] What would have happened had the fight been prolonged and a civil war ensued is a matter for speculation, but the obvious fact is that actual intervention should not be confused with potential or desired intervention. "Operation Brother Sam" is a clear example of US willingness, interest, and capability to intervene in South America. Its outcome is a clear example of its needlessness.

The second argument presented for making the case for US influence on the 1964 military coup in Brazil asserts that the United States was actually not too late because it had helped to create the conditions for the coup through earlier covert operations designed to strengthen anti-communist forces and through its supposed indoctrination of Brazilian military officers. This is the line with the argument made by Agee immediately after the coup, when he attributed it to US "careful planning and consistent propaganda campaigns."[24] Likewise, Jan Black and Ruth Leacock mention US assistance to opposition candidates in the Brazilian 1962 elections as having played a central role.[25] Leacock points out that the United States funded "some of the anticommunist literature" in Brazil and provided an opposition candidate for governor in the northeast state of Pernambuco with "anticommunist films, comic books, and pamphlets."[26] The author regards such activities as examples of "extensive American interference."[27] Nevertheless, the results of aforesaid US support were virtually fruitless since the US-funded opposition gubernatorial candidate mentioned by Leacock lost the election to an openly pro-communist candidate and the general outcome of US support to the opposition was extraordinarily unimpressive as it did little to alter the balance of political forces prevailing before the 1962 election. In fact, in that election, leftist forces gained more space in the Brazilian political landscape.[28] Given these results, Moniz Bandeira concludes that the monies spent to influence Brazilian elections "were not good for the CIA."[29] As Robert Wesson notices, "[t]he concrete actions taken [by the United States] seem to have been trivial in their effects."[30]

If the support for opposition candidates was anything but effective, on the other hand there is the argument that at least the United States was successful in indoctrinating the Brazilian military into anti-communist ideology and teaching them the intricacies of counterinsurgency tactics. Here, the role of the Brazilian ESG—*Escola Superior de Guerra* (commonly translated to English as Superior School of War) is regarded as central, since many of the coup plotters attended that institution, which was inspired by the National War College in the United States. For Leacock, "under American guidance," the ESG "stressed anticommunism and the American view of the Cold War."[31] Black also emphasizes the US influence in that institute and thus over the coup plotters and concludes that "support of, association with, and training by the U.S. military reinforced the anti-democratic biases of the Brazilian military elite."[32] A more careful examination would demonstrate that such allegations seem exaggerated at best. Besides the fact that Black presents no evidence that association with the US military would supposedly reinforce the "anti-democratic biases of the Brazilian military elite," which sounds somewhat counterintuitive, a more important question is whether the Brazilian military needed to be educated by the United States as to the alleged perils of communism. After all, the army in Brazil was concerned about communism even before the Cold War. One Brazilian diplomat argues that anticommunism in the Brazilian army dates back at least to 1935, when military officials linked to the Brazilian Communist Party staged a revolt in order to overthrow the president and establish a communist government.[33] This episode led to the persecution of individuals associated with communism in Brazil, and was used as a justification for giving dictatorial powers to

President Getulio Vargas in 1937. By 1939, the Chief of Staff of the Brazilian army exteriorized concerns with the "Bolshevik menace."[34] Interestingly enough, in view of what later happened in the United States in the 1950s, US ambassador to Brazil Adolf Berle Jr. asked in 1945 for an end to the persecution of communists in Brazil.[35] Against the advice of US Secretary of State George Marshall, Brazil was the first country in the western world to break relations with Moscow, and a Brazilian general is reported to have criticized the Truman administration for its "excessive tolerance" of communism.[36] When Truman visited Brazil, it was Brazilian President Dutra who asked him to put anti-communism at the top of his agenda.[37] By 1951, the Brazilian army had produced a report entitled "Communism in Brazil" in which it expressed special worries about communist infiltration in the army.[38] Hence, when the United States became concerned with the advancement of communism in Latin America in the early 1960s, after the Cuban Revolution, the Brazilian generals needed no indoctrination. In fact, the Brazilian army's annual report in 1961 already expressed concern with Cuba and its "subversive ideas" as well as with communist activities in Brazil.[39] As had been the case with Truman years earlier, when the Nixon administration developed the policy of détente, some in the Brazilian military criticized the US President for being too "soft" on communism.[40]

However, it could be argued that even if there was no need to teach anti-communism to the Brazilian army, "American guidance" and "training," particularly through the ESG, would constitute central factors in the development of the counterinsurgency strategy that was employed to fight domestic subversion. Here again, closer examination of domestic dynamics put these allegations in perspective. Brazilian General Cordeiro de Farias, who was responsible for the organization of the ESG during its initial years—in the late 1940s, it should be noted—recounts the episode when the US government sent three military officers to provide advising for the establishment of the school, which was, after all, inspired by the National War College. According to Farias, the US officers

> came in with the statute of the National War College and tried to make us adopt it without restrictions, claiming that what had worked in the United States would work for Brazil. I fought against them but I could not convince them. I defended the proposition that the ESG, as a center of studies, could not be disconnected from our national concerns.[41]

General Farias concludes that after he took the US officers on a trip throughout Brazil, they were finally convinced of the need to adapt the school to the particularities of the country. In fact, as Alfred Stepan remarks, the Brazilian institution had two fundamental differences in relation to its US model. The first was that, because of Brazil's condition as a developing country, "the question of a strong armed force could not be separated from the question of economic development" and therefore there was the need to put greater "emphasis on internal aspects of development and security."[42] It should be noted that the United States would only incorporate the notion of development in the concept of security during the 1960s. Hence, when the Kennedy administration came up with the Alliance for Progress linking instability with poverty, it was not launching a revolutionary new idea but responding to a demand that existed previously. The second difference between the National War College and the *Escola Superior de Guerra* relates to the first. Because of the central focus on development, in contrast to the largely military-oriented National War College, civilian participation would be a key aspect in the Brazilian institution.[43]

As for US training of Brazilian officers in counterinsurgency strategies, this is also an argument that loses some of its appeal when the researcher is curious enough to investigate its actual validity. When one examines the origins of the so called "counterrevolutionary theory," the original contributions of the French become evident. While in the United States the notion of "counterinsurgency" acquired relevance only with the war in Vietnam, the French, who had already fought and been defeated in Indochina, had by then developed the notion of *"guerre révolutionnaire,"* and were applying it in the Algerian war during the 1950s.[44] It is revealing that when US Lieutenant-Colonel Donn A. Starry drew attention in 1967 to the fact that the United States had only been giving serious consideration to the problem of "wars of liberation" since 1961, he entitled his article as *"La Guerre Révolutionnaire."*[45] In comparison to the French approach, John Shy and Thomas Collier regard the US counterinsurgency strategy developed during the Vietnam War as "shallow" with an inadequate "almost purely military approach."[46] Armand Mattelart remarks that although the US military had to deal with counterinsurgency strategies before, it had not been translated into a formal doctrine, since the "strategic consciousness" in the United States "was totally absorbed in deterrence and the debate between partisans of 'massive retaliation' and those who favored 'flexible response' . . . There was a prevailing belief in technological determinism, conductive to viewing the future from the perspective of nuclear apocalypse."[47]

This is the basic reason why the Brazilian army did not look for inspiration in the US strategy in Vietnam, which did not fit the domestic reality in Brazil, but to the French experience in Algeria. The libraries of the Brazilian army were indeed filled with French literature on the Algerian War.[48] Commenting on the development of counterinsurgency strategies in ESG, a Brazilian general singles out the "French military literature" as a decisive influence.[49] Certainly, Brazilians generals had no problems reading in French, as many of them attended schools in France, including the first president of the military regime, Castelo Branco. The inauguration speech of General Gois

Monteiro as Chief of Staff of the Brazilian army in 1937 is permeated with quotes from French Generals, all in the original French.[50] A Brazilian military officer commented that "the boasted American influence" in the doctrines adopted by the Brazilian army was "practically null" and adds that "the future historian, in a serene examination of this episode, will certainly find a certain French influence."[51]

The French influence was not restricted only to Brazil. Ernesto López demonstrates that the biggest foreign influence in the development of the Argentinean National Security Doctrine also came from France.[52] Several translations to Spanish from books written by French generals were published in Buenos Aires,[53] and the French Colonel Patrice de Naurois wrote several articles for the magazine of the Argentinean *Escuela Superior de Guerra*.[54] Thus, the problem of revolutionary war and the strategies to fight it were in the minds of Brazilian as well as Argentinean militaries before the Kennedy administration shaped its counterinsurgency doctrine in the 1960s. While López points out that by 1958 the Argentinean military was already in the final stages of the development of its counterrevolutionary doctrine,[55] Stepan observes that "[e]ven before the emphasis in the cold war shifted in the United States from atomic to revolutionary warfare, the ESG became the center of ideological thought concerning counterrevolutionary strategy in Brazil."[56]

Although the CIA collaborated with Brazilian intelligence services, there is no evidence of any US official who participated in torture sessions in Brazil. Indeed, the most noteworthy case of a relationship between foreign torturers and the Brazilian dictatorship was during 1973 when the French government sent to Brazil General Paul Aussaresses, a prominent leader of the repression and torture operations in Algeria.[57] By that year, the School of the Americas, regarded by many as a center for indoctrination of Latin American military coup plotters,[58] had received about 30,000 students, with just a little over 300 from Brazil.[59] Obviously, as Stepan observes, "the United States, as the major anti-Communist country, was viewed as a natural ally,"[60] and Brazil sought as much collaboration as it could—and the United States was willing to provide it, particularly after the Cuban Revolution. This was true only to the extent that it was understood by the Brazilian military government to serve Brazilian interests—when the Carter administration in 1977 required a report on human rights performance by the recipients of military assistance, the Brazilian government interpreted it as constituting interference in its domestic affairs, and it simply revoked a military assistance agreement that it had had with the United States since 1952, virtually ending any formal military collaboration between the two countries.[61] Brazil and United States would only sign another military agreement in 2010.[62]

BRAZIL'S "REGIONAL IMPERIALISM" IN THE COLD WAR

Those who neglect the regional subsystemic perspective in favor of an international systemic perspective tend to interpret every episode of the Cold War from the point of view of Washington or Moscow. The reality is that the advancement of communism in the world—or what was perceived as such—threatened the interests of the United States as a global power, but the advancement of communism in South America—but not elsewhere in Latin America—also threatened the interests of Brazil as a regional power, and this had been true even before the inauguration of the military regime in 1964. Even President Janio Quadros, whose resignation in 1961 originated the crises that led to the overthrow of his vice-president Joao Goulart in 1964, is described as being "viscerally anticommunist."[63] In 1961, Quadros considered the possibility of annexing Guyana because of what he saw as communist infiltration in that country.[64] The fact that Quadros famously received Che Guevara in Brazil and bestowed a medal of honor on him has equivocally been interpreted as a signal of sympathy for communism by those who tend to reason in binary terms, thus failing to understand Brazilian political intricacies. These and other symbolic gestures became part of Quadros' foreign policy, which was termed "independent" and it was seen in many ways an alibi for his "reactionary" domestic policy.[65] In summary, understanding the role of Brazil in the South American subsystem during the Cold War begins by deconstructing the myth that anticommunism was exclusively a US cause that was somehow incorporated by its "client" states through diligent work from Washington.

Because the typical analyses of the relationship between the United States and South America neglect the fact that—for economic, security, and political reasons—the advancement of governments that were seen as identifying with communism in South America were perceived as a threat to Brazilian interests, the existence of overlapping interests is confounded with mere subordination. This interpretation is undoubtedly reinforced by the fact that the majority of the declassified documents available for research comes from US sources, since many of the Brazilian and South American sources remain classified or are simply unavailable because, for example, not many South American presidents kept records of their conversations. Without this discernment between subordination and overlapping interests, it becomes difficult to understand how regional dynamics influenced the extent of US involvement in South America, in comparison to elsewhere in Latin America and other parts of the world, beyond the argument that it was somehow a matter of lack of interest or neglect. If there is anything that the official declassified documents and the sheer amount of money spent in trying to influence the political landscape in South America show is that lack of interest is a weak explanation. The United States did try to help a coup succeed in Brazil and, as will be shown below, actively planned a coup in Chile, but the fact was that the planning was never translated into decisive action, that is, the kind of action that the United States as a global superpower could easily have taken, as it did so many times in Central America, the Caribbean, and other parts of the world during the Cold War. The United States did send money and equipment, provided training, moral support, and helped anti-communist forces throughout South America in order to defend its interests, but it was just supplying an existent demand and never went beyond that relatively modest role of supplier, which is a far cry from an imperial policy, particularly in its own "backyard." This chapter's argument is that one reason for this imperial absence during the Cold War is that the United States did not need to adopt a costly imperial policy in South America because its major interests coincided with those of Brazil, a country which was willing to actively prevent the emergence of governments associated with communism in the South American subsystem.

The reasons for this Brazilian willingness can be found in a combination of rapid economic growth with the authoritarian character of the military regime. According to Moniz Bandeira, this combination allowed Brazil to take an "offensive, imperialist" posture in South America.[66] Similarly, Robert Wesson notices that Brazilian "economic muscle" in the seventies "permitted Brazil to indulge in a little imperialism of its own."[67] Indeed, the Brazilian military regime was heavily influenced by a geopolitical view that stressed the role of Brazil in South America. The role of the United States was described by the most prominent geopolitical theorist of the Brazilian military regime as being part of a *"barganha leal"* or "fair bargain" with Brazil: Brazil would support the United States in the global East-West conflict and the United States would support Brazil to fulfill its own "manifest destiny" in South America.[68] This geopolitical perspective, not very different from the old idea of an "unwritten alliance," led to the development of the notion of "ideological frontiers" and the "encirclement theory." Together, these conceptions meant that the advancement of communist regimes in South America would isolate Brazil, and thus the challenge should be to "reverse the wave of international subversion" on its borders.[69] In 1971 Bolivia became the first target, after leftist General Juan Jose Torres took power in 1970, the same year Salvador Allende became president in Chile and the Brazilian consul in Uruguay was kidnapped by the *Tupamaros*, a Marxist guerrilla organization that operated in that country.

It is well known that the coup that toppled Torres in Bolivia counted with "logistical, political, and ideological support from Brazil, both in the planning stage as well as in the process of execution."[70] Brazil helped the coup plotting with "money, arms, aircrafts, and even mercenaries" as well as by providing "open logistical support" for the coup itself.[71] Brazilian airplanes landed in Bolivian airports to bring equipment without concern of concealing their identification. As James Dunkerley observes, "Brazil's intervention was scarcely discreet."[72] In case the coup failed, the Brazilian government is thought to have considered the possibility of direct military intervention.[73] The Bolivian coup was also supported by the United States and, to a lesser degree, by the Argentine military government.[74] The Bolivian Minister of Interior during the Torres government refers to Argentina and Brazil as the "two proimperialist partners," but focuses mostly on the US and Brazilian participation, which he defines as a "dark organization of the political police in Brazil and the CIA."[75] A few days after the coup, the Brazilian government granted Bolivia ten million dollars in credit and an average of forty-six million for the following years.[76] To Brazil, the successful coup in Bolivia represented "the end of its regional isolation" and led to a "reverse Domino Theory" in South America—Uruguay and Chile would come next.[77]

In Uruguay, US and Brazilian concerns with the guerilla groups in that country became more salient after the head of the US Public Safety program in Uruguay, Dan Mitrione, and the Brazilian Consul Aloisio Gomide were kidnapped by the *Tupamaros* in the early 1970s. While Gomide was released after seven months, Mitrione was executed after the US and Uruguayan government refused to comply with the guerillas' demands. Therefore, when the leftist coalition *Frente Amplio* gained ground in the 1971 elections, both countries were apprehensive, especially in the view of the victory of the *Unidad Popular* in Chile a year earlier. For the United States a victory of the *Frente Amplio* would represent a dangerous trend in South America, while for Brazil it would confirm the view of the "encirclement theory," in addition to representing more immediate threats of subversion along its strategic southern border. US documents declassified in 2002 make clear the concern of US officials with the situation in Uruguay, but do not show any direct involvement or plans to intervene in that country in order to avoid a victory of the *Frente Amplio*. One of the documents is a secret telegram of the State Department to US embassies in Brazil and Argentina asking for their likely reaction to a strong showing of the *Frente Amplio* and mentioning speculations of the Latin American press about the "possible Brazilian plan for action in Uruguay to frustrate the *Frente* from taking over, including use of armed force."[78] Another relevant document is a "Preliminary Analysis and Strategy Paper" on Uruguay recommending US action in five areas: psychological, economic assistance, political, labor, and security. However, this paper was explicitly written for the subsequent 1972-1976 period, "based on the premise that the *Frente Amplio* will not win the 1971 elections." The major concern of the paper was how the United States should proceed to work with the new government and to "increase support for the democratic political parties in Uruguay and lessen the threat of a political takeover by the *Frente*." In the security area, the analysis suggested that it would be "especially desirable that such neighboring countries as Argentina and Brazil collaborate effectively with the Uruguayan security forces and where possible we should encourage such cooperation."[79]

The US documents released to date thus show a combination of concern with the situation in Uruguay, and hope that Brazil, or perhaps Argentina, would ultimately take action. These US concerns are in line with the expectation of this chapter that the role played by Brazil allowed the United States to limit its involvement in South America during the Cold War. In fact, the most notorious document released on this issue shows President Nixon at a meeting with British Prime Minister Edward Heath commenting that "[t]he Brazilians helped rig the Uruguayan election," in a reference to the supposed fraud that would have happened in the 1971 election, won by the incumbent party.[80] The Brazilian government was clearly satisfied with the outcome of the elections and the then recently elected president of Uruguay immediately declared that he had "ideological affinities" with Brazil.[81]

What the Nixon administration did not know, besides speculations in the South American press, was that the Brazilian army had in place a plan to invade Uruguay in case the *Frente Amplio* won the elections. This plan was called "Operação Trinta Horas" ("Operation Thirty Hours") in reference to the time frame estimated by the Brazilian military to take over the country.[82] As noted above, the unavailability of declassified documentation pertaining to the Brazilian military period complicates the task of the investigator. Therefore, the evidence must generally be sought in testimonies by people involved in the operation or through researchers who had access to them.[83] Perhaps the most explicit testimony from someone directly involved in the plans to invade Uruguay came from Brazilian Colonel Dickson Grael, who was a supporter of the 1964 coup but later became disillusioned with the course of the military regime. Grael participated in the formulation of the plans to invade Uruguay and he makes clear how closely the Brazilian army was from actually intervening. He further claims that Brazilian military units were mobilized and put on alert, just waiting for the result of the Uruguayan elections "to execute the plan."[84] It is noteworthy that while Brazil explicitly took into consideration the Argentinean reaction to a possible invasion of Uruguay, it apparently made no mention of the United States' reaction.[85] Indeed, a report from the State Department expressed that the major concern for the United States in relation to the situation in Uruguay "may well not be the outcome of Uruguayan election" but the deterioration of relations between Brazil and Argentina or a major change in the regional balance of power in the case of a unilateral action from any of them in Uruguayan affairs.[86]

CHILE AND THE "BRAZILIAN CONNECTION"

It is within the context exposed above that Brazilian attitudes toward Chile should be understood. Brazil's clear disposition to intervene in Uruguay and Bolivia denoted a low level of tolerance for regimes that were identified with communism, both for reasons of ideological incompatibility as well as because of a spillover of the domestic repressive apparatus. The coincidence in goals with those expressed by US foreign policy during the Cold War meant this Brazilian "regional imperialism" allowed the United States to exert what one could call a sort of "soft imperialism" in South America.[87] Although it is commonly ignored in many studies, the United States was not the only country in the hemisphere concerned with Allende's ascension to power in Chile, and Brazilian involvement may provide an important part of the explanation when it comes to assessing the role of foreign influences in the 1973 coup. Here again, the problem of insufficient records on the Brazilian side contrasted with abundant documentation on the US side may create the impression of a monologue when there may be in fact more voices present. While circumstantial evidence already strongly suggested a "Brazilian connection" in the military coup that overthrew Allende,[88] documents declassified in 2009 present the clearest evidence to date corroborating these suspicions. But before analyzing these documents, a brief overview of US actions in Chile is needed.

Undoubtedly, the best account of US involvement in Chile up until the 1973 coup is the 1975 US Senate "Staff Report of the Select Committee to Study Governmental Operations with Respect to Intelligence Activities," also known as the "Church Report" since it was chaired by Senator Franck Church of Idaho.[89] Although it was produced only two years after the fall of Allende, no new information since then has significantly changed the assessments of the Church Report, which remains as the main source of information for the majority of the analyses of US activities in Chile. A more recent report by the CIA produced in 2000, known as the "Hinchey Report," after US Congressman Maurice Hinchey of New York, basically corroborates and complements the findings of the 1975 Senate report, adding little new information that would drastically transform what is currently known about the actual extent of US involvement in Chile in the events leading to the downfall of Allende.[90] These two reports offer a detailed and comprehensive account of US activities in Chile and will thus be used as the basic sources for the analysis that follows.

There are at least two aspects of the US actions in Chile that deserve careful consideration in order to produce an accurate analysis. The first is the fact that the overwhelming majority of the money spent in covert action in Chile—more than ninety percent—was in propaganda, including support for mass media and for political parties. From the analyst's point of view, the problem with this kind of strategy is that, in spite of some assumptions equating investment in propaganda with actual influence, it is obviously complicated to assess its real impact on the overall political process. Nevertheless, while it is hard to infer a perfect causal relationship when there is a coincidence between the political outcome and the objectives of propaganda action, if the first differs from the latter it seems reasonable to assume that the latter was unproductive. CIA support for opposition candidates in Brazil's 1963 elections, for example, was largely fruitless, which made evident the limits of such assistance. Likewise, the period that the CIA spent more money in Chile was between 1964 and 1969, during the Johnson administration, and despite this support the Chilean left gained ground during these years. One could argue that had the United States not helped with money, the left would have made even more gains, but, aside from this speculation, the reality shows that the actual results could hardly be considered a case of success, as will be further explored below. The second aspect of US actions in Chile that deserves special attention is the fact that the bulk of CIA activities in Chile, including an attempt to encourage a military coup, was concentrated in the period before Allende became president in 1970 and were thus aimed to prevent him from taking office. Consequently, the eventual inauguration of Allende as president of Chile is another indication of the actual (in)effectiveness of the operations undertaken by the United States in the South American country.

As noted above, the peak of US propaganda actions in Chile was during the period between 1964 and 1969. In spite of the high investment, it is hard to conclude that the results were satisfactory. The Church Report remarks that CIA help in 1964 "enabled Eduardo Frei to win a clear majority in the 1964 election, instead of merely a plurality," but adds that it is not clear "why it was necessary to assure a majority, instead of accepting the victory a plurality would have assured."[91] The same report also notices that, in the years between 1965 and 1969, the portion of the vote of the CIA-backed Christian Democrats fell from forty-three to thirty-one percent. CIA efforts were not only concentrated on political parties, but also on influencing Chilean institutions, particularly those related to labor and peasants. The CIA evaluation of these projects, according to the Church Report, concluded that they were "rather unsuccessful in countering the growth of strong leftist sentiment and organization among workers, peasants and slum dwellers."[92] All in all, the most optimistic definition would characterize the outcome of CIA covert operations in Chile during the period between 1964 and 1969 as a limited success, but a case could also be made that the outcome was largely ineffective.

In 1970, the CIA spent around one million dollars to affect the outcome of that year's election by "undermining communist efforts to bring about a coalition of leftist forces which could gain control of the presidency" and "strengthening non-Marxist political leaders and forces in Chile in order to develop an effective alternative to the Popular Unity coalition in preparation for the 1970 presidential election."[93] On the other hand, the Church Report indicated that "the Cubans provided about $350,000 to Allende's campaign, with the Soviets adding an additional, undetermined amount."[94] The Soviet figures were later disclosed by KGB senior archivist Vasili Mitrokhin, who had access to extensive documentation in the USSR that reveals a close and regular association between Allende and the Soviets, picturing him as "the most important of the KGB's confidential contacts in South America."[95] The documents, which are part of the so called "Mitrokhin Archive," show that "Allende made a personal appeal . . . for Soviet funds" and that the KGB provided the Chilean Communist Party with $400,000 plus a "personal subsidy of $50,000 to be handed directly to Allende" and $18,000 to persuade a left-wing senator to remain within Allende's coalition and not to stand as presidential candidate in order to prevent splitting the leftist vote.[96] Additional funding, including money handed directly to Allende, continued to be sent throughout his term in office.[97]

The fact that Allende won a plurality—though a very narrow one—of the 1970 election made obvious that US efforts to prevent a leftist coalition from gaining a plurality of the votes "did not succeed."[98] Indeed, if one seeks to attribute every political outcome of 1970 Chile as a result of foreign influence, the conclusion should be that it was the KGB who was successful, and in fact, "[i]n its report to the Central Committee, the KGB claimed some credit for Allende's victory."[99] By the time Allende was elected, "little was left of the CIA-funded propaganda apparatus."[100] Yet, Allende's victory was a significant blow to US foreign policy in an age of Cold War and President Nixon decided not to let him come to power. Nixon informed the CIA that "an Allende regime in Chile would not be acceptable to the United States,"[101] and it was decided that "a more aggressive covert action initiative" was necessary, which included a plan to form a coup to prevent Allende from actually taking office.[102] In order to block Allende's accession to the presidency, the Nixon administration considered taking action in two different "tracks." "Track I" included political, economic, and propaganda activities "designed to induce Allende's opponents in Chile to prevent his assumption of power," while "Track II" went a step further and included actions "directed toward actively promoting and encouraging the Chilean military to move against Allende."[103] Because Allende had won a plurality, but not a majority, of the votes, the Chilean constitution required that he should be confirmed as president by the Congress. Track I failed to gather support from opposition forces to intervene in the Chilean political process in order to challenge Allende and also failed to generate an economic crisis strong enough to impact the votes in the Congress. Allende's victory was not only approved by the Congress, but was approved by such a wide margin—153 to 35—that labeling Track I as a complete failure may be an understatement.

When it became clear that Track I was shipwrecking, Track II was intensified. The CIA made several contacts with the Chilean military in order "to convince them to carry out a coup" and met Chilean officers "who were actively involved in coup plotting."[104] According to the Hinchey Report, the CIA met with three different groups of coup plotters and all of them indicated that the success of the coup required the kidnapping of Chilean Army Commander Rene Schneider, who favored Allende's confirmation as president. The CIA therefore provided arms and ammunition to one of the groups in order to abduct Schneider. However, the group that eventually kidnapped Schneider did not have the CIA's support and acted "independently of the CIA," which had concluded a few days before the operation that that particular group of plotters could not successfully carry out the coup.[105] The weapons that the CIA had provided to its preferred group "were later returned unused to the Station." Schneider was mortally wounded during the attack and his death "provoked a strong reaction in Chile," ruining the prospects for the execution of a coup against Allende, and making Track II as unsuccessful as Track I.[106] On November 3, 1970, Salvador Allende was inaugurated as president of Chile, making it plainly obvious that "U.S. efforts, both overt and covert, to prevent his assumption of office had failed."[107]

Hence, if the ultimate outcome of the 1970 Chilean elections demonstrates anything, it is the limits of US influence in certain areas of Latin America. Despite the explicit orders by a US President to carry out plans to overthrow a Latin American leader seen as an important threat to US interests, Allende was inaugurated in accordance with the precepts of the Chilean constitution. Perhaps the closest instance of a comparable failure is the 1961 Bay of Pigs Invasion in Cuba, but if in the case of Chile the US imperial toolbox included relatively "soft" measures such as propaganda actions and "encouragement" within the existent Chilean institutions for a military coup, the Cuban case could hardly be classified under the category of "soft imperialism." The Bay of Pigs was indeed an outright case of intervention through invasion, including the use of US aircraft and a US-trained and equipped mercenary army to invade Cuba and topple the government. While both are equivalent instances of failure, the Chilean case differs from the Cuban case in the relative timidity of the actions undertaken in order to fulfill similar objectives. If historians and political scientists want to classify both events under the same category of "US intervention in Latin America" to make the case for US imperial thrust in the region, they may not be conceptually wrong depending on the definitions used for "intervention," but they surely miss distinctions that are not negligible.

When Allende was finally overthrown by a military coup, it was not the CIA who brought him down. There is a reasonable consensus that domestic factors played the biggest role in the fall of Allende, and he would probably have been overthrown at about the same time even "without the slightest encouragement from the United States."[108] When it comes to foreign influences leading to the 1973 coup, there seems to be strong indication that Brazilian actions played an important role, as will be explored later. Obviously, having actively tried to prevent Allende from taking office, it would be surprising if the Nixon administration made his life any easier, especially considering events during his first twelve months in office such as the expropriation of US copper companies with no compensation (in fact, these companies were told that they actually owed Chile money due to "excess profits") and Fidel Castro's highly publicized month-long visit to Chile. Although covert operations continued to be undertaken after 1970, the major official action to influence the course of Chilean politics in that period was economic pressure. Nevertheless, Washington's actions to affect the Chilean economy after Allende was inaugurated president, in spite of claims of intervention, can be interpreted as being perfectly legitimate. Withholding support for loans, reducing investments, commercial credits, and bilateral aid to a government identified as opposed to US interests and that had actually taken steps in an anti-American direction could only be considered as intervention under the most vague definitions of the term. After the United States had badly lost the bet to prevent Allende from coming to power in Chile, it would be unrealistic given the Cold War environment to expect it to finance the so-called "Chilean path to socialism," which was the political platform of the coalition that supported Allende.

Indeed, Allende's term as president was characterized by enormous economic and political difficulties. However, attributing which part of the difficulties was the direct result of US policies and which part lies within domestic factors and other international conditions is a challenging endeavor. It is beyond the scope of this research to conduct an extensive examination of Allende's management of the economy in order to assess its effectiveness, but, when it comes to international factors, it should come as no surprise that the socialist reforms carried out by Allende would scare some of the international capitalist investors, particularly in the United States. In addition, in terms of international conditions, perhaps more important than any individual US action was the drop in the price of copper in 1971, which has historically represented a significant share of Chilean exports. In terms of access to international credit, Paul Sigmund comments that Chile "had surprising success in securing loans from countries other than the United States—and these were by no means restricted to the Soviet Union, Eastern Europe and China."[109] Sigmund maintains that loans from communist countries, plus Canada, Argentina, Mexico, Australia, and Western Europe "more than counterbalanced reductions from U.S. and U.S.-influenced sources" and that by August of 1973, "Allende had more short-term credits available to him ($574 million) than at the time of his election to office ($310 million)."[110] Likewise, Whitaker observes that cuts in loans and credits by the United States were counterbalanced by alternative sources from other parts of the world.[111] Juan Batista Yofre informs that, from Argentina alone, Chile had secured a line of credit of one hundred million dollars.[112] Commenting on the US strategy of economic pressure, the Church Report noticed that while it could work on the long term, in the short term Chile "was not immediately vulnerable to investment, trade or monetary sanctions imposed by the United States."[113] Indeed, the Foreign Minister of the Allende administration, Clodomiro Almeyda, commented that even though US economic actions may have contributed to the deterioration of the economic situation in Chile, "it cannot be said that they were the primary cause of these difficulties."[114] These statements help to put into perspective the notion that the United States was responsible for all misfortunes of the Chilean economy during the presidency of Salvador Allende. In any case, the important theoretical question remains as to the effectiveness of external economic pressure, especially if exerted unilaterally, in order to bring about political change.[115] The example of Castro's Cuba, which was even more economically dependent on the United States than Allende's Chile, seems to demonstrate the limits of such influence.

But the state of the economy tells only part of the story, as Allende's political situation was not any better. Elected by a margin of around just one percent over the candidate that came in second place, Allende presided over a divided country, and Chilean political life became increasingly polarized as the economy floundered. His own coalition quickly came apart as the left and the "ultra-left" split, the latter reproaching Allende for being "more reformist than revolutionary."[116] The economic problems, including shortages and growing inflation, exacerbated the political problems and brought unrest to several sectors of the country.[117] As time went by, there was a growing notion that Allende was losing control of the situation and it was a common saying in Chile that "the president does not govern."[118] US covert support to the opposition—combined, incidentally, with the far less researched Soviet covert support to the other side—may have contributed to aggravating political tensions but it is implausible to assume they were the major factor in creating them. This assessment is identical to the one made by Allende's Foreign Minister, who remarked that "U.S. activities designed to destabilize the UP [*Unidad Popular*] Government—activities which the U.S. authorities have cynically acknowledged—did not create the factors which caused the UP Government to fall but rather increased and intensified the impact of those factors."[119] The Chilean forest was burning and, while the United States threw in a few gallons of fuel, it definitely did not start the fire.

As for direct US involvement in the military coup that eventually over-threw Allende, the evidence to date seems to be conclusive in indicating that there was no such participation. After extensive investigation, the Church Report found "no hard evidence of direct U.S. assistance to the coup, despite frequent allegations of such aid."[120] Likewise, the Hinchey Report concluded that the CIA "was aware of coup-plotting by the military" but that it "did not instigate the coup that ended Allende's government on 11 September 1973," given that "the consensus within the US government was that the military intended to launch a coup at some point, that it did not need US support for a successful coup, and that US intervention or assistance in a coup should be avoided." In fact, continues the report, after Allende was inaugurated presi-dent, "the US government's long term objective" was not a military coup but "to keep the opposition active in the hope that it could defeat Allende in the 1976 election."[121] These conclusions corroborate US ambassador to Chile Nathaniel Davis' allegation that he "did not engage in coup plotting" and that he was "unaware of any of my U.S. colleagues having done so, including the personnel of the CIA station, the attaché offices, and the Military Advisory Group."[122] As Whitaker observed, the responsibility of the United States in the coup that overthrew Allende seems to be very limited "to the disappoint-ment, no doubt, of the makers of U.S. policy towards Allende who flattered themselves on their success."[123]

But if is true Davis did not engage in coup plotting, there is strong evi-dence that his Brazilian colleague in Chile apparently did not share the same behavior. While refuting the notion that the United States helped in coup plotting, Davis remarked that "there is no real doubt in my mind that allega-tions of a Brazilian connection are true."[124] Davis' predecessor in Santiago, Edward Korry, who served as ambassador from 1967 to 1971, was even more explicit when he stated in 1981 that "[t]he CIA did not overthrow Al-lende . . . It played almost no role. The actual technical and psychological support came from the military government of Brazil."[125] Earlier, Korry had mentioned that the Brazilian support for the coup was a "well-kept secret" in Washington.[126] Davis recounts an episode of March 1973, six months before the military coup, when the Brazilian ambassador to Chile met him and "made a series of leading suggestions (which I turned aside), trying to draw me into cooperative planning, interembassy coordination, and joint efforts toward the Allende government's demise."[127] Indeed, there are several indi-cations that "Brazil's complicity was, actually, more extensive than it ap-peared"[128] and that Brazilian ambassador to Chile, Camara Canto, was in fact actively involved in coup plotting. Yofre, who conducted extensive research on the Argentinean ambassador to Santiago during the Allende years, re-counts the episode of a meeting between the Argentinean and the Brazilian ambassador in 1969 when they discussed the possibility of a coup in Chile in the case of an Allende victory in the following year. Yofre emphasizes that this meeting made evident the close connections between Camara Canto and the Chilean military.[129] Likewise, Bandeira comments that Canto was "intimately related with those who conspired against Allende's ascension to the presidency of Chile."[130] Before Allende's election, Camara Canto was informed by Santiago that the army would not accept him as president, and when a coup failed to materialize, he attributed that to "the lack of a leader."[131] The Argentinean ambassador reported to Buenos Aires that Brazil saw Allende's election as a "headache" and "a source of disturbances to all countries in the Southern Cone."[132] During a busy reception hosted by the Brazilian embassy in Santiago a couple of days before the decision for the coup was made, the main topic was the military coup that was about to happen.[133] In fact, a week before the coup, the Brazilian Minister of War told the Paraguayan ambassador to Brazil that Chile was "already in military hands."[134] A Brazilian congressman close to Allende said that the Chilean president had told him two days before the coup that "the Brazilian embassy in Santiago was one of the main focuses of subversion against his administration, having a more ostensive activity than the US embassy" and that a week before the coup, Allende was actually preparing to denounce the "Brazilian connection" internationally.[135]

Besides official governmental participation, there is also evidence that private sectors in Brazil helped with the coup. Marlise Simons, who interviewed Brazilian businessmen and politicians, reports that "private business and interests" in Brazil "gave money, arms and advice on political tactics" to coup plotters. Simons points out that the Brazilian businessmen who helped to plot the 1964 military coup in Brazil "were the same people who advised the Chilean right on how to deal with Marxist President Allende," and that Chilean businessmen met with Brazilian businessmen to learn how "to prepare the ground for the military to move."[136] Brazilian political advice included instructions on how to create chaos and mobilization, particularly in exploring the role of women in mobilizing society and marching through the streets. A Brazilian politician reportedly said that "we taught the Chileans how to use their women against the Marxists. Once we saw Chilean women were marching, we knew that Allende's days were numbered."[137] A member of Brazil's Anti-Communist Movement claimed that he took money to anticommunist organizations in Chile and that the money came "from Sao Paulo and there was a lot of it."[138] In addition, there is strong indication that the experience of the 1964 coup in Brazil was used as a model for civilian and military sectors in Chile.[139] One Brazilian historian interviewed by Simons commented that "[t]he first two days I felt I was living a Xerox copy of Brazil 1964. The language of Chile's military communiqués justifying the coup . . . was so scandalously identical to ours, one almost presumes they had the same author."[140] In sum, although far less documented than the US participation, these evidences indicate that Brazilian participation in the events in Chile also contributed fuel to the fire that was consuming the Chilean political forest.

Furthermore, while Argentina was "passive" during the coup,[141] and there is no evidence that the United States was informed of the date beforehand,[142] Brazil knew about the beginning of the coup with "several hours of antecedence."[143] A representative of the Brazilian Minister of Foreign Affairs said that "Allende's overthrow was not a surprise" for the Brazilian government.[144] Five days after the coup, the first trip abroad of a Chilean official was to Brazil.[145] General Augusto Pinochet, the chief of the military junta who substituted for Allende in the presidency, is reported to have said that "[w]e were still shooting when the [Brazilian] ambassador communicated the recognition."[146] Indeed, Brazil was the first country to recognize the new government and Ambassador Camara Canto was apparently so pleased that he is reported to have answered the phone on the day of the coup with the phrase: "We won."[147] Soon after the coup, Camara Canto "coordinated measures of support to the new authorities"[148] and Brazil sent food and medication in addition to political and military help and a credit of $200 million to Chile.[149] During the first year after the coup, Brazil provided $150 million in direct economic aid to Chile, more than the United States.[150] When the Pinochet regime captured people accused of subversion, several accounts indicate that a number of the captors spoke Portuguese.[151] One of the Brazilians tortured by the Chilean military regime reports that Brazilian agents wrote the questions, and the medicine he took had a label that stated "donated by the Brazilian Navy."[152]

In regional terms, the Chilean coup d'état, combined with the previous coups in Uruguay and Bolivia, meant an end to the feeling of isolation and "encirclement" in Brazil and indicated in fact "an enlargement of Brazilian regional influence."[153] Undoubtedly, the Brazilian military government "was pleased with the shift to the right in the Southern Cone" since "it would remove many of the political obstacles to Brazil's goals" in the region.[154] On the other hand, Argentina, Brazil's main competitor for regional influence, became increasingly isolated, which was one of the contributing factors for the 1976 military coup in that country.[155] In fact, after Allende was overthrown, Argentinean official communication reported that Brazil was "the biggest beneficiary" from the coup and expressed concerns about the balance of power in the region.[156]

All the above evidence was already fairly well known and was by and large based on interviews, testimonies, and foreign governments' official communication. As has been suggested, the student interested in exploring the role of Brazil in Chile in detail will have to wait until Brazil makes available a larger part of the classified documentation related to its military period. Nevertheless, recently declassified documents in the United States present perhaps the strongest evidence to date of Brazil's official involvement in Chile. These documents, declassified in July 2009, refer to a meeting between US President Richard Nixon and Brazilian President Emilio Garrastazú Médici in December 1971. The records of the meeting show that Nixon and Médici got along really well, shared basically the same views about hemispheric issues, and overall the meeting took place in a particularly friendly atmosphere. General Vernon Walters, who was then the US military attaché in Paris and spoke several languages, served as interpreter for the meeting. Walters reports twice in the same memorandum that Nixon "was greatly impressed with Medici." He adds that the US president was "delighted at the personal rapport they had established and the closeness of their views. With only very few chiefs of state had he developed so quickly a close relationship."[157] The record of the meeting states that since Nixon had felt that he and Médici "had gotten along so well and found that their views were so close together . . . it was important that they maintain close contact and have a means of communicating directly outside of normal diplomatic channels when this might be necessary."[158] While Nixon appointed National Security Advisor Henry Kissinger as the representative for such private channels, Médici appointed Brazilian Foreign Minister Gibson Barboza. More importantly, and what is certain to make the life of the future researcher of the subject even more difficult, is the fact that, according to Médici, Barboza kept a "special file in which all items were handwritten, instructions or questions from the President and Gibson Barboza's replies all handwritten, so that not even typists had knowledge of them."[159] In his memories, Barboza made no reference to this episode,[160] and asked years later about Brazilian involvement in Chile, he denied the file's existence.[161]

Nixon and Médici discussed several topics and basically agreed on all of them, from the policy toward Cuba to the difficulty, expressed by Médici, in "dealing with and understanding the Spanish-American mentality."[162] Subsequently, when Nixon asked Médici about the situation in Chile, the Brazilian president replied categorically that "Allende would be overthrown for very much the same reasons that Goulart had been overthrown in Brazil." However, the most relevant passage for the purposes of the argument made in this chapter came after Nixon asked Médici about his assessment of the capability of the Chilean armed forces to overthrow Allende. Médici replied to Nixon that not only did he think the Chilean forces were capable, but also that "Brazil was exchanging many officers with the Chileans." More significantly, Médici acknowledged that "Brazil was working towards this end."[163] This passage is of great importance because it is perhaps the first document to show an official confirmation that the Brazilian government was actively working to help Allende's fall. Nixon's response is also germane, since he remarked that "it was very important that Brazil and the United States work closely in this field" but added that the United States "could not take direction." Nixon continued, saying that "if the Brazilians felt that there was something we could do to be helpful in this area, he would like President Médici to let him know. If money were required or other discreet aid, we might be able to make it available." The Brazilian president expressed satisfaction in seeing "that the Brazilian and American positions and views were so close."[164] This exchange is a perfect illustration of the notion that the coincidence in US and Brazilian views coupled with Brazilian willingness to prevent the spread of governments associated with communism in South America made it possible for the United States to "not take direction" and exercise a "soft imperialism" of, in the words of Nixon, "discreet aid" in South America. Had Brazil, Bolivia, Uruguay, and Chile fallen into the hands of communist governments, it is very unlikely, given the international environment of the Cold War, that the United States would remain so discreet.

Further passages of the meeting report and other associated documentation reinforces the notion of Brazil's "regional imperialism" as a South American surrogate for US "imperialism" during the Cold War. The conclusion of the report on the White House meeting suggested that Médici "hoped that we could cooperate closely, as there were many things that Brazil as a South American country could do that the U.S. could not."[165] In his memorandum to Kissinger, Walters noticed that "Médici wanted to do everything he could to lighten the President's burden."[166] A CIA memorandum on the four-day visit of the Brazilian president to the United States mentioned that Médici "personally believes the Brazilian government must assume a greater role in defending neighboring, friendly governments" and that he had "proposed that the United States and Brazil cooperate in helping other democratic countries in Latin America counter the trend of Marxist/leftist expansion." The memorandum adds that Nixon "took great interest in this proposal and promised to assist Brazil when and wherever possible."[167] A few months after Médici's visit to the United States, a National Intelligence Estimate entitled "The New Course in Brazil" concluded that

> Brazil will be playing a bigger role in hemispheric affairs and seeking to fill whatever vacuum the US leaves behind. It is unlikely that Brazil will intervene openly in its neighbors' internal affairs, but the regime will not be above using the threat of intervention or tools of diplomacy and covert action to oppose leftist regimes, to keep friendly governments in office, or to help place them there in countries such as Bolivia and Uruguay. While some countries may seek Brazil's protection, others may work together to withstand pressures from the emerging giant.[168]

Given the tone of these documents, it is somewhat astonishing that much of the repercussion in the media at the time of their declassification interpreted them as an attempt by the part of Nixon to "enlist Brazil in a coup"[169] in view of the fact that "cultivation of Medici fits Nixon and Kissinger's pattern of recruiting conservative heads of state to the U.S. Cold War cause."[170] However, these views should not be especially surprising since they merely reflect the traditional approach to the study of US-Latin America relationship during and beyond the Cold War. Without an alternative framework to interpret the relationship between the United States and South America, these analysts tend to shape the facts according to their preconceived notions in which the United States has virtually complete and homogenous control over the weaker countries south of the Rio Grande. Therefore, even though the aforementioned documents indicate that it was actually the Brazilian president who was "enlisting" or "recruiting" a very hospitable Nixon to the cause of fighting "the trend of Marxist/leftist expansion" in South America, the conventional international-system approach centered on the great powers hinders a more accurate analysis of those primary documents, thus reinforcing a cycle that affects the perception of researchers who only had access to secondary sources.

SURINAME: A FORGOTTEN EPISODE

As the examples of Bolivia and Uruguay indicated above suggest, the existence of a Brazilian connection regarding the 1973 Chilean military coup should come as no surprise, since it should be clear by now that the Brazilian military government was at least as concerned as the US government about the ascension of political forces viewed as having an association with communism. Ten years later, with the Cold War still in full force, events in another South American country would demonstrate what a difference a regional subsystem makes.

On October 25, 1983, the United States conducted its first major military operation since the Vietnam War when eight thousand US troops invaded the Caribbean island of Grenada under the traditional Cold War rationale of preventing the spread of communism. Due to the nature of this operation—an open and armed intervention—the case of Grenada is thoroughly studied and mentioned in the literature as an example of US interventionist disposition in the Western Hemisphere. Nevertheless, a very similar case at about the same point in time and in a country only a few hundred miles from Grenada had a very different outcome, and because of that outcome it is virtually ignored by the literature. Like Grenada, Suriname was also a country governed by a dictator with affinities with the Castro government in Cuba. Like Grenada, Suriname was also regarded as in a strategic position due to its geographic location near the Caribbean Sea. Consequently, like Grenada, Suriname was also an important concern for the Reagan administration in the hemisphere.

Unlike Grenada, Suriname shared a border with Brazil, and by the eighties it could be considered part of the South American regional subsystem. Examining how the case of Suriname unfolded in contrast to the case of Grenada provides a good illustration of how subsystemic factors contributed to avoiding a US military intervention in the South America subsystem, thus keeping the US absent.

After 1980, when a military coup under the leadership of Dési Bouterse overthrew the government of Suriname and declared the country to be a socialist republic, the CIA started closely monitoring the situation in that country. In December 1982, fifteen people who identified with the opposition were arrested and executed, which drew world attention to Suriname and led the CIA to develop plans to invade the country. These plans and the events that followed were kept in secrecy by all the participants until recently. Perhaps the best source to date on this issue is Paul Kengor and Pat Clark Doerner's book *The Judge: William P. Clark, Ronald Reagan's Top Hand.*[171] Kengor and Doerner describe the events in Suriname as "the best kept secret in Washington" at the time.[172] They add that the participants "took almost no notes and kept few written records of their involvement."[173] Therefore, in order to write the chapter on Suriname, Kengor and Doerner interviewed several of the participants in that event, but most importantly William P. Clark, who was one of the central figures in the first Reagan administration, serving as Deputy Secretary of State from 1981 to 1982, National Security Advisor from 1982 to 1983, and Secretary of the Interior from 1983 to 1985. Clark was a key participant in the Suriname case; he indicates that he was sent on a secret trip to Brazil and Venezuela in1983 to develop, as Ronald Reagan recorded in his diaries, a plan to "oust the dictator" of Suriname which "required their [Brazil and Venezuela] cooperation."[174]

The case of Suriname illustrates the notion developed throughout this chapter that the role of Brazil in the South American subsystem affected the structure of costs and benefits of US action during the Cold War. The option to count on Brazil to deal with the situation allowed the United States to limit its participation in that subsystem, which is made even clearer when contrasted with the outcome in Grenada. As Kengor and Doerner point out, the main hope of Clark's secret trip to South America "was that the Venezuelans and Brazilians could be encouraged to clean up their own neighborhood rather than face some form of U.S. military intervention."[175] The first stop of Clark's trip was in Caracas, where the US plan to count on their cooperation was turned down. On the other hand, Clark's meeting with Brazilian President Figueiredo yielded very different results. While the Venezuelans were unwilling to help, in Brasilia Clark found "an extremely helpful and unheralded Brazil."[176] With Venezuela out of the equation, Clark's main goal in Brasilia "was to persuade the Brazilians to take care of the Bouterse problem on their own, to make it unnecessary for the United States to organize and orchestrate a major deployment,"[177] and he presented the Brazilians with detailed scenarios for the invasion of Suriname. As Kengor and Doerner comment, the presentation of the plan had an important effect on the Brazilian generals as "Brazil's brass was taken aback at the specter of U.S. forces crashing into South America."[178] Following Clark's presentation of the issue, the Brazilians came up with a plan that did not include an invasion force, since Figueiredo "did not want a military operation, either Brazilian or American. Yet, he and his colleagues also dreaded a Soviet presence next door."[179] The Brazilian strategy included a package of assistance and cooperation, including military aid, in order to substitute Cuban and Soviet presence with Brazilian influence. The Reagan administration called this operation "Operation Giminich," in reference to the name of a horse that Figueiredo had given to Reagan after a meeting between them. As it turned out, the Brazilian proposal was "enough to keep Suriname from going Marxist and becoming a Soviet-Cuban base of operation in the Atlantic."[180] As Bandeira argues, while Brazil developed its northern region during the seventies and the eighties, it sought to avoid the penetration of foreign powers in the Amazon region.[181] Therefore, concludes Bandeira, "once it could not simply negate collaborating with the United States, the Figueiredo administration, in order to avoid the invasion of Suriname, which was already decided by Washington, took the responsibility to solve peacefully the issue."[182] The whole deal was kept secret and both sides promised to maintain its confidentiality, which explains why this event is largely unaccounted for.

One of the main participants in the Brazilian mission sent to Suriname to offer the package was diplomat Luiz Felipe Lampreia, who later became ambassador to that country under Figueiredo and eventually Foreign Minister between 1995 and 2001 throughout the Cardoso administration. In 2010, Lampreia published his memoirs, which helped to bring additional information to the events in Suriname. Lampreia recalls that during the meeting between Clark and Figueiredo, the Brazilian president "refused the invitation" to participate in the invasion of Suriname, "but said that, since it was a neighboring country, Brazil considered that the situation in Suriname required an adequate and exclusively Brazilian reaction," because the Brazilian government "considered the issue to be their own responsibility."[183] Thus, the plan to offer technical, economic, and material support in exchange for removing the Cubans—which, according to Lampreia, totaled fifty million dollars—was born. For Lampreia, Bouterse and the Surinamese military were more opportunistic than ideological, and therefore the plan had a high chance of succeeding without the need for a military intervention. Indeed, even though Reagan was skeptical about the Brazilian proposal and offered US help "if you wish, and whenever you ask for it," he acquiesced to the Brazilian proposal and wished Figueredo luck.[184] Fearing the possibility of a Brazilian invasion, Bouterse gladly accepted the plan, the Cuban presence in

Suriname was greatly reduced, and the operation was deemed a success. "Not a shot was fired!" celebrated Clark in a memorandum to Reagan.[185] As the Brazilian package was implemented in Suriname, the United States was ready to send troops to Grenada.

CHAPTER CONCLUSION

The period of the Cold War provides perhaps the better opportunity to test the hypothesis of this research that the specific dynamics of the South American subsystem contributed to keeping the United States an absent empire in that part of the hemisphere. Because of the particular characteristics of the bipolar period, the incentives for the United States to intervene in countries in faraway places like Korea or Vietnam were much higher. Within this context, it is unlikely to expect that any US administration would tolerate countries in Latin America to fall in the hands of communist governments, especially given the symbolism that it would represent. Therefore, usual justifications for US relative lack of involvement or interest in South America, such as geographic distance or strategic irrelevance, have perhaps their weakest explanatory power during this period, which was strongly characterized by an ideological confrontation that did not necessarily follow purely strategic calculations. Indeed, successive US administrations demonstrated great concern with the progress of events in South America, and at least two presidents came close to intervening and toppling South American governments that were perceived as being associated with communism. Such actions would come as no surprise, since they would replicate a pattern of behavior that had been pretty clear in Central America and the Caribbean. Nevertheless, in spite of the interest in South America and the disposition to intervene and resort to imperial solutions, the best the United States could do was to exert a sort of "soft imperialism." This difference between intentions and outcomes must be explained, and this chapter intended to offer an explanation by employing the regional subsystemic perspective.

Hence, following the framework laid out in chapters 2 and 3, this chapter explains the United States' relative absence from South America during the Cold War by looking at how Brazil affected the structure of costs and benefits of subsystemic change for the United States in that period. In other words, Brazil's foreign policy objectives in the South American subsystem basically coincided with US objectives, thus raising the benefits for the United States for the maintenance of the status quo and likewise decreasing the incentives for resorting to imperial solutions, such as an invasion to topple particular governments. Brazil's economic growth at the time, combined with the authoritarian character of the military regime, created the conditions

for a Brazilian "regional imperialism" that worked actively to contain the
spread of governments associated with communism in South America. As
this chapter intended to demonstrate, this policy was a result of Brazil's view
of its national interests and was not directed from Washington. An important
part of the argument made here was the deconstruction of the myth that anti-
communism was a US prerogative that should somehow be incorporated by
South American countries through the diligent work of indoctrination designed from offices in Washington. Obviously, the United States was willing
to take action, but the actions taken did not go beyond supplying an existing
demand for things like money, equipment, and armaments. Because of Brazil's willingness to play a regional imperial role during the period under
study in this chapter, as clearly demonstrated by the cases of Bolivia, Uruguay, and Suriname, there was no need for an imperial policy from the part
of the United States in South America. As demonstrated in the previous
chapter, Brazil has considered South America to be its area of influence, and
this perception continued to be very much present during the period under
study here.

It is within this context that the case of the 1973 military coup in Chile
should be understood. The Chilean coup is an especially hard case to test the
hypothesis presented here because it is widely mentioned in the literature as
following the same pattern of US interventions elsewhere in Latin America.
To make a counterpoint to this view, this chapter examined the extension of
US involvement in Chile. Because the United States worked to avoid Salvador Allende's ascension to power, and because he was eventually toppled by
a military coup, the temptation to connect the dots and establish a causal
relationship is high. This kind of temptation is helped by the usual framework of US hegemony in Latin America and, although it can explain with
reasonable adequacy similar cases in Central America and the Caribbean
during the Cold War, it does not provide a satisfactory explanation for the
case of Chile. The puzzle presented by Chile is why the United States
stopped short of an imperial solution, in contrast to what it had done in other
places in the world. As this chapter proposed to show, every step taken by the
United States—during both Democratic and Republican administrations—to
prevent Allende from being elected and later to prevent him from taking
office failed miserably. Given the outcome in 1970, if one wishes to offer an
interpretation attributing it to the works of foreign intelligence agencies, the
merit should probably go to the KGB and not to the CIA. The remaining
explanation to link Allende's fall to actions taken by the United States, since
there is no clear evidence of US direct involvement in the coup that eventually overthrew him, is the fact that the United States attempted to destabilize
Allende's government through economic measures. This explanation has at
least two main weaknesses: one is that it tends to attribute to the United

States all misfortunes of the Chilean economy, which is debatable, and the other that it makes a direct connection between US economic actions and the political outcome in Chile, which is unclear.

The overemphasis of US actions, which is greatly helped by the abundance of documentation available from US sources, blurs the focus on other countries that also may have played a role in Chile. Because of Brazilian foreign policy at the time, which was illustrated by its actions in Bolivia and Uruguay, one would suspect that Chile would also be a concern for the Brazilian military regime. Indeed, there are a number of circumstantial evidences—confirmed by two US ambassadors to Santiago—that Brazil was actively working with coup plotters in Chile. The lack of documentation from Brazilian sources of Brazil's involvement in Chile, though, complicates the life of the researcher interested in demonstrating its extension. Nevertheless, recently declassified documents in the United States seem to provide the clearest evidence to date that Brazil was in fact taking actions in order to help the overthrown of Allende. These documents refer to a meeting between Brazilian President Médici and US President Nixon which shows Médici acknowledging that Brazil was working to overthrow Allende, and Nixon demonstrating satisfaction that he could count on Brazil to limit US involvement in Chile. To put it in terms of the theoretical framework developed here, the Nixon-Médici interchange is a clear demonstration of how Brazil successfully affected US cost-benefit calculations, which made the US less likely to resort to an imperial strategy in the South American subsystem.

NOTES

1. Arthur Preston Whitaker, *The Western Hemisphere Idea: Its Rise and Decline* (Ithaca, NY: Cornell University Press, 1954), 154-77.

2. For interpretations of the United States as an empire during the Cold War, see for example: Liska, *Imperial America*: 113, 21; De Riencourt, *The American Empire*; Steel, *Pax Americana*; Steel, *Imperialists and Other Heroes: A Chronicle of the American Empire*, 1st ed. (New York: Random House, 1971); Lens, *The Forging of the American Empire*; Lundestad, "Empire by Invitation? The United States and Western Europe, 1945-1952"; May, *Imperial Democracy*.

3. See for example: Edwin Lieuwen, *U.S. Policy in Latin America: A Short History* (New York: Praeger, 1965), 134-35; Child, *Unequal Alliance*: 16; Abraham F. Lowenthal, *Partners in Conflict: The United States and Latin America in the 1990s*, rev. ed. (Baltimore: Johns Hopkins University Press, 1990), 39; Pastor, *Whirlpool*: 35; Joseph Smith, *The United States and Latin America: A History of American Diplomacy, 1776-2000* (London: Routledge, 2005), 112.

4. Katzenstein, *A World of Regions*: 226.

5. Ibid., 225.

6. Ibid.

7. Ibid., 226.

8. Mares, "Middle Powers under Regional Hegemony," 454.

9. Cole Blasier, *The Giant's Rival: The U.S.S.R and Latin America* (Pittsburgh: University of Pittsburgh Press, 1987), 156.

10. Grace Livingstone, *America's Backyard: the United States and Latin America from the Monroe Doctrine to the War on Terror* (London: Zed Books, 2009), 2.

11. Black, *United States Penetration of Brazil*: 2.

12. Black, *Sentinels of Empire: The United States and Latin American Militarism*: 4.

13. William Blum, *Killing Hope: U.S. Military and C.I.A Interventions since World War II*, 2., updated ed. (Monroe, ME: Common Courage Press, 2004), 163.

14. Phillip Agee, *Inside the Company: C.I.A Diary*, American ed. (New York: Stonehill, 1975), 362.

15. Peter Kornbluh, "Brazil Marks 40th Anniversary of Military Coup," *The National Security Archive*, March 31, 2004. http://www.gwu.edu/~nsarchiv/NSAEBB/NSAEBB118/index.htm#docs (accessed December 1, 2010).

16. Lincoln Gordon, *Brazil's Second Chance: En Route toward the First World* (Washington, DC: Brookings Institution Press, 2001), 68.

17. Carlos Fico, *O grande Irmão: da Operação Brother Sam aos Anos de Chumbo* (Rio de Janeiro: Civilização Brasileira, 2008), 101-02.

18. Cordeiro de Farias, Aspásia Camargo, and Walder de Góis, *Meio Século de Combate: Diálogo com Cordeiro de Farias* (Rio de Janeiro: Editora Nova Fronteira, 1981), 571.

19. Fico, *O Grande Irmão*:101.

20. Gordon, *Brazil's Second Chance*: 67.

21. Lester D. Langley, *America and the Americas: The United States in the Western Hemisphere*, 2nd ed. (Athens: University of Georgia Press, 2010), 220.

22. Phyllis R. Parker, *Brazil and the Quiet Intervention, 1964* (Austin: University of Texas Press, 1979), 104.

23. Gordon, *Brazil's Second Chance*: 64.

24. Agee, *Inside the Company*: 362.

25. Black, *United States Penetration of Brazil*: 66-67; Ruth Leacock, *Requiem for Revolution: The United States and Brazil, 1961-1969* (Kent, Ohio: Kent State University Press, 1990), 119.

26. Black, *Requiem for Revolution*: 113; 21.

27. Ibid., 121.

28. Bandeira, *Presença dos Estados Unidos no Brasil*: 430.

29. Bandeira, *Formula para o Caos: a Derrubada de Salvador Allende (1970-1973)* (Rio de Janeiro: Civilizacao Brasileira, 2008), 86.

30. Robert G. Wesson, *The United States and Brazil: Limits of Influence* (New York: Praeger, 1981), 48.

31. Leacock, *Requiem for Revolution*: 183.

32. Black, *United States Penetration of Brazil*: 178.

33. M. Pio Corrêa, *O Mundo em que Vivi* (Rio de Janeiro, RJ: Expressão e Cultura, 1995), 812.

34. Esteves, *Documentos Históricos do Estado-Maior do Exército*: 228.

35. Elio Gaspari, *A Ditadura Derrotada* (São Paulo, Brazil: Companhia das Letras, 2003), 124-25.

36. Ibid., 126-27.

37. Ibid., 127.

38. Esteves, *Documentos Históricos do Estado-Maior do Exército*: 325-26.

39. Ibid., 353-54.

40. Paulo R. Schilling, *O Expansionismo Brasileiro: A Geopolítica do General Golbery e a Diplomacia do Itamarati* (São Paulo: Global, 1981), 81.

41. Farias, Camargo, and Góis, *Meio Século de Combates*: 416-17.

42. Alfred C. Stepan, *The Military in Politics: Changing Patterns in Brazil* (Princeton, NJ: Princeton University Press, 1971), 175.

43. Ibid., 175-76.

44. John Shy and Thomas W. Collier, "Revolutionary War," in *Makers of Modern Strategy: from Machiavelli to the Nuclear Age*, ed. Peter Paret, Gordon Alexander Craig, and Felix Gilbert (Princeton: Princeton University Press, 1986).

45. Armand Mattelart, *The Globalization of Surveillance*, trans. Suzan Taponier and James A. Cohen (Cambridge: Polity Press, 2010), 86.

46. Shy and Collier, "Revolutionary War," 856.

47. Mattelart, *The Globalization of Surveillance*: 80.

48. Elio Gaspari, *A Ditadura Escancarada* (São Paulo, Brazil: Companhia das Letras, 2002), 31.

49. Maria Celina Soares d' Araújo, Gláucio Ary Dillon Soares, and Celso Castro, *Os Anos de Chumbo: a Memória Militar sobre a Repressão* (Rio de Janeiro: Relume Dumará, 1994), 77-78.

50. Esteves, *Documentos históricos do Estado-Maior do Exército*: 186-93.

51. Joaquim Xavier da Silveira, *A FEB por um Soldado* (Rio de Janeiro: Nova Fronteira, 1989), 264.

52. Ernesto López, *Seguridad Nacional y Sedición Militar* (Buenos Aires: Editorial Legasa, 1987).

53. Joseph Comblin, *A Ideologia da Segurança Nacional: o Poder Militar na America Latina* (Rio de Janeiro: Civilização Brasileira, 1978), 14.

54. López, *Seguridad Nacional y Sedición Militar*: 187.

55. Ibid., 145-46.

56. Stepan, *The Military in Politics*: 179.

57. Gaspari, *A Ditadura Escancarada*: 304.

58. For example, Lesley Gill, *The School of the Americas: Military Training and Political Violence in the Americas* (Durham: Duke University Press, 2004).

59. Mattelart, *The Globalization of Surveillance*: 100.

60. Stepan, *The Military in Politics*: 179.

61. *Jornal do Brasil*, "Brasil Denuncia Acordo Militar com EUA," March 12, 1977, 1; 19-22.

62. *Reuters*, "U.S and Brazil Sign Defense Pact, No Decision on Jets," April 12, 2010. http://www.reuters.com/article/idUSTRE63B5YV20100412 (accessed December 19, 2010).

63. Corrêa, *O Mundo em que Vivi*: 741.

64. Gaspari, *A Ditadura Derrotada*: 71-72.

65. Corrêa, *O Mundo em que Vivi*: 741.

66. Moniz Bandeira, *Estado Nacional e Política Internacional na América Latina: O Continente nas Relações Argentina-Brasil, 1930-1992* (São Paulo, SP: Ensaio, 1993), 228.

67. Wesson, *The United States and Brazil*: 67.

68. Golbery do Couto e Silva, *Geopolítica do Brasil* (Rio de Janeiro: Livraria J. Olympio, 1967), 50-52.

69. Leonel Itaussu Almeida Mello, *Argentina e Brasil: A Balança de Poder no Cone Sul* (São Paulo, SP, Brasil: Annablume, 1996), 124.

70. Ibid., 128.

71. Bandeira, *Brasil, Argentina e Estados Unidos*: 416-17.

72. James Dunkerley, *Rebellion in the Veins: Political Struggle in Bolivia, 1952-82* (London: Verso, 1984), 198.

73. Schilling, *O Expansionismo Brasileiro*: 65-66.

74. J. Patrice McSherry, *Predatory States: Operation Condor and Covert War in Latin America* (Lanham, MD: Rowman & Littlefield Publishers, Inc., 2005), 55.

75. Jorge Gallardo Lozada, *De Torres a Banzer* (Buenos Aires: Ediciones Periferia, 1972), 403,15.

76. Dunkerley, *Rebellion in the Veins*: 205.

77. Mello, *Argentina e Brasil*: 128.

78. U.S. National Archives and Records Administration, "Secret Department of State Telegram to U.S. Embassies in Brazil and Argentina" (Subject-Numeric Files 1970-73. August 20, 1971).

79. U.S. State Department. Reading Room., "Secret U.S.Embassy Preliminary Analysis and Strategy Paper—Uruguay " (Microfiche on Human Rights in Uruguay 1971-1983. August 25, 1971).

80. U.S. National Archives and Records Administration, "Top Secret Memorandum from Henry Kissinger on a meeting between the U.S. President and British Prime Minister Edward Heath " (VIP Visits boxes 910-954, Nixon National Security Council Materials. December 20, 1971).

81. Bandeira, *Formula para o Caos*: 247.

82. Schilling, *O Expansionismo Brasileiro*; Bandeira, *Estado Nacional e Política Internacional na América Latina: o Continente nas Relações Argentina-Brasil, 1930-1992*: 226-27; Bandeira, *Brasil, Argentina e Estados Unidos*: 417; Leonel Itaussu Almeida Mello, *A geopolítica do Brasil e a Bacia do Prata* (Manaus: Editora da Universidade do Amazonas, 1997), 194-202; Enrique Serra Padros, "A Ditadura Brasileira de Segurança Nacional e a Operação 30 horas: Intervencionismo ou Neocisplatinização do Uruguai? ," *Ciências&Letras [Porto Alegre]* jan/jun, no. 37 (2005); McSherry, *Predatory States*: 56.

83. For example, Helio Contreiras, *Militares Confissões: Historias Secretas do Brasil* (Rio de Janeiro: Mauad, 1998), 59; Gaspari, *A Ditadura Derrotada*: 194; Marco Antônio Villalobos, *Tiranos Tremei! Ditadura e Resistência Popular no Uruguai (1968-1985)* (Porto Alegre: EDIPUCRS, 2006), 100-08.

84. Dickson M. Grael, *Aventura, Corrupção e Terrorismo: À Sombra da Impunidade* (Petrópolis: Vozes, 1985), 18-19.

85. Schilling, *O Expansionismo Brasileiro*: 63.

86. U.S. National Archives and Records Administration, "Secret Department of State Memorandum from Theodore Eliot Jr. to Henry Kissinger," (Department of State Subject-Numeric Files 1970-73, National Archives. November 27, 1971).

87. Some authors have employed the term "subimperialism" to characterize Brazilian policies in South America during the military regime. Nevertheless, the concept of subimperialism is connected with the Leninist concept of imperialism, which is distinct from the argument made in this book. Moreover, the notion of subimperialism implies a condition of subordination, which is also not the argument made here. For the notion of Brazilian subimperialism see: Ruy Mauro Marini, "Brazilian Subimperialism," *Monthly Review* 23, no. 9 (1972); Gustavo V. Dans and North American Congress on Latin America., *NACLA's Brasil a la Ofensiva: La Estrategia Continental del Imperialismo* (Lima: Editorial Dipsa, 1975); Daniel Zirker, "Brazilian Foreign Policy and Subimperialism During the Political Transition of the 1980s: A Review and Reapplication of Marini's Theory," *Latin American Perspectives* 21, no. 1 (1994).

88. Marlise Simons, "The Brazilian Connection," *The Washington Post*, January 6, 1974.

89. U.S. Congress. Senate. Select Committee to Study Governmental Operations with Respect to Intelligence Activities, "Covert Action in Chile, 1963-1973: Staff Report of the Select Committee to Study Governmental Operations with Respect to Intelligence Activities, United States Senate," (Washington: U.S. Govt. Print. Off., 1975).

90. To produce the report, the authors "reviewed relevant CIA records of the period predominantly from recent document searches; studied extensive Congressional reports regarding US activities in Chile in the 1960s and 1970s; read the memoirs of key figures, including Richard Nixon and Henry Kissinger; reviewed CIA's oral history collection at the Center for the Study of Intelligence; and consulted with retired intelligence officers who were directly involved." U.S. CIA. General Reports., "C.I.A. Activities in Chile," September 18, 2000. http://www.cia.gov/library/reports/general-reports-1/chile/index.html#1 (accessed December 1, 2010).

91. U.S. Congress. Senate. Select Committee to Study Governmental Operations with Respect to Intelligence Activities, "Covert Action in Chile, 1963-1973"

92. Ibid.

93. Ibid.

94. Ibid.

95. Christopher M. Andrew and Vasili Mitrokhin, *The World Was Going Our Way: The KGB and the Battle for the Third World* (New York: Basic Books, 2005), 69.

96. Ibid., 72.

97. Ibid., 75, 80, 81.
98. U.S. Congress. Senate. Select Committee to Study Governmental Operations with Respect to Intelligence Activities, "Covert Action in Chile, 1963-1973."
99. Andrew and Mitrokhin, *The World Was Going Our Way*: 72.
100. U.S. Congress. Senate. Select Committee to Study Governmental Operations with Respect to Intelligence Activities, "Covert Action in Chile, 1963-1973."
101. Ibid.
102. U.S. CIA. General Reports, "C.I.A. Activities in Chile."
103. U.S. Congress. Senate. Select Committee to Study Governmental Operations with Respect to Intelligence Activities, "Covert Action in Chile, 1963-1973."
104. U.S. CIA. General Reports, "C.I.A. Activities in Chile."
105. Ibid.
106. Ibid.
107. U.S. Congress. Senate. Select Committee to Study Governmental Operations with Respect to Intelligence Activities, "Covert Action in Chile, 1963-1973."
108. Whitaker, *The United States and the Southern Cone: Argentina, Chile, and Uruguay*: 415.
109. Paul E. Sigmund, "The 'Invisible Blockade' and the Overthrow of Allende," *Foreign Affairs* 52, no. 2 (1974): 336.
110. Ibid., 336-37.
111. Whitaker, *The United States and the Southern Cone*: 415. Also, William F. Sater, *Chile and the United States: Empires in Conflict* (Athens: University of Georgia Press, 1990), 184-85.
112. Juan Bautista Yofre, *Misión Argentina en Chile, 1970-1973* (Providencia Chile: Editorial Sudamericana, 2000), 297.
113. U.S. Congress. Senate. Select Committee to Study Governmental Operations with Respect to Intelligence Activities, "Covert Action in Chile, 1963-1973."
114. Clodomyro Almeyda, "The Foreign Policy of the Unidad Popular Government," in *Chile 1970-1973: Economic Development and its International Setting: Self-Criticism of the Unidad Popular Government's Policies*, ed. Sandro Sideri (The Hague: Nijhoff, 1979), 127.
115. On this issue, see, for example, R. Harrison Wagner, "Economic Interdependence, Bargaining Power, and Political Influence," *International Organization* 42, no. 3 (1988).
116. Yofre, *Misión argentina en Chile, 1970-1973*: 257.
117. A detailed account of economic and political problems faced by Allende is provided by the US ambassador to Chile during the Allende years: Davis, *The Last Two Years of Salvador Allende*.
118. Yofre, *Misión Argentina en Chile, 1970-1973*: 162.
119. Almeyda, "The Foreign Policy of the Unidad Popular Government," 129.
120. U.S. Congress. Senate. Select Committee to Study Governmental Operations with Respect to Intelligence Activities, "Covert Action in Chile, 1963-1973."
121. U.S. CIA. General Reports, "C.I.A. Activities in Chile."
122. Davis, *The Last Two Years of Salvador Allende*: 348.
123. Whitaker, *The United States and the Southern Cone*: 415.
124. Davis, *The Last Two Years of Salvador Allende*: 332.
125. Edward Korry, "Confronting our Past in Chile," *Los Angeles Times*, March 8, 1981.
126. Korry, "The Sell-Out of Chile and the American Taxpayer," *Penthouse*, March 1978, 116.
127. Davis, *The Last Two Years of Salvador Allende*: 363.
128. Bandeira, *Estado Nacional e Política Internacional na América Latina*: 227; Bandeira, *Brasil, Argentina e Estados Unidos*: 418.
129. Yofre, *Misión Argentina en Chile, 1970-1973*: 33.
130. Bandeira, *Formula para o Caos*: 172.
131. Ibid., 177.
132. Yofre, *Misión Argentina en Chile, 1970-1973*: 77.
133. Ibid., 413.
134. Simons, "The Brazilian Connection."

135. *Veja*, "Pagina Negra: As Tenebrosas Transações do Itamarati no Chile," November 13, 1985.
136. Simons, "The Brazilian Connection."
137. Ibid.
138. Ibid.
139. Ibid; Bandeira, *Formula para o Caos*: 484.
140. Simons, "The Brazilian Connection."
141. Yofre, *Misión Argentina en Chile, 1970-1973*: 424.
142. Davis, *The Last Two Years of Salvador Allende*: 363.
143. Yofre, *Misión Argentina en Chile, 1970-1973*: 426.
144. *Brazilian Information Bulletin.*, "Chilean Coup: Brazil Goes Over the Andes," Fall 1973.
145. Ibid.
146. Gaspari, *A Ditadura Derrotada*: 355.
147. Ibid, *Veja*, "Pagina Negra: As Tenebrosas Transações do Itamarati no Chile."
148. Bandeira, *Estado Nacional e Política Internacional na América Latina*: 228.
149. Bandeira, *Formula para o Caos*: 558-59.
150. Mello, *Argentina e Brasil*: 131.
151. Gaspari, *A Ditadura Derrotada*: 356.
152. Bandeira, *Formula para o Caos*: 560.
153. Mello, *Argentina e Brasil*: 130.
154. Robert D. Bond, "Brazil's Relations with the Northern Tier Countries of South America," in *Brazil in the International System: The Rise of a Middle Power*, ed. Wayne A. Selcher (Boulder, CO: Westview Press, 1981), 165.
155. Bandeira, *Estado Nacional e Política Internacional na América Latina*: 229; Mello, *Argentina e Brasil*: 131-32.
156. Yofre, *Misión Argentina en Chile, 1970-1973*: 435.
157. U.S. State Department. Foreign Relations of the United States, "Memorandum From the Senior Department of Defense Attaché in France (Walters) to the President's Assistant for National Security Affairs (Kissinger)," (Washington: Undated. Volume E–10, Documents On American Republics, 1969–1972, Document 144, 1971).
158. U.S. State Department. Foreign Relations of the United States, "Memorandum for the President's File," Foreign Relations of the United States (Washington: December 9. Volume E–10, Documents On American Republics, 1969–1972, Document 143, 1971).
159. Ibid.
160. Mario Gibson Barboza, *Na Diplomacia, o Traço Todo da Vida* (Rio de Janeiro: Record, 1992).
161. *Veja*, "Pagina Negra: As Tenebrosas Transações do Itamarati no Chile."
162. U.S. State Department. Foreign Relations of the United States, "Memorandum for the President's File."
163. Ibid.
164. Ibid.
165. Ibid.
166. U.S. State Department. Foreign Relations of the United States, "Memorandum From the Senior Department of Defense Attaché in France (Walters) to the President's Assistant for National Security Affairs (Kissinger)."
167. U.S. State Department. Foreign Relations of the United States, "Memorandum From the Acting Director of Central Intelligence (Cushman) to the President's Assistant for National Security Affairs (Kissinger)," (Washington: December 29. Volume E–10, Documents On American Republics, 1969–1972, Document 145, 1971).
168. U.S. State Department. Foreign Relations of the United States, "National Intelligence Estimate 93–72," (Washington: January 13. Volume E–10, Documents On American Republics, 1969–1972, Document 146, 1972).
169. Andrew Zajac, "Nixon Offered Brazil Money to Undermine Allende, Records Show," *Los Angeles Times*, August 16, 2009.

170. Alexei Barrionuevo, "Memos Show Nixon's Bid to Enlist Brazil in a Coup," *New York Times*, August 16, 2009.

171. Paul Kengor and Patricia Clark Doerner, *The Judge: William P. Clark, Ronald Reagan's Top Hand* (San Francisco: Ignatius Press, 2007).

172. Ibid., 212.

173. Ibid., 203.

174. Ronald Reagan and Douglas Brinkley, *The Reagan Diaries*, 1st ed. (New York: Harper-Collins, 2007), 141, 43.

175. Kengor and Doerner, *The Judge*: 211.

176. Paul Kengor, "Secrets of Suriname," *National Review Online*, April 30, 2008. http://www.nationalreview.com/articles/224326/secrets-suriname/paul-kengor (accessed January 15, 2011).

177. Kengor and Doerner, *The Judge*: 216.

178. Ibid.

179. Ibid., 217.

180. Kengor, "Secrets of Suriname."

181. Bandeira, "O Brasil como Potência Regional e a Importância Estratégica da América do Sul na Sua Política Exterior," 7.

182. Bandeira, *Brasil, Argentina e Estados Unidos*: 458.

183. Luiz Felipe Lampreia, *O Brasil e os Ventos do Mundo: Memórias de Cinco Décadas na Cena Internacional* (Rio de Janeiro: Objetiva, 2010), 110-11.

184. Ibid., 111.

185. Kengor and Doerner, *The Judge*: 218.

Chapter Six

Negotiating the FTAA: The South American Subsystem after the Cold War

The disintegration of the USSR and the end of the bipolar system that characterized the Cold War combined with the proliferation of democratically elected regimes in South America would once again create new opportunities for the development of new patterns of relationships in the Western Hemisphere, which could eventually lead to subsystemic change. With the United States as the sole remaining superpower in a reconfigured international system, and with the fears of a Soviet-influenced communist takeover in Latin America out of policy makers' calculations, economic issues tended to eclipse the earlier predominance of security issues. Hence, the main prospects for the development of comparatively new patterns of relationships in the Americas in the immediate post-Cold War period were through the establishment of an all-encompassing regional trading bloc which would be relevant enough to create new patterns of trade and interdependence among the countries in the hemisphere and possibly spill over to other arenas including political and security ones.[1]

Indeed, the nineties began with such promise, after the completion of the North American Free Trade Agreement (NAFTA) and the beginning of the negotiations for a Free Trade Area of the Americas (FTAA) in 1994. But after many years of debate, the FTAA never came into existence and, instead of the creation of radically new patterns of relationships, what actually happened was the reinforcement and deepening of previous patterns along regional subsystemic lines. In fact, the analysis of the process leading to the rise and fall of the negotiations over the FTAA presents yet another opportunity to observe the functioning of regional subsystemic pressures contributing to affect the outcome of US foreign policies toward South America.

This chapter's choice in focusing on the FTAA negotiations as a case study does not mean that the political perspective that characterized the previous chapters will be abandoned in favor of a more economic approach based on trade analysis. Instead, in order to preserve a certain level of homogeneity across the chapters, this section will focus on the political dimension of processes of regional integration based on trade liberalization.[2] Therefore, the analysis will move away from the specific effects that the FTAA would have on patterns of trade in order to explore the political aspect of an increased economic interdependence that such agreement would likely generate, or, at least the policy makers' perception of such increased interdependence. The underlying assumption is that the conclusion of a free trade area in the Western Hemisphere would conceivably strengthen US political leverage, particularly in South America, since Mexico, the Caribbean states and Central America are by and large already dependent on the US market to a much higher degree than is the case in the rest of Latin America. In other words, the establishment of a Free Trade Area of the Americas could represent an important step in merging the North and South American subsystems through the creation of new patterns of interaction.

The main argument of this section is that the outcome of the negotiations concerning the establishment of a Free Trade of the Americas replicates the historical pattern exposed in the previous chapters in which the role of Brazil was key to understanding the relative absence of the United States in the South American regional subsystem. Although keeping with the overall theme of the United States as an "absent empire" in South America, there is no suggestion in this chapter that the institution of a free trade area in the Western Hemisphere should necessarily correspond to an "imperial offensive" on the part of the United States.[3] As a matter of fact, both NAFTA and the FTAA could be understood more as push from Latin American states than as an exclusively US idea, since the first began as a Mexican initiative (and was approved by the US House of Representatives by a relatively narrow margin of 234-200) and the proposal for the latter was met with enthusiasm in most of the Latin American capitals. This caveat is important because it marks a difference in tone from the previous chapters, and the notion of absence becomes now more salient than the notion of empire as defined in the introduction of this book. What matters for the purposes of the present chapter is the fact that the developments of the negotiations for a Free Trade Area in the Americas offer a good opportunity to investigate yet another instance when U.S. policy makers demonstrated a clear interest in expanding

US presence in South America—now in a completely different international environment from both of the periods analyzed earlier—but again the outcome ended up being the same relative absence.

This chapter examines the origins of the FTAA proposal, showing that the idea of a hemispheric free trade area was launched at the same time that each of the regional subsystems in the hemisphere were consolidating their own regional institutions around core regional states: NAFTA in North America, and Mercosur in South America. I show that the United States saw a hemispheric free trade agreement as an extension of NAFTA and consequently Mercosur was soon perceived as a nuisance by US policy makers. Likewise, Brazil demonstrated clear reservations regarding the establishment of a free trade area in the Americas since the beginning, a feeling that was not initially shared by its neighbors. Therefore, contrary to earlier periods examined by this research, the interests of Brazil and the United States now clashed, and given the disparities in power between the two countries, it would be reasonable to expect that the final outcome would favor the latter's view. Brazil's strategy was to lead the formation of a South American bloc, thus raising the costs for the United States to push for an agreement that could have the potential to affect the status quo in South America. I argue that Brazil's strategy of leadership was facilitated by the United States' lack thereof. I also show that one economic crisis in each of regional subsystems in the Americas—Mexico in North America, and Argentina in South America—acted as catalysts that reinforced subsystemic dynamics and made even more evident the separation between these two regional subsystems. The combination of these factors led to the eventual demise of the FTAA, with Brazil increasingly seeking to institutionalize the South American subsystem and the United States resorting to bilateral agreements with like-minded countries in that regional subsystem.

NAFTA AND MERCOSUR

A few months after the United States signed a free trade agreement with Canada in the late 1980s, Mexican President Carlos Salinas approached his US counterpart George Bush in the beginning of 1990 with the idea of a free trade agreement between the two countries. Initially, this proposal "came as a surprise" to the Bush administration,[4] since its top trade policy priority was the conclusion of the so-called Uruguay Round of the General Agreement on Tariffs and Trade (GATT), which would eventually lead to the creation of the World Trade Organization (WTO). In spite of the initial hesitation, the Bush administration soon embraced the idea, as an agreement with Mexico was seen from Washington's point of view as "part of an overall strategy of building" a "continental base" centered on the United States.[5] Therefore, in August of 1990, President Salinas officially requested a free trade agreement with the United States. The Canadians, who had just fought a fierce domestic battle over the conclusion of their own free trade agreement with the United States, did not initially want to get involved, but realizing that it had little to gain by staying on the sidelines, the Canadian government later decided that it would be better to participate and consequently they joined the negotiation in early 1991. Hence, what was initially a bilateral negotiation became a trilateral one, and thus was created the basis for the treaty known as North American Free Trade Agreement (NAFTA). More than just a free trade agreement, at the political level NAFTA allowed the US government to reaffirm the principles of international free trade "as a symbol and a reality of a new economic order ushered by the United States as part of its victory in the Cold War."[6] Indeed, in the midst of the negotiations with Mexico, the Bush administration unveiled its Enterprise for the Americas Initiative (EAI), a hemispheric program of which one of the central aims was the extension of free trade to the whole of the Americas. Within the framework of a "new world order," NAFTA would thus be just a strategic "continental base" from which the United States would lead the post-Cold War world, beginning by reaffirming its leadership in the Western Hemisphere. Therefore, US interest in hemispheric integration could be interpreted as going beyond the notion of economic benefits given the "possibilities it offers for the reinforcement of the structural and ideological foundations of US hegemony, consistent with its parallel global strategies."[7]

The vision of a hemispheric free trade area put forth by President Bush was embraced by subsequent US administrations until its demise in the mid-2000s during the second President Bush administration. While the first President Bush launched the overall idea and initiated NAFTA, the Clinton administration wrapped up NAFTA and made the FTAA one of its top foreign policy priorities in Latin America, an approach that was followed by his successor. According to one of the participants in the initial stages of FTAA, there was a growing feeling in the Clinton administration in 1992 that a hemispheric summit "would be a logical follow-up to NAFTA."[8] President Clinton had the expectation that the conclusion of NAFTA would enable the United States to "use the Mexican precedent to go into the whole rest of Latin America."[9] Accordingly, in 1993, the Clinton administration announced that a summit would take place in Miami in December 1994 to discuss a number of hemispheric issues. During the Miami Summit, which was attended by all countries in the hemisphere except Cuba, the participating countries announced the goal of a hemispheric free trade area to be established by the year 2005, thus marking the beginning of the negotiations of the FTAA.

The year the Miami Summit convened was particularly relevant for matters of hemispheric integration. In January of 1994, the North American Free Trade Agreement, which had been approved by the US Congress in late 1993, came into force. In December of that year, a few days after the Miami Summit, Argentina, Brazil, Paraguay, and Uruguay signed in Brazil the Protocol of Ouro Preto, which complemented the 1991 Treaty of Asunción and established the institutional basis of the Southern Common Market (Mercosur) thus giving Mercosur legal personality of international law and providing it with effective actor capabilities in the international arena.[10] On the first day of 1995, the four countries of Mercosur introduced a common external tariff covering about eight-five percent of the goods traded within the bloc, thus transforming Mercosur into a customs union, although an imperfect one given the fact that some of the goods were outside the scope of the tariff. From an economic standpoint, Mercosur has been the second largest trading bloc in the hemisphere after NAFTA in terms of combined GDP, and the fourth in the world behind the European Union, NAFTA, and the Association of South East Asian Nations (ASEAN). Therefore, any meaningful regional integration in the Western Hemisphere would have to accommodate the reality of Mercosur—to deal with it or to do away with it. From the point of view of the United States, hemispheric integration meant the absorption of Mercosur into an enlarged NAFTA with the United States at the center. In fact, members of the Clinton administration expressed a number of times that Mercosur was seen as "harmful" to the FTAA and "a threat to hemispheric regionalism."[11] As pointed out above, the ideal design for the Clinton administration would be basically to extend the NAFTA model southward. Given US economic weight, such an arrangement could have the potential to eventually absorb the South American regional subsystem if it ended up creating new patterns of relationship in the hemisphere relevant enough to bring about a relative homogenization of a Latin American periphery arranged around a US center.

Because of the prospects of altering the status quo in the South American subsystem, this scenario was feared by Brazil, which held suspicions regarding the establishment of free trade in the Americas since the beginning and saw it as an "obstacle to the designs of Brazilian leadership within the regional order" in South America.[12] In fact, the Brazilian foreign minister during the Cardoso administration described the FTAA as a tool to consolidate US "economic preponderance in the continent" and as a "potential threat" to Brazil, therefore mirroring verbatim the Clinton administration's view of Mercosur.[13] When the Enterprise for the Americas Initiative was unveiled in 1991, Brazil was clearly "the least enthusiastic among the participating countries to move forward on hemispheric integration."[14] In fact, Brazilian official position towards hemispheric free trade has been, like the US official position, considerably consistent through time, permeating four different administrations from different political outlooks. Basically, Brazil's strategy has been one of securing and reinforcing its position within the South American subsystem in order to avoid its absorption by an all-encompassing hemispheric subsystem. Within this context, the establishment of Mercosur with the Treaty of Asuncion in 1991 was a key strategic component. As soon as George Bush announced his Enterprise for the Americas Initiative, the administration of Collor de Mello in Brazil responded that it would only negotiate a hemispheric agreement within the 4+1 framework, that is, the four countries of the recently created Mercosur would take a joint position when negotiating with the United States. In 1993, the same year that NAFTA was approved by the US Congress, the administration of Itamar Franco made a proposal for a SAFTA—South American Free Trade Area.[15] These early efforts demonstrate the Brazilian concern in securing a "continental base" for itself in order to counter the prospects of a US commercial offensive in South America. In fact, when Cardoso was the Brazilian foreign minister, he spoke about the notion of a "South American platform,"[16] and later, as president, Cardoso referred to Mercosur as "a pole from which we will organize the South American space."[17] Mercosur was thus seen as a hub from which Brazil would build an alternative pole of attraction in the hemisphere, and as a result would attempt to create obstacles for greater US penetration in the South American subsystem. As will be shown below, these efforts were continued and then deepened in subsequent Brazilian administrations.

Brazilian official strategy towards hemispheric free trade was, not surprisingly, far from enjoying unanimity in South America. As a matter of fact, two of the biggest powers in the region, Argentina and Chile, were very enthusiastic about the possibility of coming to an agreement with the United States as early as possible, ideally before the 2005 deadline. In a complete reversal of its historically contentious stance towards the United States, the Argentine government became one of its most fervent supporters during the greater part of the nineties. Distant and often confrontational towards US foreign policy initiatives during most of its history, Argentina undertook a complete shift in that historical position under the administration of Carlos Menen and sought to establish, in the now legendary words of Menen's foreign minister, "carnal relations" with the United States.[18] Perhaps the best indication of this renewed relationship is the fact that Argentina dispatched naval vessels to the 1991 Gulf War, the only Latin American country to do so. In 1998, the United States reciprocated Argentinean cooperation by designating Argentina as a "major non-NATO ally," also the only Latin American country to have this distinction.[19] Within this context, a trade agreement with the United States was a logical extension of Argentinean foreign policy, which even entertained the possibility of an accession to NAFTA. However, Argentina could not freely sign a bilateral agreement with the United States without leading to the demise of Mercosur as a customs union and creating problems with Brazil, which was a more important market for Argentina than the United States: in 1994, the year before the Ouro Preto Protocol took effect, Argentina exported twice as much in value to Brazil than to the United States.[20] Therefore, by locking in Argentina through Mercosur, Brazil could with reasonable success contain Argentinean initial enthusiasm during the early stages of the FTAA negotiations. On the other hand, Argentinean and other South American countries' eagerness for such an agreement was an important reason why Brazil could not simply negate to negotiate the US-proposed FTAA, as it would leave Brazil isolated in the region it aspired to influence.

Conversely, the constraints that applied to Argentina were not valid for Chile. Chile was not part of Mercosur and the United States was a much more important market for Chilean exports than Brazil. Moreover, Chile has had a relatively open economy and international trade has been a key component of its development strategy. In fact, Chile had been seeking a free trade agreement with the United States since the early nineties, and after Mexico it was next in line to negotiate such an agreement. During the Miami Summit in 1994, Chile was officially invited to join NAFTA and was hailed by the Canadian Prime Minister as the fourth "amigo" in the North American agreement.[21] Following the official invitation, negotiations for Chilean accession to NAFTA were formally initiated in 1995. Nevertheless, the Clinton administration had one important domestic obstacle after 1994—the lack of the so-called "fast track" authority to negotiate free trade agreements. This bureaucratic detail that, up until then, was little known outside the circle of trade experts, turned out to be the centerpiece of the problems facing the United States during the negotiations of the FTAA, and made it considerably easier for Brazil to enforce its agenda in South America.

According to the US Constitution, it is the responsibility of the Congress to regulate matters of foreign trade. Because of the possibility that Congress may change an agreement previously signed by the executive to the point that it becomes entirely distinct from what was originally agreed upon by the parts, Congress may grant the president a special authority that became known as "fast track," which gives greater autonomy to the executive to sign free trade agreements, leaving Congress the possibility to either accept or reject it without amendments. Additionally, fast track rules require the Congress to vote within ninety days after the bill is submitted by the president. NAFTA was approved by the US Congress under fast track provisions, but that expired in 1994. For the remainder of his administration, President Clinton unsuccessfully tried to reinstate fast track authority after 1994 in order to promote the FTAA agenda. As it became clear the difficulty that the Clinton administration had in obtaining fast track, the agreement with Chile lost momentum and by 1996 Chile had all but abandoned any hopes of joining

NAFTA. The Chilean President Eduardo Frei was reported to have "considered the United States an unreliable ally."[22] As the difficulties in joining NAFTA became clear, "Chilean advocates of expanding ties with the Southern Cone gained ground."[23] Indeed, in October of 1996, Chile joined Mercosur as an associated member, as it became, in the words of Henry Kissinger, "tired of waiting for the long-promised access to NAFTA."[24] By 1997, after Chile had already signed free trade agreements with both Mexico and Canada, as well as with Mercosur and other South American countries, the Chilean foreign minister declared that NAFTA ascension no longer had "either the urgency or the importance it had in 1994."[25]

Therefore, whereas Brazilian leadership was an important factor to explain the lack of an early agreement in the case of Argentina, in the case of Chile the main explanation should lie with US lack of leadership; not so much because of an unwillingness to lead, but more because of incapacity to do so due to domestic dynamics. It is this combination of Brazilian obstructionism and US inability to provide the necessary leadership that provides the better explanation for the failure of the FTAA. In other words, Brazilian strategy of leading a South American bloc was greatly facilitated by US lack of leadership in the process. The cases of Argentina and Chile during the first couple of years of FTAA negotiations provide a clear illustration of this claim.

LAUNCHING THE FTAA

As indicated above, since the very beginning of the negotiations for the establishment of a Free Trade Area of the Americas two major views regarding the character of hemispheric integration clashed. These two views were represented by the two biggest economies in the hemisphere and the two major powers within their respective regional subsystems: the United States and Brazil. These different perspectives were rooted in the fact that the US view of the international system after the Cold War clashed with the Brazilian view of preserving its role in the South American regional subsystem. As noted above, while for the United States an expansion of NAFTA to the whole hemisphere formed the basis of its approach to hemispheric integration and was seen as part of the broader US view of a new world order, the Brazilian priority was to consolidate its position in the South American subsystem which, from the point of view of Brazilian policy makers, would be jeopardized by a hemispheric free trade area.

Brazil's concern about regional leadership was unsurprisingly not shared by the other South American countries, which, as exemplified by the cases of Argentina and Chile mentioned above, generally greeted the 1994 Miami

Summit with great enthusiasm. In contrast, the Brazilian Foreign Minister signalized Brazilian skepticism regarding the Miami meeting and "warned that the region had overly high expectations of the summit."[26] These dynamics were already patently clear when US Vice President Al Gore made a trip to Argentina, Bolivia, and Brazil in 1994 to promote the Miami Summit, scheduled for the end of that year. Like Argentina, Bolivia also demonstrated great interest in the proposal for a hemispheric free trade area and even suggested that it should be reached by the year 2000 instead of by the original 2005 goal. On the other hand, Gore's meeting with Brazilian representatives revolved around recognizing Brazil's "stature in hemispheric affairs" and "little discussion of the summit agenda as such."[27] The themes that Gore discussed in Brazil evidently reflected what the true Brazilian concerns were at the time.

As the preparations for the Miami Summit went forward, it became increasingly clear that accommodating the different views of the United States and Brazil would be a central issue in the negotiations for a free trade area in the hemisphere. Because it could not simply block the negotiations as it was in a relatively isolated position, Brazilian strategy was to "render the plan of action more modest in its ambitions, less exact in its objectives, less specific in its timetables, and less accountable in its implementation."[28] In fact, not only did Brazil actively participate in the negotiations, its delegation in Miami was second in number only to the United States, which is an indication of the interest that the Brazilian government had in the issue. According to one US negotiator, "the heart of the drama of Miami was Brazil's struggle to establish itself as the interlocutor for South America,"[29] and a major concern of Brazil was to introduce changes in the final text "aimed at lessening future US influence and leaving the integration process less carefully scripted."[30] Contrary to most of the other countries, Brazil wanted to gain time in order to consolidate and enlarge Mercosur, in order to strengthen its own position vis-à-vis the United States, and only then attempt to strike a "grand bargain between NAFTA and Mercosur (that is, between the United States and Brazil)."[31] In spite of Brazilian efforts to bypass the mention of a date certain, the Miami Declaration stuck with the 2005 goal of hemispheric free trade, reflecting the view of the majority of the countries in Latin America.

Therefore, by the end of the Miami Summit, even though the differences between Brazil and the United States were clear, it was the latter that got the upper hand and dictated the pace of the negotiations at the onset. This could obviously be understood as a logical corollary of the overwhelming disparities in all dimensions of power between the two countries, which seemed to offer support for the conventional analysis of US hegemony in Latin America predicting that "[b]ecause of US power, NAFTA is probably a closer approximation to the evolving FTAA than is Mercosur."[32] In fact, many studies that attempted to forecast the "economic and business outcomes of the FTAA" commonly accepted the apparently obvious premise that the FTAA "is going to build on the basic principles of NAFTA."[33] As soon as it was established, NAFTA was quickly presented even as a theoretical model of "hemispheric regionalism" as opposed to a "Latin American regionalism."[34] However, the actual facts do not corroborate the assumption that US power would inevitably bring into being the US view of hemispheric integration. This gap between a proposed US policy and the actual outcome begs for an explanation. Evidently, one could once again concentrate only on domestic factors and conclude that this gap can be adequately explained by the troubles that the Clinton administration had in obtaining fast track authority from Congress. Although one can be satisfied with this explanation—and domestic factors were certainly critical—it can also be argued that it is an incomplete one. Indeed, even when the Bush administration finally got the fast track—then renamed "Trade Promotion Authority" (TPA)—between 2002 and 2007, thus including the 2005 deadline for the completion of the FTAA, still no hemispheric NAFTA came into being. Instead, the Bush administration used the TPA to negotiate a series of bilateral trade agreements with countries in the region, hence outside the scope of a comprehensive hemispheric framework. The argument of this book is that taking into consideration the regional subsystemic level can help explain this outcome. In order to do that, it is necessary to understand how interactions at the regional subsystemic level contributed to the developments of the FTAA negotiations after the Miami Summit.

MEXICO AND ARGENTINA: A TALE OF TWO CRISES

A few days after the Miami Summit, on December 20, 1994, and following a series of political shocks during that year that put Mexico's political and economic stability in question, a sudden devaluation of the Mexican peso caused a profound economic crisis in that country, with impacts all over Latin America. Having just signed a free trade agreement with Mexico and with high stakes in its financial stability, the United States acted swiftly in leading the elaboration of an international rescue plan for its southern neighbor. The final package totaled about fifty billion dollars, with the United States and the International Monetary Fund (where the United States has the largest share of votes) contributing with more than two-thirds of this value.[35] Although the rescue package ended up being successful and the Mexican economy recovered from the crisis by 1996, the costs of rescuing Mexico reduced much of the enthusiasm in Washington for further agreements with other Latin American countries, which greatly contributed to the difficulties of the Clinton administration in obtaining fast track authority after 1994.

Indeed, according to some analyses, the Mexican crisis represented a "lethal blow" for the FTAA.[36] This US paralysis offered an opportunity for Brazil to push its agenda in South America, and while "U.S. congressional approval of any post-NAFTA trade agreements had been put in jeopardy by the Mexican crisis, Mercosur initiated negotiations with Bolivia, Venezuela, and Chile."[37] By 1997, both Chile and Bolivia—which were two of the most enthusiastic countries regarding the FTAA—had been added to Mercosur as associate members, thus starting a process of regional institutionalization that, as will be shown below, would eventually lead to something resembling the original Brazilian scheme of a South American Free Trade Area.

Therefore, by the time of the Second Summit of the Americas in 1998, in Santiago, Chile, which officially launched the negotiations of the FTAA, there was a clear change in the mood from four years earlier. While in North America the United States had been intimately involved in rescuing Mexico from financial collapse, in South America, Brazil, as President Cardoso had remarked, was actively seeking to "organize the South American space" by using Mercosur as "the pole of attraction for a future South American Free Trade Area." As the United States, for better or for worse, became more involved in Mexican affairs and faced the domestic consequences of such involvement, a "leadership vacuum" was created in South America which "was quickly filled by Brazil reaching out to other South American countries so as to establish SAFTA to accumulate negotiating power" in order to deal with the United States. A clear illustration of this change in mood that facilitated Brazilian strategy is the fact that Chile was aligned with Mercosur at the negotiating table in Santiago.[38]

Consequently, at the Santiago Summit in 1998, the scenario was much more favorable to Brazil in comparison to Miami in 1994, as Brazil had achieved its key objective of negotiating the FTAA not on a country-by-country basis but "between a South American bloc, led by Brazil, and a North American bloc, led by the United States."[39] This notion of the FTAA as following the principle of "building blocs," that is, integration within the existent regional blocs, had been a key component of the Brazilian strategy, which was clearly much more focused on first securing its position in South America before reaching any agreement that included the United States. Hence, as the negotiations were formally launched in Santiago, what initially seemed a process of hemispheric integration centered on NAFTA increasingly became a process of hemispheric integration with two poles of attraction, one in North America and the other in South America. In a matter of just four years, "the roles of US and Brazil in the FTAA negotiations had been reversed."[40] According to one US analyst at the time, "[t]he balance of hemispheric power shifted at the Santiago summit" as "the United States had lost the initiative in the FTAA negotiations" and had "become a mere bystander in a hemispheric process of trade liberalization in which Brazil now is setting the pace and direction of negotiations."[41]

Another financial crisis would soon have an impact on the negotiations of hemispheric integration in the Americas. Similarly to what had happened to Mexico after the Miami Summit, a few months after the Santiago Summit, Brazil would also be forced to abruptly devalue its currency at the beginning of 1999. Argentina, which at the time had a currency regime fixed by law to the value of the US dollar, soon suffered the consequences of the Brazilian devaluation and, after a brutal economic, political, and social crisis, was also eventually forced to abandon its fixed exchange rate in January 2002. Therefore, between 1999 and 2001, while Brazil had a flexible exchange rate, Argentina stuck to a fixed exchange rate, which created significant macroeconomic imbalances between the two major Mercosur members. These events had dreadful economic effects on Mercosur and created a series of bitter trade disputes between Brazil and Argentina, with Argentina resorting to a number of protectionist measures incompatible with Mercosur rules in order to compensate for the disparities in the exchange rates between the two countries, which had made Argentinean exports to Brazil less competitive. Intra-Mercosur exports, which had quadrupled between 1994 and 1998, from around six to twenty billion dollars, dropped to ten billion dollars in 2002.[42] Thus, while Mercosur was seen as a great success by the time of the Santiago Summit in 1998, at the next gathering of the heads of state and government of the Americas, which was held in Quebec, Canada, in 2001, the South American bloc had effectively lost much of its economic rationale and faced its darkest period, with many analysts proclaiming its imminent demise.[43] However, while the 1999-2001 crises underlined the economic limitations of Mercosur, the eventual survival of the bloc and the subsequent events underscored the importance of its political dimension, particularly to Brazil.

But before examining the factors behind the survival of Mercosur even after it seemed to have collapsed, it is crucial to investigate how the Argentinean crisis made evident pressures at the regional subsystemic level. Similarly to the Mexican crisis, which brought Mexico and the United States closer together and at the same time decreased US eagerness for hemispheric integration, the Argentinean crisis ended up having comparable political effects in respect to the South American subsystem—as Argentina recovered from its economic crisis, it became closer to Brazil and far less enthusiastic about the FTAA. In other words, both the Mexican and the Argentine crises worked as catalysts for reinforcing patterns of relationships within their respective regional subsystems, thus demonstrating the difficulties of overcoming such patterns based on regular interactions and geography and, consequently, in bringing about subsystemic change. This assessment becomes even more apparent when one considers that both Mexico and Argentina had similar foreign policy trajectories in their relations with the United States—from a generally cool and sometimes confrontational policy during most of their history, to an abrupt shift in the late 1980s and early 1990s as both sought to develop a close-as-possible policy. While this shift may be explained both by domestic factors as well as a response to the changes in the international system, the regional subsystemic approach can help explain the differences in outcome of these two similar policies. Examining the distinct interactions that followed the Argentinean economic crisis in contrast to the Mexican economic crisis a few years earlier uncovers how subsystemic dynamics were at play.

At least two factors can be pointed out to explain why the Argentinean crisis had the effect of bringing Brazil and Argentina closer together instead of further apart, as seemed to be the trend during the several trade disputes between Argentina and Brazil after 1999. One factor was that the economic crisis led Argentinean policy makers to the realization that the policy of "carnal relations" with the United States announced in the early 1990s seemed to have produced few tangible results. In contrast to its behavior during the Mexican crisis a few years earlier, when the United States quickly acted to bail out its southern neighbor, Argentina was treated with "indifference and lack of assistance" by Washington.[44] This evident dissimilarity in US attitudes accelerated a process of reorientation in Argentina's foreign policy towards a gradual distancing from Washington, which had in fact been taking place since 1997, by the end of the Menem administration.[45] With the short-lived era of automatic alignment with the United States over, Brazil emerged as the "principal beneficiary" of US unresponsiveness to Argentina's economic debacle, as Argentina openly refocused its foreign policy in improving relations with its most important neighbor.[46] Realizing an opportunity to reinforce its position in South America, Brazil, "in stark contrast to the perceived callous indifference of the United States to Argentina's plight," took a series of unilateral measures beginning in 2002 in order to facilitate Argentinean exports.[47] In addition, all the Mercosur countries, including the associated members Chile and Bolivia, convened an extraordinary meeting in Buenos Aires to offer their support and request financial assistance to Argentina from international institutions. Therefore, as Mario Carranza asserts, in spite of the negative effects of the Argentinean crisis on Mercosur, it "had a positive political impact" since the "absence of US leadership to deal with the crisis strengthened political solidarity among the Mercosur partners."[48]

The second factor accounting for why the Argentinean crisis ultimately had the effect of bringing Argentina closer to Brazil while it simultaneously became far less enthusiastic about the need for a FTAA is, in a sense, intimately related to the first: the fact that the extension and depth of the crisis that hit Argentina led to a "significant reassessment of the country's power position in the regional, hemispheric and multilateral systems." The immedi-

ate effect of this "downward revision of Argentina's power potential" was
that it increased the "incentives for bandwagonning with its stronger neigh-
bour in order to increase its leverage in external negotiations."[49] In other
words, the Argentinean crisis had such a psychological impact on policy
makers and civil society alike as to remove Argentinean pretensions of joining the developed North—as symbolized by its inconsequential granting as a
"major non-NATO ally" during the early 1990s—and to "South-American-
ize" Argentinean foreign policy. This reorientation meant that Argentina's
foreign policy had become closer to Brazil's, which had been constantly
seeking to establish a united South American front to negotiate the FTAA.

The above discussion helps to understand Mercosur's endurance in spite
of its near collapse. The basic reason seems to be the fact that Mercosur has
never been just about trade liberalization, but also had important political and
also military dimensions. While Argentina, as well as Paraguay and Uruguay, initially saw the commercial aspects of Mercosur as the major factor
for joining the regional trading bloc, for Brazil, whose economic benefits
from Mercosur are less significant, the main motivation "would appear to be
its ambition to be a regional power."[50] Successive Brazilian administrations
have consistently valued Mercosur not merely for its potential economic
benefits, but as a "potent symbol of Brazil's ambition to be a leader of South
American unity."[51] Before the Quebec meeting in 2001, at the height of the
crisis between Brazil and Argentina, President Cardoso set the tone of Brazil's position declaring that "'Mercosur is a destiny for us, while the FTAA is
an option."[52] Without accounting for the strategic considerations behind Brazilian support for Mercosur, in terms of the consolidation of a sphere of
influence in South America, it becomes definitely problematic to explain its
resilience. In fact, the survival of Mercosur after bitter trade disputes between
Brazil and Argentina following their financial crises can only be understood
in the context of the political approximation that they contributed to bring
about, even as it accelerated the shift in Argentinean foreign policy away
from Washington and closer to Brasilia. In other words, Mercosur's survival
"reflected a convergence of foreign policy or 'strategic' incentives between
the governments of Argentina and Brazil" that had been initiated in the late
1990s.[53] Also important is the fact that after both countries were forced to
adopt a fluctuating exchange rate, this "strategic convergence" was followed
by a gradual macroeconomic convergence, which removed much of the rationale behind their trade disputes. Indeed, intra-Mercosur exports grew every
single year after hitting the bottom in 2002, from ten billion dollars to a
record forty-one billion dollars in 2008.[54]

In regional subsystemic terms, the resilience of Mercosur is explained
because it is not an artificial arrangement with no basis on actual interactions
but an institutional translation of a regional subsystemic reality—the same
way that NAFTA is.[55] A putative FTAA, on the other hand, would have to

either reflect or create new patterns of relationships in order to overcome subsystemic pressures and be an effective and enduring institution. Because the FTAA did not reflect actual patterns of interactions between the North and South American regional subsystems, it would have probably required a combination of specific political circumstances in order to bear the necessary costs to make it happen. Another possibility was that an unexpected disturbance in the regional subsystems in the hemisphere—such as a financial crisis in a key regional state—could set in motion potentially self-reinforcing subsystemic dynamics, making it even more difficult or costly to create new patterns of relationship necessary for the establishment of an enduring hemispheric arrangement.

BRAZIL AS THE LEADER OF A SOUTH AMERICAN BLOC

Therefore, during the course of their interactions following the goals enunciated at the Miami Summit in 1994, it became clear that neither US power nor the enthusiasm with which the FTAA proposal was initially received in Latin America would necessarily translate into a comprehensive hemispheric integration scheme centered on the United States. The difficulties in obtaining fast track authority and the discrepancies in behavior between the Mexican and Argentinean crises seemed to signal that the United States was either unwilling or unable to bear the costs of subsystemic change through the establishment of fundamentally new patterns of interactions. On the other hand, contrary to its past strategies aimed at preventing the United States to undertake such change and preserving the stability of the South American subsystem—when Brazil raised the benefits of subsystemic stability for the United States—now the Brazilian strategy was basically one of increasing the costs of subsystemic change through the consolidation of a South American bloc centered on Mercosur.

By the time of the Third Summit of the Americas in April of 2001 in Quebec, in spite of the apparent collapse of Mercosur at the time, the Brazilian strategy, in great part because of the context explained above, was reasonably secured. As a new administration was inaugurated in the United States that openly proclaimed its commitment to free trade and to the establishment of the FTAA, the process of consolidation of a South American space had already been set in motion.[56] As the preparations for the Quebec meeting began in 2000, Brazil launched a historic initiative: it brought all of South America's leaders together for the first time to a conference in Brasilia in order to discuss a variety of issues pertaining to that regional subsystem. The significance of this event was that it was the first exclusive meeting of all South American presidents. The Mexican president, like every other Latin

American leader outside South America, was not invited for the summit and declared that he "would like to have been invited," adding that "our geographical situation in North America in any way impedes us from having an intense relationship with Latin America."[57] However, this was not to be another "Latin American" meeting, but explicitly a South American one. It was a concrete symbol of the realization that South America was in fact a distinct regional subsystem, one in which Brazil played a central role. As Sean Burges commented, the 2000 meeting was "the first exclusive gathering of South American presidents, giving symbolic gravitas to South America as a viable geopolitical entity" and its outcome suggested "an implicit acceptance of the consensual leadership role that Brazil had been accruing over the previous six years."[58]

For Burges, who places particular emphasis on the above-mentioned concept of "consensual leadership," this kind of leadership is based not on "coercion or imposition" but on "coordination, consultation, and discussion."[59] Since it requires fewer resources than relying on coercion, it is particularly fitted for a country that occupies a key position in its region but at the same time has limited power resources, as is the case of Brazil. The concept alluded to by Burges is based on the notion of "co-operative hegemony" developed by Thomas Pedersen. In contrast to the hegemonic stability theory, which focuses only on powerful states,[60] the co-operative hegemony approach "centres around the proposition that major states which are militarily weak or weakened may seek to maximise or stabilise their influence through non coercive means by pursuing a strategy of co-operative hegemony within a multilateral structure."[61] Thus, Pedersen's theory of co-operative hegemony seeks to explain the formative processes of regional institutionalization based on the long-term strategies of major regional powers, while at the same time it highlights the importance of geopolitical and security elements, rather than economic factors, leading to regional institutionalization. A key element of the grand strategy of co-operative hegemony is what Pedersen denominates "power aggregation capacity," which "refers to the capacity of a regional big power to make a number of neighbouring states rally around its political project." The author adds that even though "this capacity is constrained by external structural factors at the regional and global level, it also depends upon psychological factors and leadership skills."[62] Pedersen's cooperative hegemony approach provides a particularly appropriate framework to understand the role of Brazil during the FTAA negotiations, which became especially evident after the year 2000.

By bringing together all twelve presidents of South America to Brasilia, the Brazilian government officially signaled its attempt to rally the South American states around Brazil's political project of organizing a South American space as a means of inserting the region in the post-Cold War international system. President Cardoso described the 2000 summit as a "moment of reaffirmation of South America's identity as a region" adding that a "free trade agreement between Mercosur and the Andean Community will be the dorsal spine of South America as an extended economic space." Therefore, he concluded, "it should be seen as a political objective of immediate concern."[63] These statements make plainly clear the goal as well as the means to accomplish it. The immediate goal was the construction of South America as a distinct economic and political space. In order to achieve it, it was necessary to act in two dimensions—at the ideational level, it was essential to affirm a South American identity, while at the practical level it was necessary to merge Mercosur and the Andean Community, which was the second major trading bloc in South America and at the time included Bolivia, Peru, Ecuador, Colombia, and Venezuela. This Brazilian proposal—which was clearly an upshot of the original scheme of a South American Free Trade Area unveiled almost a decade before—is especially significant if considered within the context of the acute crisis that Mercosur was going through at the time, as pointed out above.

The principle behind this policy was consistently supported by the administrations that preceded Cardoso as well as by the administrations that have succeeded him. In fact, the administration of Lula da Silva, which was inaugurated in 2003, saw the integration of South America as a top foreign policy priority[64] and in 2004, during the third meeting of South American presidents in Peru, Mercosur and the Andean Community formalized a cooperation agreement thus creating the "South America Community of Nations," which later became the "Union of South American Nations," or Unasur. In May 2008, the Unasur countries met in Brasilia to sign its constitutive treaty, establishing its juridical and political components and including the Brazilian proposal of a South American Defense Council. The Brazilian defense minister, when asked on a visit to Washington how the United States could help, said that the best way the United States could collaborate would be to "watch from the outside and keep its distance."[65] Colombia, which has had strong military ties with the United States and was then in the middle of an acute diplomatic crisis with Venezuela and Ecuador, was the only country not to sign the pact that created the Defense Council. However, after intense negotiations led by Brazil and a growing fear of political isolation in the region, Colombia decided to join the Council a couple of months later. In 2009, the South American Defense Council held its first meeting in Santiago, Chile, and was attended by all defense ministers of the region. The main significance of this body is that it excludes the United States and overlaps with functions that were previously performed by hemispheric bodies such as the Organization of American States (OAS). In particular, it represents a challenge to the security counterpart of the FTAA launched at the 1994 Miami

Summit: the Defense Ministerial of the Americas, which assembled for the first time in 1995, in Williamsburg, Virginia, and have met roughly every two years since then in different countries.[66]

By explicitly articulating the concept of a South America as a distinct regional subsystem, successive Brazilian administrations after the end of the Cold War were basically recuperating a recurrent theme of Brazil's foreign policy that, as indicated in chapter 5, was present since the early days of independence: the notion that in contrast to rest of Latin America, where Brazil would seek not to get involved and would—sometimes tacitly, sometimes explicitly—recognize US preeminence, South America was understood by Brazilian policy makers as being a Brazilian sphere of influence where US interference should be kept at arm's length since it could easily overtake Brazil as the predominant player in the region. The meeting of South American presidents in 2000 made explicit the concept of South America once again as a key component of Brazilian diplomacy, a reality that turned out to be even more salient during the Lula da Silva administration. One noteworthy change that was marked by the 2000 meeting was that, while initially the Brazilian view of South America had been mostly restricted to the Southern Cone, now it unequivocally incorporated the northern tier countries of South America, including Guiana and Suriname.[67] This reflected a process that had began since at least the late 1970s, and had become apparent by the Brazilian behavior during the case of Suriname in the 1980s recounted in the previous chapter. The agreements between Mercosur and the Andean Community and the successive meetings of South American presidents that led to the creation of a Union of South America Nations are thus the institutional translation of these earlier interactions.

Consequently, by the time the Bush administration finally got fast track authority from Congress in 2002, the Brazilian strategy was already clearly underway. Between 1994 and 2002, the years that US administrations had no fast track and therefore could not provide clear leadership to the FTAA process, Brazil had achieved its goal of forging a South American bloc by using Mercosur as an alternative hub to NAFTA with reasonable success, and was also in the process of bringing Argentina closer to the Brazilian camp. With this basic framework in place, Brazil could shift the focus away from the US lack of fast track and concentrate on more substantive issues such as agriculture liberalization, particularly regarding non-tariff barriers, which had been a focal point of disagreement between the United States and Brazil throughout the negotiations. Again, the United States helped the Brazilian case by providing the necessary ammunition when the US Congress passed a one-hundred-billion-dollar farm bill that significantly increased agricultural subsidies in the same year that President Bush got fast track authority, in 2002.[68] The passing of the 2002 farm bill signaled the US unwillingness to liberalize a sector that was central to Brazilian interests in the FTAA and allowed President Cardoso to frame the United States, and not Brazil, as the real problem for the establishment of hemispheric free trade.[69] In addition, the Bush administration after September 2001 was primarily focused on the Middle East, which dominated the US domestic political debate at the time.

Within this context, the results of a ministerial meeting in Miami in 2003, at the final phase of the FTAA negotiations, was considered a Brazilian victory—the final outcome of Miami was termed as a "FTAA à la carte" or a "FTAA-light," that is, a non-comprehensive FTAA with different levels of commitment.[70] The Ministerial Declaration of Miami stated that the "Ministers recognize that countries may assume different levels of commitments" and that the "negotiations should allow for countries that so choose, within the FTAA, to agree to additional obligations and benefits."[71] These statements meant that the notion that the FTAA should be negotiated as a comprehensive "single undertaking," which was a basic principle until then, had come to an end. Each country was free to negotiate which areas to put in a FTAA agreement and with the interests of the United States and Brazil "very much at opposite ends of the spectrum," (since the first was interested mainly in liberalization of services and investments and the latter on the agricultural sector) they did not have any incentives to compromise.[72] It was the beginning of the end of the FTAA.

As the American heads of state convened for the Fourth Summit of the Americas in Mar del Plata, Argentina, in 2005, the long process of FTAA agony that had become evident by the Miami Ministerial Declaration two years earlier came to an end. Since 2005 marked the original deadline for a final agreement on the FTAA and no agreement was eventually reached, the ailing FTAA was virtually buried in Mar del Plata. The 2005 summit was a perfect illustration of how Mercosur was efficiently used by Brazil as the core of its strategy to fend off the establishment of a hemispheric free trade area. Among the thirty-four participants of the summit, twenty-nine were in favor of moving forward on the FTAA negotiations.[73] The five dissenting nations were composed of the four full members of Mercosur plus Venezuela, which a month later was officially invited to join Mercosur as a full member. It is noteworthy that these five nations together represent about seventy-five percent of the total GDP of South America. With the possibility of a comprehensive hemispheric agreement off the table, and with the Trade Promotion Authority in hand, the Bush administration sought to establish bilateral free trade agreements with individual countries, including Chile, Peru, Colombia, and Ecuador, at the same time that Brazil sought to establish South America as an "extended economic space," as President Cardoso had declared at the beginning of the decade. The biggest difference between the two strategies seems to be that while the United States relies on specific and detailed agreements with individual countries, Brazil seeks a higher degree of multilateral institutionalization though a regional framework coupled with the attempt to construct a South American identity. These two approaches seem to be "on a collision course"[74] and point toward a situation of what Henry Kissinger had termed at the beginning of the last decade as a "tacit competition" between Brazil and the United States in South America since the end of the Cold War.[75]

CHAPTER CONCLUSION

The process involving the rise and fall of the FTAA negotiations is a clear illustration of Brazil's main regional strategy of keeping the United States at arm's length in the South American subsystem. However, while earlier periods were characterized by a general coinciding of core goals between the two biggest countries in the hemisphere—which made Brazilian strategy less apparent and often confounded with subordination to US policies—the reorganization of hemispheric relations brought about by the end of the Cold War created the conditions for a clash in views and objectives between the United States and Brazil. This made evident that the generally cooperative attitudes of earlier times were contingent on US support to Brazilian broader regional goals. As Brazil perceived the United States as competing with its goal of keeping the status quo in the South American regional subsystem, Brazilian strategy adapted to this perception. Therefore, if earlier strategies were aimed at increasing the benefits of regional subsystemic stability for the United States, now Brazil sought to increase the costs of subsystemic change. This was done through intense participation in the FTAA process, even though Brazil had clearly no enthusiasm for it, while in parallel leading the formation of a South American bloc by creating political and economic incentives that in many ways competed with the FTAA goals. Whereas the United States sought to use an extended NAFTA as a continental base from which it would lead the post Cold War world, Brazil sought to build a South American platform organized around Mercosur. Because these two objectives tended to collide, both the United States and Brazil saw each other's project as a threat to their own policies from the beginning.

As it turned out, in spite of the disparities in power between the United States and Brazil, time was on the latter's side. Domestic and regional subsystemic pressures tended to favor the maintenance of the status quo, and all Brazil had to do was work to delay the conclusion of the FTAA in order to give time for these pressures to make themselves felt. Whereas the launching of the FTAA negotiations reflected the weight of US power in the hemisphere, the actual interactions among the American states following the Miami Summit in 1994 reinforced subsystemic dynamics and made power discrepancies less relevant to the outcome of the negotiations. In fact, in a matter of four years, between the Miami Summit in 1994 and the Santiago Summit in 1998, it became clear that two poles of attraction were being constituted in the hemisphere—one centered on the United States-NAFTA core and the other centered on Brazil-Mercosur. Focusing on the international system and on power imbalances would be of little help to explain this configuration. In order to provide an effective explanation for this outcome, it is necessary to take into account the interplay between domestic and regional subsystemic dynamics.

Domestically, the difficulties of the Clinton administration in obtaining fast track authority to negotiate the FTAA made it clear that the United States was not willing to pay the costs of regional subsystemic change. This lack of effective leadership was a key element in enabling Brazil to push its agenda in South America more successfully. The case of Chile, which had gone from considering NAFTA membership to embracing Mercosur, provides a clear illustration of this claim. In regional subsystemic terms, the outbreak of the economic crises first in Mexico and later in Argentina acted as catalysts that helped to set in motion regional subsystemic dynamics by bringing closer together the two major actors of each regional subsystem—the United States and Mexico in North America, and Brazil and Argentina in South America. While the outcome of the Mexican crisis made it clear that NAFTA had definitively North-Americanized Mexico, the Argentinean crisis contributed to the South-Americanization of Argentina's foreign policy. Both of these processes reinforced interactions at the regional level making even more difficult the establishment of new patterns of interactions necessary for the reconfiguration of the regional subsystems in the hemisphere.

These interactions favored the Brazilian strategy of consolidating a South American bloc around the Mercosur core, and when the United States eventually overcame some of its domestic obstacles as the US Congress granted fast track authority (then renamed Trade Promotion Authority) to the Bush administration in 2002, the original FTAA goals of a genuine hemispheric integration had lost much of its impulse. As a result, even with fast track authority in hands, the Bush administration was not able to conclude the FTAA by the original 2005 target date. The immediate consequence of the FTAA debacle was that the United States resorted to the establishment of bilateral trade agreements with individual countries in South America, while Brazil hoped to accelerate the process of institutionalization of the South American space, thus incorporating issues going beyond trade, such as security.

In contrast to the US strategy, which relies mostly on specific trade agreements and therefore is much more restricted, Brazil seems to pursue a strategy of co-operative hegemony in which it attempts, within a multilateral structure and by stressing a common identity, to make all South American states rally around the political project of establishing South America as a distinct region within the hemisphere, thus increasing the costs of a more significant US involvement in that subsystem. The Brazilian strategy of leading a South American bloc seems to have been working so far, as indicated by a 2010 public opinion poll taken on eighteen Latin American countries which shows Brazil as being perceived as the country with greatest leadership in the region by 19 percent of the population in Latin America followed by the United States with 9 percent.[76] It is interesting to notice that the same report shows that 67 percent of the Latin American population sees the United States as a positive influence, contrasted to Brazil's 61 percent, which seems to indicate that US numbers are not related to an anti-US feeling. Since Brazilian leadership perception decreases as one moves from Argentina to Mexico, when considering only the nine South American countries in the sample (excluding Brazil), Brazil's average goes up to around 27 percent, with half of the Argentinean population indicating Brazil as the regional leader.[77] These numbers seem to indicate that Brazilian strategy of co-operative hegemony has achieved a considerable degree of success, which at the same time seems to depend to a great extent on keeping the United States as a relative absent empire in the South American regional subsystem.

NOTES

1. For the politico-security implications of the FTAA see, for example, Georges A. Fauriol and William Perry, *Thinking Strategically About 2005: The United States and South America* (Washington, DC: Center for Strategic and International Studies, 1999); and Patrice M. Franko, *Toward a New Security Architecture in the Americas: The Strategic Implications of the FTAA* (Washington, DC: Center for Strategic and International Studies, 2000).

2. The relationship between economic interdependence and political influence is explored in Albert Hirschman's pioneering work "National Power and the Structure of Foreign Trade": Albert O. Hirschman, *National Power and the Structure of Foreign Trade* (Berkeley and Los Angeles: University of California Press, 1945). Later, this notion was famously taken up by Robert Keohane and Joseph Nye in Robert O. Keohane and Joseph S. Nye, *Power and Interdependence: World Politics in Transition* (Boston: Little, Brown, 1977).

3. An example of this perspective can be found in James Petras, "U.S. Offensive in Latin America: Coups, Retreats, and Radicalization," *Monthly Review* 54, no. 1 (2002). This viewpoint is usually connected to the notion of imperialism rather than to the notion of empire as explained in the introductory chapter.

4. Frederick Mayer, *Interpreting NAFTA: The Science and Art of Political Analysis* (New York: Columbia University Press, 1998), 41.

5. Ibid., 42.

6. Jorge I. Domínguez and Rafael Fernández de Castro, *The United States and Mexico: Between Partnership and Conflict*, 2nd ed. (New York: Routledge, 2009), 26.

7. Nicola Phillips, "Hemispheric Integration and Subregionalism in the Americas," *International Affairs (Royal Institute of International Affairs 1944-)* 79, no. 2 (2003): 331.

8. Richard E. Feinberg, *Summitry in the Americas: A Progress Report* (Washington, DC: Institute for International Economics, 1997), 58.

9. Ibid., 66.

10. Even though the personal preferences of the author of this book would advise him to use the Portuguese term "Mercosul," the use of the Spanish form "Mercosur" is more widely employed in the literature in English.

11. Bernier and Roy, "NAFTA and Mercosur: Two Competing Models?," 69; Mario E. Carranza, *South American Free Trade Area or Free Trade Area of the Americas?: Open Regionalism and the Future of Regional Economic Integration in South America* (Aldershot, UK: Ashgate, 2000), 124; Moniz Bandeira, *As Relações Perigosas: Brasil-Estados Unidos (de Collor a Lula, 1990-2004)* (Rio de Janeiro: Civilização Brasileira, 2004), 133-35; Smith, *Brazil and the United States*: 189.

12. Amado Luiz Cervo and Clodoaldo Bueno, *História da Política Exterior do Brasil*, 3 ed. (Brasília: Editora UnB, 2008), 488.

13. Lampreia, *O Brasil e os Ventos do Mundo*: 183, 89.

14. Jan van Rompay, "Brazil's Strategy Towards the FTAA," in *Free Trade for the Americas?: The United States' Push for the FTAA Agreement*, ed. Paulo Gilberto Fagundes Vizentini and Marianne Wiesebron (London: Zed Books, 2004), 120.

15. Carranza, *South American Free Trade Area or Free Trade Area of the Americas?*: 1, 84; Paulo Gilberto Fagundes Vizentini, "The FTAA and US Strategy: A Southern Point of View," in *Free Trade for the Americas?: The United States' Push for the FTAA Agreement*, ed. Paulo Gilberto Fagundes Vizentini and Marianne Wiesebron (London: Zed Books, 2004), 17; Cervo and Bueno, *História da Política Exterior do Brasil*: 487.

16. Fernando Henrique Cardoso, *Política Externa em Tempos de Mudança: A Gestão do ministro Fernando Henrique Cardoso no Itamaraty (5 de Outubro de 1992 a 21 de Maio de 1993): Discursos, Artigos e Entrevistas* (Brasília: Fundação Alexandre de Gusmão, 1994), 185.

17. Fernando Henrique Cardoso and Roberto Pompeu de Toledo, *O Presidente Segundo o Sociólogo: Entrevista de Fernando Henrique Cardoso a Roberto Pompeu de Toledo* (São Paulo: Companhia das Letras, 1998), 127.

18. Ronaldo Munck, "The Democratic Decade: Argentina Since Malvinas," *Bulletin of Latin American Research* 11, no. 2 (1992): 210.

19. Brazil, "wary of Washington's potentially overbearing influence" in South America, had a "notably negative" reaction: Fauriol and Perry, *Thinking Strategically About 2005*: 33.

20. By 2009, Argentina exported to Brazil four times more than to the United States. Data from: Interamerican Development Bank, "Dataintal—Comercio Bilateral," http://www.iadb.org/dataintal/ (accessed February 1, 2011).

21. "We have been the Three Amigos. Now we will be the Four Amigos," proclaimed Canadian Foreign Minister Jean Chretien: Larry Rohter, "Free Trade Goes South With or Without U.S.," *New York Times*, January 6, 1997.

22. Feinberg, *Summitry in the Americas*: 177.

23. Stephan Haggard, "The Political Economy of Regionalism in the Western Hemisphere," in *The Post-NAFTA Political Economy: Mexico and the Western Hemisphere*, ed. Carol Wise (University Park, PA: The Pennsylvania State University Press, 1998), 318.

24. Henry Kissinger, *Does America Need a Foreign Policy?: Toward a Diplomacy for the 21st Century* (New York: Simon & Schuster, 2001), 96.

25. Rohter, "Free Trade Goes South With or Without U.S."

26. Feinberg, *Summitry in the Americas*: 115.

27. Ibid., 109.

28. Ibid., 146.

29. Ibid., 195.

30. Ibid., 134.

31. Ibid., 180.

32. Katzenstein, *A World of Regions*: 233.

33. Alan M. Rugman, "Economic Integration in North America: Implications for the Americas," in *Free Trade in the Americas: Economic and Political Issues for Governments and Firms*, ed. Sidney Weintraub, Alan M. Rugman, and Gavin Boyd (Cheltenham, UK ; Northampton, MA: Edward Elgar, 2004), 90.

34. Hurrell, "Regionalism in the Americas"; Atkins, *Latin America and the Caribbean in the International System*: 16.

35. *New York Times*, "Aid for Mexico Gives Economy Shot in the Arm," February 2, 1995.

36. Riordan Roett, "U.S. Policy Toward Mercosur: From Miami to Santiago," in *Mercosur: Regional Integration, World Markets*, ed. Riordan Roett (Boulder, CO: Lynne Rienner, 1999), 112.

37. Mônica Hirst, "Mercosur's Complex Political Agenda," in *Mercosur: Regional Integration, World Markets*, ed. Riordan Roett (Boulder, CO: Lynne Rienner, 1999), 40.

38. Carranza, *South American Free Trade Area or Free Trade Area of the Americas?*, 106.

39. Ibid., 127.

40. Ibid., 131.

41. John Sweeney, "Clinton's Latin America Policy: A Legacy of Missed Opportunities," *The Heritage Foundation*, July 6, 1998 http://www.heritage.org/research/reports/1998/07/clintons-latin-america-policy (accessed February 8, 2011).

42. Interamerican Development Bank, "Dataintal—Comercio Bilateral."

43. See, for example: *Stratfor*, "Members' Policies Spell Mercosur's Demise," October 10, 2001, www.stratfor.com/memberships/3653/analysis/members_policies_spell_mercosurs_demise (accessed February 9, 2011); Mario E. Carranza, "Can Mercosur Survive? Domestic and International Constraints on Mercosur," *Latin American Politics and Society* 45, no. 2 (2003); Heinz G. Preusse, "The Future of Mercosur," in *Free Trade in the Americas: Economic and Political Issues for Governments and Firms*, ed. Sidney Weintraub, Alan M. Rugman, and Gavin Boyd (Cheltenham, UK ; Northampton, MA: Edward Elgar, 2004).

44. Larry Rohter, "Argentina and the U.S. Grow Apart Over a Crisis," *New York Times*, January 20, 2002.

45. Juan Gabriel Tokatlian, "Politica Exterior Argentina de Menem a de la Rua: La Diplomacia del Ajuste," *Escenarios Alternativos* 4, no. 9 (2000).

46. Rohter, "Argentina and the U.S. Grow Apart Over a Crisis."

47. Thomas Andrew O'Keefe, *Latin American and Caribbean Trade Agreements: Keys to a Prosperous Community of the Americas* (Leiden: Martinus Nijhoff Publishers, 2009), 96-97.

48. Mario E. Carranza, "Mercosur and the End Game of the FTAA Negotiations: Challenges and Prospects after the Argentine Crisis," *Third World Quarterly* 25, no. 2 (2004): 326.

49. Laura Gomez Mera, "Explaining Mercosur's Survival: Strategic Sources of Argentine-Brazilian Convergence," *Journal of Latin American Studies* 37, no. 1 (2005): 134.

50. Sidney Weintraub, *Development and Democracy in the Southern Cone: Imperatives for U.S. Policy in South America* (Washington, DC: Center for Strategic and International Studies, 2000), 28.

51. Stephen Handelman, "Special Report: Summit of the Americas," *Time*, April 19, 2001.

52. Larry Rohter, "South American Trade Bloc Under Siege," *New York Times*, March 24, 2001.

53. Mera, "Explaining Mercosur's Survival: Strategic Sources of Argentine-Brazilian Convergence," 129.

54. Interamerican Development Bank, "Dataintal—Comercio Bilateral."

55. As Jeffrey Schott remarks: "When US-Mexico free trade talks were first broached in 1990, few realized how closely integrated the two economies already were, or how closely US interests coincided with the promotion of economic growth and political stability in the region." Schott, *Prospects for Free Trade in the Americas*: 93-94.

56. Indeed, the George W. Bush administration came to Quebec willing to move up the deadline for the FTAA to 2003 from 2005: Handelman, "Special Report: Summit of the Americas."

57. *Veja*, "O Brasil diz não," September 6, 2000, 49.

58. Sean W. Burges, *Brazilian Foreign Policy After the Cold War* (Gainesville: University Press of Florida, 2009), 59.

59. Ibid., 54.

60. For the hegemonic stability theory see Robert O. Keohane, *After Hegemony: Cooperation and Discord in the World Political Economy* (Princeton, NJ: Princeton University Press, 1984); Gilpin, *War and Change in World Politics*.

61. Thomas Pedersen, "Cooperative Hegemony: Power, Ideas and Institutions in Regional Integration," *Review of International Studies* 28, no. 4 (2002): 696.

62. Ibid., 689.

63. Fernando Henrique Cardoso, "O Brasil e uma nova América Do Sul," *Valor Economico*, August 30, 2000.

64. Bandeira, *As Relações Perigosas*: 289.

65. Eliane Catanhede, "EUA Ajudam Quando Ficam Longe, Diz Jobim," *Folha de Sao Paulo*, March 22, 2008.

66. After Williamsburg, the Defense Ministerial of the Americas met in Bariloche, Argentina (1996); Cartagena, Colombia (1998); Manaus, Brazil (2000); Santiago, Chile (2002); Quito, Ecuador (2004); Managua, Nicaragua (2006); Banff, Canada (2008); and Santa Cruz de la Sierra, Bolivia (2010). Uruguay will host the tenth meeting, in 2012.

67. Cardoso, "O Brasil e Uma Nova América do Sul."

68. Elizabeth Becker, "Accord Reached on a Bill Raising Farm Subsidies," *New York Times*, April 27, 2002.

69. Rompay, "Brazil's Strategy Towards the FTAA," 128.

70. Simon Romero, "Hemisphere Trade Talks in Miami Are Reported to Hit a Bump," *New York Times*, November 17, 2003.

71. Ministerial Declaration: Free Trade Area of the Americas. Miami., "FTAA. Eighth Ministerial Meeting," November 20, 2003. http://www.ftaa-alca.org/ministerials/miami/Miami_e.asp (accessed February 10, 2011).

72. Sherry M. Stephenson, "New Trade Strategies in the Americas," in *Economic Integration in the Americas*, ed. Joseph A. McKinney and H. Stephen Gardner (London: Routledge, 2008), 29.

73. *New York Times*, "Negotiators Fail to Agree on Free Trade Proposal at Americas Summit," November 6, 2005.

74. Stephenson, "New Trade Strategies in the Americas," 41.

75. Kissinger, *Does America Need a Foreign Policy?*:98.

76. Latinobarómetro, "Annual Report 2010," (Santiago: Latinobarómetro Corporation, 2010), 111.

77. In decreasing order of Brazil's leadership perception: Argentina, Uruguay, Paraguay, Chile, Colombia, Bolivia, Peru, Venezuela, and Ecuador.

Chapter Seven

Conclusions

This book aimed to fundamentally address two broad sets of questions. First, it sought to challenge the notion that the concept of Latin America should take preeminence over other possible regional subdivisions within the field of international relations. For that reason, the first set of questions asks if there is such a thing as South America and, if so, what makes it distinctive from the rest of Latin America. The second set of questions builds upon the first and asks if, from the perspective of international relations, the fact that there is indeed a South American regional subsystem matters. In a nutshell, it was argued that geography and patterns of interactions justify the existence of a North and a South American regional subsystem in the Western Hemisphere, and that this is important so that one may understand the distinct interactions that characterize US relations with each of these subsystems.

In order to answer these two sets of question, this book employed an approach based on the notion of regional subsystems. Hence, chapter 2 laid out a conceptualization of regional subsystems that was both regional (geographic proximity) and systemic (patterns of interaction). A regional subsystem was thus defined as a *subset of the international system reflecting the outcome of actual patterns of interactions—including the whole spectrum between conflict and cooperation—among countries in condition of geographic proximity*. By focusing on geography and patterns of interaction as necessary and sufficient conditions for the establishment of a regional subsystem, other variables, such as culture or level of development, were deemed irrelevant.

Following this characterization, chapter 3 demonstrated that, if geography and patterns of interactions are considered as necessary and sufficient conditions for the determination of a regional subsystem, it logically follows that dividing the Western Hemisphere between a North American (including

Mexico, Central America, and the Caribbean) and a South American regional subsystem makes more sense from the point of view of the study of international relations than dividing it between Latin America (including the Caribbean) and United States/Canada. While the first subdivision follows the regional subsystemic criteria laid out by this book, the second is based on variables that have little utility for the purposes of this research. Nevertheless, it is the latter categorization that has been most widely used by scholars of international relations.

As this research argued, the concept of Latin America is clearly not a geographic one, even though it has been used as such. Indeed, making the case for a Latin American regional subsystem based solely on geography is far more complicated than making the case for a South American regional subsystem. Conversely, chapter 3 sought to offer the rudiments of a possible way to operationalize patterns of interactions based on the variables war/armed conflicts, trade, and international organizations. I suggested that North and South American countries fight more within their own respective subsystems, trade more within their own subsystems, and create more enduring and relevant international organizations within their own subsystems. A central preoccupation of the present book was to demonstrate that subdividing the Western Hemisphere between a North and a South American regional subsystem can provide relevant insights and uncover a number of important interactions that are neglected both by using the international-domestic dichotomy as well as by employing the concept of Latin America to explain the international relations of the Americas. In summary, that is why it does matter that there is such a thing as a South American regional subsystem.

Chapter 3 suggested that a key interaction that a regional subsystemic perspective for the study of South America helps to uncover is the relationship between that regional subsystem and the United States. While a number of students of Latin America have acknowledged that "the United States has treated South America somewhat differently than it has Mexico, Central America, and the Caribbean," this differentiation has not been sufficiently theorized and explained.[1] Basically, those who dedicated some time to explain this differentiation have been content to point to two main variables: distance and stability, which combined would make South America strategically irrelevant for the United States. Although these variables can provide compelling explanations for the relative absence of the United States in South America vis-à-vis the rest of Latin America, the best they can do is perhaps explain a supposed lack of interest, or neglect, toward South America vis-à-vis Mexico, Central America, and the Caribbean. However, relying on distance and stability to explain US relative absence in South America has a number of shortcomings. First, it does little to satisfactorily explain why South American states would be more "stable" than other Latin American states. Second, these variables become less relevant in instances when the

United States demonstrated a clear interest in South American affairs, and yet the outcome was the same relative absence. Finally, they tend to be a pretext to transform this US relative absence from South America in a relative absence of studies of US foreign policy toward South America.

The alternative explanation offered by this book to account for the distinct interactions that have characterized the relations between the United States and South America in contrast to the rest of Latin America focuses on the role of Brazil within the South American regional subsystem. Hence, in making the case for a subsystemic approach to the study of South America, this book also makes the case for emphasizing the role of Brazil in that subsystem. It follows that a central argument of this research is that Brazil is a status quo power that has affected the calculations of costs and benefits of subsystemic change in South America for the United States. This book maintains that without understanding the role of Brazil in the South American subsystem, any explanation for US relative absence from South America is incomplete at best. Under this perspective, South America's allegedly strategic irrelevance would not provide a sufficient explanation for this phenomenon; instead, it may have worked in favor of Brazil in the sense that it gave more room for the South American country to pursue its regional objectives by spending fewer resources than would have been the case had South America been considered a region of higher strategic value.

In order to assess the validity of the hypothesis that Brazil has affected the calculations of US statesmen when interacting with the South American regional subsystem, chapters 4, 5, and 6 explored case studies including instances when a clear interest in South America was demonstrated—thus the argument of neglect could be discarded—and yet the outcome was consistently the same: an absence of imperial policies of the kind that often characterized US policies towards the rest of Latin America. Chapter 4 dealt with the early interactions between the United States and the newly independent Latin American countries in order to demonstrate that there was a clear differentiation, both in actions and discourse, between South America and the rest of the region from the beginning of their mutual interactions. This differentiation is hardly acknowledged by the literature, which interprets the Monroe Doctrine as an all-encompassing policy that was applied homogeneously to the whole of Latin America. Nevertheless, an examination that goes beyond the 1823 declaration and investigates how the Monroe Doctrine was actually applied throughout history as well as the interpretation given to it by subsequent administrations makes clear the scope and extent of that policy. This examination is what chapter 4 attempted to accomplish. It sought to demonstrate that successive US administrations made progressively clear the Caribbean character of the doctrine. Distance from the United States and relative stability of core South American countries are just part of the explanation in the sense that these factors made possible the early development of a system of power politics in South America around the ABC countries: Argentina, Brazil, and Chile. It is noteworthy that the two most interventionist U.S. administrations in Latin America—Theodore Roosevelt's and Woodrow Wilson's—were also the two administrations that most clearly made a distinction between the North and South American regional subsystems. This view was utterly reciprocated by Brazil, which pursued an "unwritten alliance" with the United States, meaning "a tacit accord whereby Brazil acknowledged the hegemony of the United States in North America and the United States respected Brazilian pretensions to the hegemony of South America."[2] This arrangement became even more relevant at the beginning of the twentieth century, when Chile declined in power and Argentina developed a foreign policy with a clear anti-United States component. Brazil's willingness to be the defender of the status quo in South America allowed the United States to concentrate its actions in the circum-Caribbean area, and there was no compelling reason for the United States to change this state of affairs. In other words, Brazil played a role in South America that increased the benefits of subsystemic stability for the United States.

The investigation of the early developments of the South American subsystem and its interaction with the United States helped to put in context the case studied in chapter 5. The overthrow of the Salvador Allende government in Chile is an especially relevant case for at least two reasons. First, it is a clear instance when both a Democrat and a Republican administration in the United States demonstrated a strong interest in employing imperial policies in South America, such as the ones previously implemented elsewhere in Latin America during the Cold War, such as in Guatemala or in the Dominican Republic. This was so because the Cold War environment increased the incentives for the United States, now a true global superpower, to intervene in several regions of the world in order to contain the spread of communism. This was particularly true, even if for symbolic reasons, in Latin America, which was considered the US's most immediate sphere of influence where its power should be uncontested. The second reason that makes the case of Chile particularly important is the fact that this has been widely mentioned as an example of a homogeneous imperial Latin American policy on the part of the United States. Because there is an abundance of evidence regarding US involvement in Chile, the usual interpretation is that this equals an evidence of abundance. On the other hand, there is much less evidence of involvement from third countries in the Chilean case, such as the Soviet Union and Brazil, and this lack of evidence seems to be interpreted as an evidence of lack. The result is that when it comes to the assessment of foreign influences leading to the military coup that eventually overthrew Allende, there is a virtual monologue when in fact there may have been more voices present.

Therefore, congruent with the central argument made in this book, chapter 5 intended to emphasize the role played by Brazil during this process. By using both primary and secondary sources, I sought to put the specific case of Chile into context by demonstrating the Brazilian military government's willingness to take action in order to prevent South American countries from tilting towards communism. In other words, I suggested that Brazil played a role in Chile that allowed the United States to limit its involvement to that of a great power, instead of having to resort to truly imperial solutions which would have involved taking decisive actions to topple Allende. Brazil's role in the Chilean case was far from being an isolated one during the Cold War, as demonstrated by the cases of Bolivia and Uruguay before that, and by the case of Suriname afterwards.

Although covering different periods of time with different configurations of the international system, the cases studied in chapters 4 and 5 had one characteristic in common—they displayed a relative congruence in terms of foreign policy objectives between the United States and Brazil in regards to the South American subsystem as both sought the maintenance of the status quo there. This was not the case after the end of the Cold War, when the United States proposed a free trade area in the hemisphere that could potentially lead to the development of new patterns of interactions and, therefore, to subsystemic change by incorporating the South American subsystem into a truly hemispheric subsystem centered on the United States. Because this was perceived as a challenge to the status quo in South America, Brazil sought to increase the costs of subsystemic change for the United States. It did so by actively participating in the FTAA process while at the same time working to create a web of South American institutions in order to consolidate its position in that regional subsystem. Brazilian strategy was greatly facilitated by domestic issues in the United States that were translated into a lack of effective leadership to move forward with the FTAA. Additionally, economic crises in Mexico and Argentina acted as catalysts that reinforced regional subsystemic dynamics and brought closer together the pairs of countries that are the most relevant for each of the regional subsystems in the hemisphere: the United States and Mexico in North America, Brazil and Argentina in South America. By the end the first decade of the twenty-first century, it was more evident than ever the distinction between a North and a South American regional subsystem in the Western Hemisphere.

SOME THEORETICAL CONSIDERATIONS

This research attempted to offer an alternative framework for the study of inter-American relations in particular, and of international relations in general, based on the regional subsystemic approach. This approach was presented as a third level of analysis between—and distinct from—the customary two employed in the field of international relations. The cases studied in this book sought to apply this regional subsystemic framework to the specific case of South America by emphasizing the interactions between the two most important members of each regional subsystem in the Western Hemisphere: the United States in North America and Brazil in South America. The focus was on how US foreign policies initiatives interacted with the South American subsystem to bring about outcomes that differed from the ones often produced elsewhere in Latin America. I argued that, within this regional subsystemic framework, the role of Brazil in the South American subsystem is the key to understanding the outcome of these interactions, which has kept the United States a relatively absent empire in South America.

One criticism that could be raised regarding the explanation offered here is that each of the particular case studies could be satisfactorily explained by reference to domestic politics, without consideration to regional subsystemic dynamics. For example, the failure to reach an agreement for comprehensive free trade in the Americas could be attributed to the rise of leftist governments in South America by the early 2000s that were opposed to the FTAA project. Similarly, Brazilian policies during the military regime could be attributed to the particular characteristics of that type of government. In fact, if it could be demonstrated that the historical events studied by this book were related mostly to particular domestic configurations of individual countries, with regional dynamics playing no distinctively relevant role, then this would obviously undermine the hypothesis set forth here. Nevertheless, one preoccupation that was present throughout this research was to make clear that there has been a regional pattern of interactions that remained relatively stable regardless of particular domestic circumstances both in the United States and in Brazil. Likewise, this was also true concerning the configuration of the international system and the role of the United States in it. Even as the United States went from a regional power in a multipolar world, to a global power in a bipolar world, and finally to the remaining superpower in a unipolar world, there were certain patterns of interaction that remained relatively unchanged. On the other hand, although Brazil went from a monarchy to a republic, from a military regime to a democracy with presidents from distinct political outlooks, the basic concern with the maintenance of the status quo in the South American regional subsystem remained. In other words, changes both in the domestic environments and in the international system did not lead to change in the regional subsystem, which seems to indicate that the latter operates with a distinct logic.

Evidently, as this research also sought to make clear, the fact that the South American subsystem has shown a great deal of resilience does not mean that it is unchangeable. In fact, the possibility of subsystemic change was an overall theme present throughout this book. One possibility for sub-systemic change would be if the most powerful outside actor concluded that the benefits of change outweighed the costs, that is, if the United States decided, for example, to become a present empire in South America. This could happen through the emergence of particular international conditions and domestic circumstances in the United States combined with Brazilian inaptness to effectively affect US calculations. The result would probably be the establishment of new patterns of relationship in the Western Hemisphere, thus leading to a possible amalgamation of the North and South American subsystems which would make any differentiation between them largely ir-relevant. Likewise, the hypothesis proposed by this research only remains valid as long as Brazilian interests remain linked to the maintenance of the status quo in the South American regional subsystem. It follows that if Brazil becomes unable or unwilling to uphold the status quo, the possibility for subsystemic change increases significantly. This book sought to demonstrate that this basic interest has not changed throughout history, and that it has been present regardless of variations in domestic or international conditions. This is evidently not surprising, since it is reasonable to expect the dominant power in any given regional subsystem to favor the maintenance of the system's status quo, which perhaps explains the relative consistency in Bra-zilian regional goals as opposed to the wide variations in the foreign policies of a number of other Latin American countries. As this book intended to make clear, because US power has been perceived as a potential threat to the Brazilian position in the South American regional subsystem, keeping the United States an absent empire in that subsystem has been a central Brazilian concern.

The discussion above is germane to another important issue regarding the assumptions of this book. The attentive reader will notice the constant refer-ences to "Brazilian" or "US" interests, which would indicate that this re-search has a realist bias since it both considers states as the main actors in international relations as well as it treats them as unitary actors primarily concerned with what they perceive as their own national interest. While the first is indeed a central assumption of this book, the second is only partially so. Because this research had a systemic/structural focus of which the aim was to explain continuity rather than change, as well as the outcome of foreign policies initiatives rather than decision-making processes leading to particular policies, treating states as unitary actors was nothing but a convenient expedient for the sake of parsimony. As pointed out above, a central concern of this book was to show that there has been a broad pattern of interactions between the United States and the South American regional subsystem that has existed regardless of particular domestic circumstances. It would be difficult to make this kind of generalization and at the same time to take into consideration the complexities of domestic processes. Additionally, since this research covers a lengthy period of time, examining the peculiarities of each individual foreign policy decision would be a herculean task clearly beyond the scope of the book. Nonetheless, a convenient expedient is not necessarily an assumption. Neorealists can comfortably assume states as unitary actors in great part because they treat the international system as the independent variable, creating such dominating pressures that domestic dynamics are of little or no importance. This research assumes that states and regional subsystems are mutually constitutive and therefore domestic changes may eventually lead to subsystemic change. In fact, this book makes an important unit-level assumption when it claims that successive Brazilian governments have been concerned with the maintenance of the status quo in South America, which can also be understood as a response to a subsystemic incentive. As mentioned above, were this central concern to change, the subsystem might also change. Because this has not been the case, and the aim of this research was to explain the persistence rather than transformation of the South American regional subsystem, it was not necessary to resort to the examination of domestic dynamics.

Lastly, beyond specific issues of theory-building, some readers may notice a lack of primary sources particularly in the chapter on the Monroe Doctrine. This is due to the fact that the use of first-hand primary sources was deemed as unessential for the purposes of the book since all the necessary quotations and remarks from policy makers were available through secondary sources and the goal was not to uncover radically new findings, but rather to reinterpret the available literature through the theoretical lens employed in this book. Regarding the chapter on the Cold War, besides the aforementioned problem in getting access to the documentation concerning military regimes in South America, the most important primary sources for the purposes of the argument made here were the recently declassified (and for that reason hardly available through secondary sources) documents on the Nixon-Medici meeting. In addition, as an attempt to make up for the lack of available documentation on the Brazilian side during that period, a considerable effort was made to draw on biographies, interviews, and memoirs from key players. Probably the chapter that would have had most to gain from a wider use of primary sources, particularly interviews with key players, would be the chapter on the post-Cold War period. This book expects that future research including such material will tend to confirm the basic hypothesis put forward here.

THEORETICAL IMPLICATIONS

As pointed out above, in order to answer the questions posed by this research, it was necessary to rely on a methodology based on the concept of regional subsystem. This methodological choice was based on the grounds that neither the domestic nor the international system approaches were equipped to explain the main puzzle examined by this book. Although the main concern of this book was to analyze specifically the interaction between the United States and the South American subsystem, the methodology employed here could contribute to refining broader theoretical questions in the field of international relations. At least four major theoretical contributions can be pointed out.

The first contribution that the regional subsystemic perspective employed here could offer to the study of international relations is to provide a framework to the study of lesser powers in the international system. The international system approach, with its explicit focus on the great powers, tends to ignore the importance of middle powers. Because middle powers are likely to have mostly regional—rather than global—interests, the regional subsystem approach seems uniquely equipped to understand the role of these states both in relation to their own regional subsystem as well as in relation to outside powers. This has become increasingly more important, as it becomes clear that traditional international system approaches to international relations have limited applicability in the current world. Conventional systemic approaches based on the number of poles in the system and the formation of global balances of power tend to become less relevant in a world that is neither multipolar, bipolar, and increasingly less unipolar. In the mid-1960s, George Liska described the international system as bipolar, but "unifocal," meaning that even though there were two major poles in that system, it constituted in essence an "imperial system" centered around the United States—the relationship of individual countries with the United States was more important than the relationship those states had among themselves.[3] Drawing from Liska, one could describe the current international system as unipolar, but multifocal. That is, even though there is one clear major pole in the system, the system is not necessarily organized around this pole. It is not that the United States has lost its preeminence, or even that it will lose it in the near future, but that this preeminence is becoming increasingly irrelevant. In other words, the international system may still be characterized as unipolar but that does not seem to matter much. If during the Cold War, global pressures emanating from the bipolar configuration of the international system could explain a number of phenomena, in the current world states are increasingly subjected to pressures emanating more from their own respective regional subsystems than from the international system as a whole.

A second contribution of the regional subsystem approach to the study of international relations is the fact that it draws attention to the other fundamental feature of the international system, besides anarchy: non-mobility, that is, the fact that states are fixed in space. Applying systemic theories that were created and taking into consideration units that are mobile to a system where the major units are non-mobile may generate unsatisfactory explanations. If a system is composed by structure and interacting units, the regional subsystem approach highlights the fact that both anarchy and geography affect the interaction among states. Ignoring the role of non-mobility would mean to assume that if Brazil were located where Mexico is, little would change in Brazilian foreign policy. This seems counterintuitive for the simple fact that Brazil's foreign policy, as the foreign policy of any other state, is intimately related to its geographical situation. Therefore, the regional subsystems differ from the international system in which the first varies not only in time, but also in space. Applying the framework laid out by this book to the study of other regional subsystems would require first delineating the borders of the regional subsystem based on geography and patterns of interactions, followed by the identification of the specific characteristics of the regional subsystem under study, which is what chapter 3 attempted to do for the South American subsystem. This characterization could start by deciphering the main regional actors and the main outside powers, followed by an examination of how the main regional actors interact within their own subsystem as well as how they interact with the outside powers. If a general theory of regional subsystems is to be developed, it should probably begin by establishing criteria to classify different types of regional subsystems in order to compare and evaluate whether similar regional subsystems display similar characteristics.

Third, the regional subsystem approach deals with two fundamental theoretical issues in international relations: the level-of-analysis question and the agent-structure debate. Regarding the first, the subsystemic perspective opens up new possibilities for research since it reveals a third level of analysis located between the domestic and the international system. Thus, it seeks to avoid both the artificial homogenization associated with the latter as well as the over-differentiation associated with the first by acknowledging different degrees of interaction among states but without necessarily looking into each individual country, since the main concern is with the role of the most powerful regional players. Nevertheless, because the overwhelming majority of the literature in international relations has focused either on the total international system or the national state, the regional level has remained considerably undertheorized. In relation to the agent-structure debate, the regional subsystem approach, with its acknowledgement of different levels of interaction among states, calls for the utilization of an approach equipped to deal with the relationship between social interaction and structural effects.

Hence, a constructivist perspective, the basic premise of which is the notion that agents and structure are mutually constitutive, seems to be appropriate. But while the constructivist literature tends to stress ideational structures in detriment of material structures, the regional subsystem approach, by stressing territoriality, highlights the latter. Consequently, it assumes that interactions among states are affected not only by the role of ideas, but also by the physical reality of geographic location, which also affects how ideas are produced and reproduced.

Finally, an important comparative advantage of the theoretical framework employed here over other approaches is that it broadens the typical unidimensional explanations in which the causal direction goes only one way, that is, how US foreign policies have affected its so-called client states. This trend is even more pronounced in the case of South America, since it is considered an outright area of US influence and because its states are so comparatively weak. Some three decades ago, Geir Lundestad explored the theoretical advantages of shifting the focus away from the United States and to the objects of US foreign policy, in order to demonstrate that objects were also subjects, meaning that the periphery could directly affect the outcome of policies formulated by the center. Differing from both the traditionalist and revisionist arguments about the Cold War, Lundestad argued that the United States—like the USSR—indeed became an empire in Europe, but—unlike the USSR—it was so because the Europeans themselves invited the United States to play such a role. The United States was thus, according to Lundestad, an "empire by invitation" during the Cold War.[4] The regional subsystemic framework seeks to explore the obvious theoretical advantages of seeing objects also as subjects therefore uncovering interactions that otherwise would remain largely ignored.

POLICY IMPLICATIONS

Demonstrating the existence of a distinctive South American subsystem and examining how it has interacted with the United States has not only implications for the study of inter-American relations but also has important policy implications for US policy makers. First and foremost, it makes evident that the United States must take into account that its initiatives toward Latin America will generally tend to have different outcomes in the different regional subsystems in the hemisphere. Almost forty years ago, Thompson commented that "the foreign policy of great powers have on occasion given the impression that subsystems either do not exist or at least need not to be taken seriously."[5] Although it could be argued that overall the United States has improved in terms of designing specific foreign policies for different regional subsystems, in its own hemisphere there has been little advance, as there remains the premise that there is a Latin American regional subsystem. Therefore, it would be advisable for the United States to do away with its "Latin American" policy and design policies specifically directed to South America. In fact, the United States does not have an "African" policy that includes both Egypt and South Africa for the simple reason that this would be of little use in practical terms. The State Department has a "Bureau of African Affairs" that covers sub-Saharan Africa, while having a separate "Bureau of Near Eastern Affairs" for North Africa and the Middle East. Conversely, the "Bureau of Western Hemisphere Affairs" covers all of Latin America.

But bureaucratic subdivisions are less important than actual policy formulations, and the fact is that the United States has developed a specific set of policies for key countries in the world. Hence, successive US administrations have had to deal with the development of a China policy or a Russia policy. Likewise, within the context of a larger South American policy, a Brazil policy should be developed. This has become even more relevant given the increasing importance of Brazil in the international arena.[6] As Fareed Zakaria argues, in spite of political turmoil, the first years of the 2000s witnessed the largest period of global economy expansion, which benefited particularly the emerging economies in Asia and Latin America, and opened the way for a "tectonic power shift" in the distribution of power. For Zakaria, this redistribution of power has led to a "post-American world" characterized not necessarily by the decline of the United States, but by "the rise of the rest."[7] Within this context, even though much attention has been paid to India, and especially to China, Brazil may become a relevant player. For Leslie Gelb, the current international system is characterized by a "pyramidal" structure in which the United States occupies the top and right below it there is a second tier composed by China, Japan, India, Russia, the United Kingdom, France, Germany, and Brazil. Gelb terms these countries as "the Eight Principals," and claims that they possess "enough power to provide essential support to joint efforts with the United States and to block or seriously impede action by Washington."[8] According to Gelb, these are the key countries that the United States should take into consideration when seeking support for its actions in the different parts of the globe.

Therefore, the development of a foreign policy distinctively designed for Brazil makes sense from the point of view of the United States both because of Brazil's increasing clout in the emerging international system as well as within the specific context of South America. As long as South America in general, and Brazil in particular, remains buried in the midst of a "Latin American" or a "Western Hemispheric" foreign policy, US initiatives toward the region will be destined to have few satisfactory results. If the United States could easily afford not having a South American policy in the past, the current global trends seem to indicate that this neglect will increasingly have more important consequences for US ability to shape the post-American world.

But what kind of South American policy should the United States design? Although it is not the aim of this book to offer an answer to this question, a few lessons from what has been demonstrated here could be helpful. Chief among them is the fact that any US policy that can be interpreted by Brazilian policy makers as affecting the status quo in the South American subsystem will almost certainly face resistance in Brazil. The question is how an increasingly more powerful Brazil is going to manipulate this resistance within the context of the South American subsystem. If, on one hand, Brazil's growth may give it more resources to defend the status quo in South America and consolidate its position, on the other hand this same growth may generate suspicions among its neighbors and resurface fears of a Brazilian hegemony in the subsystem. Therefore, Brazil's ability to handle its own rise regionally will be a key component of how regional subsystemic dynamics will evolve. In any case, if the United States intends to have any significant future leverage in Brazil and consequently in South America, one feasible alternative is to increase the level of interdependence, particularly in the economic field, between them. This would require taking measures, even if unilaterally, directed at increasing the level of trade between the two countries, particularly in areas sensitive to Brazil, such as agriculture.[9] Obviously, there are domestic obstacles in the United States that must be overcome in order to undertake such initiatives. The question then is whether US policymakers will be willing to bear the costs of global and hemispheric leadership in the new emerging international environment or if domestic concerns will make the United States increasingly more absent from South America.

NOTES

1. Samuel L. Baily, *The United States and the Development of South America, 1945-1975* (New York: New Viewpoints, 1976), viii.
2. Burns, *The Unwritten Alliance*: 207.
3. Liska, *Imperial America*.
4. Lundestad, "Empire by Invitation? The United States and Western Europe, 1945-1952."
5. Thompson, "The Regional Subsystem: A Conceptual Explication and a Propositional Inventory," 97.
6. See, for example, *The Independent*, "The Rise and Rise of Brazil: Faster, Stronger, Higher," September 27, 2009; *Economist*, "Brazil Takes Off," November 12, 2009; Larry Rohter, *Brazil on the Rise: The Story of a Country Transformed* (New York: Palgrave Macmillan, 2010); *Washington Times*, "Obama: U.S. Supports Rise of Brazil's Economy," March 19, 2011.
7. Fareed Zakaria, *The Post-American World* (New York: W.W. Norton, 2008).
8. Leslie H. Gelb, *Power Rules: How Common Sense Can Rescue American Foreign Policy* (New York: Harper, 2009), 76.

9. I have discussed this topic earlier in more detail in: Carlos Gustavo Poggio Teixeira, "Brazil and United States: Fading Interdependence," *Orbis* 55, no. 1 (2011).

Bibliography

Agee, Philip. *Inside the Company: C.I.A Diary*. American ed. New York: Stonehill, 1975.

Agnew, John A., and James S. Duncan. *The Power of Place: Bringing Together Geographical and Sociological Imaginations*. Boston: Unwin Hyman, 1989.

Agor, Weston H., and Andres Suarez. "The Emerging Latin American Political Subsystem." *Proceedings of the Academy of Political Science* 30, no. 4 (1972): 153-66.

Albert, Mathias, and Lena Hilkermeier. *Observing International Relations: Niklas Luhmann and World Politics*, The New International Relations. London: Routledge, 2004.

Almeyda, Clodomyro. "The Foreign Policy of the Unidad Popular Government." In *Chile 1970-1973: Economic Development and Its International Setting: Self-Criticism of the Unidad Popular Government's Policies*, edited by Sandro Sideri, 103-34. The Hague: Nijhoff, 1979.

Alvarez, Alejandro. *The Monroe Doctrine, Its Importance in the International Life of the States of the New World*, Publications of the Carnegie Endowment for International Peace. Division of International Law, Washington. New York: Oxford University Press, 1924.

Andrew, Christopher M., and Vasili Mitrokhin. *The World Was Going Our Way: The KGB and the Battle for the Third World*. New York: Basic Books, 2005.

d' Araújo, Maria Celina Soares, Gláucio Ary Dillon Soares, and Celso Castro. *Os Anos de Chumbo: A Memória Militar Sobre a Repressão*. Rio de Janeiro: Relume Dumará, 1994.

Astiz, Carlos Alberto, ed. *Latin American International Politics; Ambitions, Capabilities, and the National Interest of Mexico, Brazil, and Argentina*. Notre Dame, IN: University of Notre Dame Press, 1969.

Atkins, G. Pope. *Latin America and the Caribbean in the International System*. 4th ed. Boulder, CO: Westview Press, 1999.

Bacevich, A. J. *American Empire: The Realities and Consequences of U.S. Diplomacy*. Cambridge, MA: Harvard University Press, 2002.

Baily, Samuel L. *The United States and the Development of South America, 1945-1975*. New York: New Viewpoints, 1976.

Bandeira, Moniz. *As Relações Perigosas: Brasil-Estados Unidos (De Collor a Lula, 1990-2004)*. Rio de Janeiro: Civilização Brasileira, 2004.

———. *Brasil, Argentina E Estados Unidos - Conflito e Integração na América do Sul: Da Tríplice Aliança ao Mercosul, 1870-2001*. Rio de Janeiro: Revan, 2003.

———. *Estado Nacional e Política Internacional na América Latina: O Continente nas Relações Argentina-Brasil, 1930-1992*. São Paulo, SP: Ensaio, 1993.

———. *Formula Para o Caos: A Derrubada de Salvador Allende (1970-1973)*. Rio de Janeiro: Civilizacao Brasileira, 2008.

————. "O Brasil como Potência Regional e a Importância Estratégica da América do Sul na sua Política Exterior." *Revista Espaço Acadêmico*, no. 91 (2008).

————. *Presença dos Estados Unidos no Brasil: (Dois Séculos De História)*, Coleção Retratos Do Brasil V. 87. Rio de Janeiro: Civilização Brasileira, 1973.

————. *Relações Brasil-EUA no Contexto da Globalização*. 2. ed. Vol. 2. São Paulo: Senac, 1997.

Barboza, Mario Gibson. *Na Diplomacia, o Traço Todo da Vida*. Rio de Janeiro: Record, 1992.

Barclay, Glen St John. *Struggle for a Continent: The Diplomatic History of South America, 1917-1945*. London: Sidgwick and Jackson, 1971.

Barrionuevo, Alexei. "Memos Show Nixon's Bid to Enlist Brazil in a Coup." *New York Times*, August 16, 2009.

Becker, Elizabeth. "Accord Reached on a Bill Raising Farm Subsidies." *New York Times*, April 27, 2002.

Becú, Carlos Alfredo. *El "ABC" y su Concepto Politico y Juridico*. Buenos Aires: Libreria "La Facultad" de J. Roldán, 1915.

Bernier, Ivan, and Martin Roy. "Nafta and Mercosur: Two Competing Models?" In *The Americas in Transition: The Contours of Regionalism*, edited by Gordon Mace and Louis Bélanger, 69-91. Boulder, CO: Lynne Rienner Publishers, 1999.

Berton, Peter. "International Subsystems—A Submacro Approach to International Studies." *International Studies Quarterly* 13, no. 4 (1969): 329-34.

Bethell, Leslie. "Brazil and 'Latin America'." *Journal of Latin American Studies* 42, no. 03 (2010): 457-85.

Binder, Leonard. "The Middle East as a Subordinate International System." *World Politics* 10, no. 3 (1958): 408-29.

Bingham, Hiram. *The Monroe Doctrine: An Obsolete Shibboleth*. New Haven: Yale University Press, 1913.

Black, Jan Knippers. *Sentinels of Empire: The United States and Latin American Militarism*. New York: Greenwood Press, 1986.

————. *United States Penetration of Brazil*. Philadelphia: University of Pennsylvania Press, 1977.

Blasier, Cole. *The Giant's Rival: The U.S.S.R and Latin America*. Pittsburgh: University of Pittsburgh Press, 1987.

Bloom, William. *Personal Identity, National Identity, and International Relations*, Cambridge Studies in International Relations. Cambridge, UK: Cambridge University Press, 1990.

Blum, William. *Killing Hope: U.S. Military and C.I.A Interventions since World War II*. 2nd updated ed. Monroe, ME: Common Courage Press, 2004.

Bond, Robert D. "Brazil's Relations with the Northern Tier Countries of South America." In *Brazil in the International System: The Rise of a Middle Power*, edited by Wayne A. Selcher, xxvii, 251 p. Boulder, CO: Westview Press, 1981.

————. "Venezuela, Brazil, and the Amazon Basin." In *Latin American Foreign Policies: Global and Regional Dimensions*, edited by Elizabeth G. Ferris and Jennie K. Lincoln, xvii, 300 p. Boulder, CO: Westview Press, 1981.

Boulding, Kenneth E. *Conflict and Defense: A General Theory*. New York: Harper, 1962.

Bowman, Larry W. "The Subordinate State System of Southern Africa." *International Studies Quarterly* 12, no. 3 (1968): 231-61.

Bradley, James. *The Imperial Cruise: A Secret History of Empire and War*. New York: Little, Brown and Co., 2009.

Brazilian Information Bulletin. "Chilean Coup: Brazil Goes over the Andes." Fall 1973.

Brecher, Michael. *The Foreign Policy System of Israel: Setting, Images, Process*. New Haven, CT: Yale University Press, 1972.

————. "International Relations and Asian Studies: The Subordinate State System of Southern Asia." *World Politics* 15, no. 2 (1963): 213-35.

Burges, Sean W. *Brazilian Foreign Policy after the Cold War*. Gainesville: University Press of Florida, 2009.

Burns, E. Bradford. *The Unwritten Alliance: Rio-Branco and Brazilian-American Relations*. New York: Columbia University Press, 1966.

Burr, Robert N. "The Balance of Power in Nineteenth-Century South America: An Exploratory Essay." *The Hispanic American Historical Review* 35, no. 1 (1955): 37-60.

———. *By Reason or Force: Chile and the Balancing of Power in South America, 1830-1905.* Berkeley, CA: University of California Press, 1967.

———. "International Interests of Latin American Nations." In *The International Politics of Regions,* edited by Louis J. Cantori and Steven L. Spiegel, 99-108. Englewood Cliffs, NJ: Prentice-Hall, 1970.

———. *The Stillborn Panama Congress: Power Politics and Chilean-Colombian Relations During the War of the Pacific,* University of California Publications in History. Berkeley, CA: University of California Press, 1962.

Buzan, Barry, and Ole Wæver. *Regions and Powers: The Structure of International Security,* Cambridge Studies in International Relations 91. Cambridge, UK: Cambridge University Press, 2003.

Cantori, Louis J., and Steven L. Spiegel. *The International Politics of Regions.* Englewood Cliffs, NJ: Prentice-Hall, 1970.

Cardoso, Fernando Henrique. "O Brasil e uma Nova América do Sul." *Valor Economico,* August 30, 2000.

———. *Política Externa em Tempos de Mudança: A Gestão do Ministro Fernando Henrique Cardoso no Itamaraty (5 de Outubro de 1992 a 21 de Maio de 1993): Discursos, Artigos e Entrevistas.* Brasília: Fundação Alexandre de Gusmão, 1994.

Cardoso, Fernando Henrique, and Roberto Pompeu de Toledo. *O Presidente Segundo o Sociólogo: Entrevista de Fernando Henrique Cardoso a Roberto Pompeu de Toledo.* São Paulo: Companhia das Letras, 1998.

Carranza, Mario E. "Can Mercosur Survive? Domestic and International Constraints on Mercosur." *Latin American Politics and Society* 45, no. 2 (2003): 67-103.

———. "Mercosur and the End Game of the FTAA Negotiations: Challenges and Prospects after the Argentine Crisis." *Third World Quarterly* 25, no. 2 (2004): 319-37.

———. *South American Free Trade Area or Free Trade Area of the Americas?: Open Regionalism and the Future of Regional Economic Integration in South America,* Political Economy of Latin America. Aldershot, UK: Ashgate, 2000.

Carvalho, José Murilo de. *A Monarquia Brasileira.* Rio de Janeiro: Ao Livro Tecnico, 1993.

Catanhede, Eliane. "EUA Ajudam Quando Ficam Longe, Diz Jobim." *Folha de Sao Paulo,* March 22, 2008.

Cervo, Amado Luiz, and Clodoaldo Bueno. *História da Política Exterior do Brasil.* 3 ed. Brasília: Editora UnB, 2008.

Chang, Yuan-Ching, Solomon W. Polachek, and John Robst. "Conflict and Trade: The Relationship between Geographic Distance and International Interactions." *Journal of Socio-Economics* 33, no. 4 (2004): 491-509.

Chapman, Charles E. "The Founding of the Review." *The Hispanic American Historical Review* 1, no. 1 (1918): 8-23.

Chevalier, Michel. *Society, Manners, and Politics in the United States,* Reprints of Economic Classics. New York: A. M. Kelley, 1966.

Child, John. *Unequal Alliance: The Inter-American Military System, 1938-1979.* Boulder, CO: Westview Press, 1980.

Comblin, Joseph. *A Ideologia da Segurança Nacional: O Poder Militar na America Latina.* Rio de Janeiro: Civilização Brasileira, 1978.

Conduru, Guilherme Frazão. "O Subsistema Americano, Rio Branco e o ABC." *Revista Brasileira de Política Internacional* 41 (1998): 59-82.

Connell-Smith, Gordon. *The Inter-American System.* London, New York: Royal Institute of International Affairs, 1966.

Contreiras, Helio. *Militares Confissões: Historias Secretas do Brasil.* Rio de Janeiro: Mauad, 1998.

Corrêa, M. Pio. *O Mundo em que Vivi.* Rio de Janeiro, RJ: Expressão e Cultura, 1995.

Crandall, Russell. *Gunboat Democracy: U.S. Interventions in the Dominican Republic, Grenada, and Panama.* Lanham [Md.]: Rowman & Littlefield Publishers, 2006.

Dans, Gustavo V., and North American Congress on Latin America. *NACLA's Brasil a la Ofensiva: La Estrategia Continental del Imperialismo*, Cuadernos De Política Mundial No. 1. Lima: Editorial Dipsa, 1975.

Davis, Nathaniel. *The Last Two Years of Salvador Allende*. Ithaca: Cornell University Press, 1985.

De Blij, Harm J. *The Power of Place: Geography, Destiny, and Globalization's Rough Landscape*. Oxford ; New York: Oxford University Press, 2009.

De Riencourt, Amaury. *The American Empire*. New York: Dial Press, 1968.

Domínguez, Jorge I., and Rafael Fernández de Castro. *The United States and Mexico: Between Partnership and Conflict*. 2nd ed. New York: Routledge, 2009.

Downie, Andrew. "A South American Arms Race?" *Time*, December 21, 2007.

Doyle, Michael W. *Empires*, Cornell Studies in Comparative History. Ithaca, NY: Cornell University Press, 1986.

Dunkerley, James. *Rebellion in the Veins: Political Struggle in Bolivia, 1952-82*. London: Verso, 1984.

Economist. "Brazil Takes Off." November 12, 2009.

Esteves, Diniz. *Documentos Históricos do Estado-Maior do Exército*. Brasília: Edição do Estado-Maior do Exército, 1996.

Etherington, Norman. *Theories of Imperialism: War, Conquest, and Capital*. London; Totowa, NJ: Croom Helm; Barnes & Noble Books, 1984.

Farias, Cordeiro de, Aspásia Camargo, and Walder de Góis. *Meio Século de Combate: Diálogo com Cordeiro de Farias*, Coleção Brasil Século 20. Rio de Janeiro: Editora Nova Fronteira, 1981.

Farrell, Mary, Björn Hettne, and Luk van Langenhove, eds. *Global Politics of Regionalism: Theory and Practice*. London: Pluto Press, 2005.

Fauriol, Georges A., and William Perry. *Thinking Strategically About 2005: The United States and South America*. Washington, DC: Center for Strategic and International Studies, 1999.

Fawcett, Louise L'Estrange, and Andrew Hurrell. *Regionalism in World Politics: Regional Organization and International Order*. New York: Oxford University Press, 1995.

Feinberg, Richard E. *Summitry in the Americas: A Progress Report*. Washington, DC: Institute for International Economics, 1997.

Feres Jr., João. "A History of the Concept of Latin America in the United States: Misrecognition and Social Scientific Discourse." PhD diss., City University of New York, 2003.

Ferguson, Niall. *Colossus: The Price of America's Empire*. New York: Penguin Press, 2004.

Ferris, Elizabeth G. "The Andean Pact and the Amazon Treaty: Reflections of Changing Latin American Relations." *Journal of Interamerican Studies and World Affairs* 23, no. 2 (1981): 147-75.

Fico, Carlos. *O Grande Irmão: Da Operação Brother Sam aos Anos de Chumbo* Rio de Janeiro: Civilização Brasileira, 2008.

Francis, Michael J., and Timothy J. Power. "South America." In *Handbook of Political Science Research on Latin America: Trends from the 1960s to the 1990s*, edited by David W. Dent, xi, 448 p. New York: Greenwood Press, 1990.

Franko, Patrice M. *Toward a New Security Architecture in the Americas: The Strategic Implications of the FTAA*. Washington, DC: Center for Strategic and International Studies, 2000.

Gaddis, John Lewis. *We Now Know: Rethinking Cold War History*. Oxford; New York: Clarendon Press; Oxford University Press, 1997.

Gallardo Lozada, Jorge. *De Torres a Banzer*. Buenos Aires: Ediciones Periferia, 1972.

Ganzert, Frederic William. "The Baron Do Rio-Branco, Joaquim Nabuco, and the Growth of Brazilian- American Friendship, 1900-1910." *The Hispanic American Historical Review* 22, no. 3 (1942): 432-51.

Gaspari, Elio. *A Ditadura Derrotada*. São Paulo, Brazil: Companhia das Letras, 2003.

———. *A Ditadura Escancarada*, As Ilusões Armadas. São Paulo, Brazil: Companhia das Letras, 2002.

Gelb, Leslie H. *Power Rules: How Common Sense Can Rescue American Foreign Policy*, 1st ed. New York Harper, 2009.

Gilderhus, Mark T. "The Monroe Doctrine: Meanings and Implications." *Presidential Studies Quarterly* 36, no. 1 (2006): 5-16.

———. *Pan American Visions: Woodrow Wilson in the Western Hemisphere, 1913-1921.* Tucson: University of Arizona Press, 1986.

Gill, Lesley. *The School of the Americas: Military Training and Political Violence in the Americas.* Durham: Duke University Press, 2004.

Gilpin, Robert. *War and Change in World Politics.* Cambridge, UK: Cambridge University Press, 1981.

Goldmann, Kjell. "The Foreign Sources of Foreign Policy: Causes, Conditions, or Inputs?" *European Journal of Political Research* 4 (1976): 291-309.

Gordon, Lincoln. *Brazil's Second Chance: En Route toward the First World.* Washington, DC: Brookings Institution Press, 2001.

Gorman, Stephen M. "Present Threats to Peace in South America: The Territorial Dimensions of Conflict." *Inter-American Economic Affairs* 33, no. 1 (1979): 51-71.

Grael, Dickson M. *Aventura, Corrupção e Terrorismo: À Sombra da Impunidade.* Petrópolis: Vozes, 1985.

Grandin, Greg. *Empire's Workshop: Latin America, the United States, and the Rise of the New Imperialism,* The American Empire Project. New York: Metropolitan Books, 2006.

Greentree, Todd R. *Crossroads of Intervention: Insurgency and Counterinsurgency Lessons from Central America.* Westport, CT: Praeger Security International, 2008.

Haas, Michael. "International Subsystems: Stability and Polarity." *The American Political Science Review* 64, no. 1 (1970): 98-123.

Haggard, Stephan. "The Political Economy of Regionalism in the Western Hemisphere." In *The Post-Nafta Political Economy: Mexico and the Western Hemisphere,* edited by Carol Wise, 302-38. University Park, PA: The Pennsylvania State University Press, 1998.

Handelman, Stephen. "Special Report: Summit of the Americas." *Time,* April 19, 2001.

Hart, Albert Bushnell. *The Monroe Doctrine: An Interpretation.* Boston: Little, Brown, and Company, 1916.

Healy, David. *Drive to Hegemony: The United States in the Caribbean, 1898-1917.* Madison, WI: University of Wisconsin Press, 1988.

———. *US Expansionism: The Imperialist Urge in the 1890s.* Madison, WI: University of Wisconsin Press, 1970.

Heiss, M. A. "The Evolution of the Imperial Idea and U.S. National Identity." *Diplomatic History* 26, no. 4 (2002): 511-40.

Hellmann, Donald C. "The Emergence of an East Asian International Subsystem." *International Studies Quarterly* 13, no. 4 (1969): 421-34.

Hendrickson, David C. *Union, Nation, or Empire: The American Debate over International Relations, 1789-1941.* Lawrence: University Press of Kansas, 2009.

Hettne, Björn, András Inotai, and Osvaldo Sunkel. *Globalism and the New Regionalism,* International Political Economy Series. New Regionalism V. 1. New York: St. Martin's Press, 1999.

Hilton, Stanley E. *Brazil and the Great Powers, 1930-1939: The Politics of Trade Rivalry,* Latin American Monographs No. 38. Austin: University of Texas Press, 1975.

Hirschman, Albert O. *National Power and the Structure of Foreign Trade.* Berkeley and Los Angeles: University of California Press, 1945.

Hirst, Mônica. "Mercosur's Complex Political Agenda." In *Mercosur: Regional Integration, World Markets,* edited by Riordan Roett, 35-47. Boulder, CO: Lynne Rienner, 1999.

Hobson, J. A. *Imperialism: A Study.* New York: J. Pott & Company, 1902.

Hoffmann, Stanley. "Discord in Community: The North Atlantic Area as a Partial International System." *International Organization* 17, no. 3 (1963): 521-49.

———. *Janus and Minerva: Essays in the Theory and Practice of International Politics.* Boulder: Westview Press, 1987.

Holm, Hans Henrik, and Georg Sørensen, eds. *Whose World Order?: Uneven Globalization and the End of the Cold War.* Boulder: Westview Press, 1995.

Hull, Cordell, and Andrew Henry Thomas Berding. *The Memoirs of Cordell Hull.* Vol. 2. New York: Macmillan Co., 1948.

Huntington, Samuel P. "The Lonely Superpower." *Foreign Affairs* 78, no. 2 (1999): 35-49.
Hurrell, Andrew. "Explaining the Resurgence of Regionalism in World Politics." *Review of International Studies* 21, no. 4 (1995): 331-58.
———. "Regionalism in the Americas." In *Regionalism in World Politics: Regional Organization and International Order*, edited by Louise L'Estrange Fawcett and Andrew Hurrell, xiii, 342 p. New York: Oxford University Press, 1995.
Ignatieff, Michael. "The American Empire." *New York Times Magazine*, May 1, 2003.
Interamerican Development Bank. "Dataintal - Comercio Bilateral." http://www.iadb.org/dataintal/ (accessed February 1, 2011).
Johnson, Chalmers A. *Blowback: The Costs and Consequences of American Empire*. New York: Henry Holt, 2004.
Jornal do Brasil. "Brasil Denuncia Acordo Militar com EUA." March 12, 1977, 19-22.
Kacowicz, Arie Marcelo. *Zones of Peace in the Third World: South America and West Africa in Comparative Perspective*, SUNY Series in Global Politics. Albany, NY: State University of New York Press, 1998.
Kaiser, Karl. "The Interaction Regional Subsystems: Some Preliminary Notes on Recurrent Patterns and the Role of Superpowers." *World Politics* 21, no. 1 (1968): 84-107.
Kaplan, Morton A. *System and Process in International Politics*. Edited by Andrew Lakoff and Stephen J. Collier, ECPR Classics. Colchester, UK: European Consortium for Political Research Press, 2005.
Katzenstein, Peter J. *A World of Regions: Asia and Europe in the American Imperium*, Cornell Studies in Political Economy. Ithaca, NY: Cornell University Press, 2005.
Kelly, Philip. *Checkerboards & Shatterbelts: The Geopolitics of South America*. 1st University of Texas Press ed. Austin: University of Texas Press, 1997.
Kengor, Paul. "Secrets of Suriname." *National Review Online*, April 30, 2008. http://www.nationalreview.com/articles/224326/secrets-suriname/paul-kengor (accessed January 15, 2011).
Kengor, Paul, and Patricia Clark Doerner. *The Judge: William P. Clark, Ronald Reagan's Top Hand*. San Francisco: Ignatius Press, 2007.
Keohane, Robert O. *After Hegemony: Cooperation and Discord in the World Political Economy*. Princeton, NJ: Princeton University Press, 1984.
———. "Between Vision and Reality: Variables in Latin American Foreign Policy." In *Latin America in the New International System*, edited by Joseph S. Tulchin and Ralph H. Espach, 207-14. Boulder, CO: Lynne Rienner Publishers, 2001.
Keohane, Robert O., and Joseph S. Nye. *Power and Interdependence: World Politics in Transition*. Boston: Little, Brown, 1977.
Kissinger, Henry. *Does America Need a Foreign Policy?: Toward a Diplomacy for the 21st Century*. New York: Simon & Schuster, 2001.
Koebner, Richard, and Helmut Dan Schmidt. *Imperialism: The Story and Significance of a Political Word, 1840-1960*. Cambridge University Press, 1964.
Kornbluh, Peter. "Brazil Marks 40th Anniversary of Military Coup." *The National Security Archive*, March 31, 2004. http://www.gwu.edu/~nsarchiv/NSAEBB/NSAEBB118/index.htm#docs (accessed December 1, 2010).
Korry, Edward. "Confronting Our Past in Chile." *Los Angeles Times*, March 8, 1981.
———. "The Sell-out of Chile and the American Taxpayer." *Penthouse*, March 1978.
Kupchan, Charles. "Regionalizing Europe's Security: The Case for a New Mittleleuropa." In *The Political Economy of Regionalism*, edited by Edward D. Mansfield and Helen V. Milner, 209-38. New York: Columbia University Press, 1997.
LaFeber, Walter. *The New Empire: An Interpretation of American Expansion, 1860-1898*. 35th anniversary ed. Ithaca, NY: Cornell University Press, 1998.
Lafer, Celso. "Brazilian International Identity and Foreign Policy: Past, Present, and Future." *Daedalus* 129, no. 2 (2000): 207-38.
Lake, David A., Patrick M. Morgan, and University of California Institute on Global Conflict and Cooperation., eds. *Regional Orders: Building Security in a New World*. University Park, PA: Pennsylvania State University Press, 1997.

Lampreia, Luiz Felipe. *O Brasil e os Ventos Do Mundo: Memórias de Cinco Décadas na Cena Internacional.* Rio de Janeiro: Objetiva, 2010.

Langley, Lester D. *America and the Americas: The United States in the Western Hemisphere.* 2nd ed. Athens: University of Georgia Press, 2010.

———. *The Banana Wars: United States Intervention in the Caribbean, 1898-1934.* Rev. ed. Lexington, KY: University Press of Kentucky, 1985.

Latinobarómetro. "Annual Report 2010." Santiago: Latinobarómetro Corporation, 2010.

Leacock, Ruth. *Requiem for Revolution: The United States and Brazil, 1961-1969,* American Diplomatic History. Kent, Ohio: Kent State University Press, 1990.

Lemke, Douglas. *Regions of War and Peace,* Cambridge Studies in International Relations 80. Cambridge, UK: Cambridge University Press, 2002.

Lenin, Vladimir Ilyich. *Imperialism, the Highest Stage of Capitalism.* New York: International publishers, 1933.

Lens, Sidney. *The Forging of the American Empire.* New York: Crowell, 1971.

———. *The Forging of the American Empire: From the Revolution to Vietnam, a History of U.S. Imperialism.* London; Sterling, VA: Pluto Press; Haymarket Books, 2003.

Leonard, Thomas M. *Central America and the United States: The Search for Stability,* The United States and the Americas. Athens: University of Georgia Press, 1991.

Lewis, Martin W., and Kären Wigen. *The Myth of Continents: A Critique of Metageography.* Berkeley: University of California Press, 1997.

Lieuwen, Edwin. *U.S. Policy in Latin America: A Short History.* New York: Praeger, 1965.

Liska, George. *Imperial America: The International Politics of Primacy.* Baltimore, MD: Johns Hopkins Press, 1967.

———. *Twilight of a Hegemony: The Late Career of Imperial America.* Dallas: University Press of America, 2003.

Livingstone, Grace. *America's Backyard: The United States and Latin America from the Monroe Doctrine to the War on Terror.* London: Zed Books, 2009.

López, Ernesto. *Seguridad Nacional y Sedición Militar.* Buenos Aires: Editorial Legasa, 1987.

Lowenthal, Abraham F. *Partners in Conflict: The United States and Latin America in the 1990s.* Rev. ed. Baltimore: Johns Hopkins University Press, 1990.

Lundestad, Geir. *The American Empire and Other Studies of US Foreign Policy in a Comparative Perspective.* Oslo: Norwegian University Press, 1990.

———. "Empire by Invitation? The United States and Western Europe, 1945-1952." *Journal of Peace Research* 23, no. 3 (1986): 263-77.

———. *The United States and Western Europe since 1945: From "Empire" by Invitation to Transatlantic Drift.* Oxford: Oxford University Press, 2003.

MacDonald, Paul K. "Those Who Forget Historiography Are Doomed to Republish It: Empire, Imperialism and Contemporary Debates About American Power." *Review of International Studies* 35, no. 1 (2009): 45-67.

Mace, Gordon, and Louis Bélanger, eds. *The Americas in Transition: The Contours of Regionalism.* Boulder, CO: Lynne Rienner Publishers, 1999.

Mansfield, Edward D., and Helen V. Milner, eds. *The Political Economy of Regionalism.* Edited by John G. Ruggie, New Directions in World Politics. New York: Columbia University Press, 1997.

Mares, David R. "Middle Powers under Regional Hegemony: To Challenge or Acquiesce in Hegemonic Enforcement." *International Studies Quarterly* 32, no. 4 (1988): 453-71.

Marini, Ruy Mauro. "Brazilian Subimperialism " *Monthly Review* 23, no. 9 (1972): 14-24.

Martz, John D. "Venezuelan Foreign Policy toward Latin America." In *Contemporary Venezuela and Its Role in International Affairs,* edited by Robert D. Bond, x, 267 p. New York: New York University Press, 1977.

Mattelart, Armand. *The Globalization of Surveillance.* Translated by Suzan Taponier and James A. Cohen. Cambridge: Polity Press, 2010.

May, Ernest R. *Imperial Democracy: The Emergence of America as a Great Power.* Chicago: Imprint Publications, 1991.

Mayer, Frederick. *Interpreting Nafta: The Science and Art of Political Analysis.* New York: Columbia University Press, 1998.

McCormick, Robert Rutherford. *The American Empire*. Chicago: Chicago Tribune, 1952.

McGann, Thomas Francis. *Argentina, the United States, and the Inter-American System, 1880-1914*, Harvard Historical Studies V. 70. Cambridge: Harvard University Press, 1957.

McSherry, J. Patrice. *Predatory States: Operation Condor and Covert War in Latin America*. Lanham, MD: Rowman & Littlefield Publishers, Inc., 2005.

Mecham, J. Lloyd. *The United States and Inter-American Security, 1889-1960*. Austin, TX: University of Texas Press, 1961.

Mello, Leonel Itaussu Almeida. *Argentina e Brasil: A Balança de Poder no Cone Sul*. São Paulo, SP, Brasil: Annablume, 1996.

———. *A Geopolítica Do Brasil E a Bacia Do Prata*. Manaus: Editora da Universidade do Amazonas, 1997.

Mera, Laura Gomez. "Explaining Mercosur's Survival: Strategic Sources of Argentine-Brazilian Convergence." *Journal of Latin American Studies* 37, no. 1 (2005): 109-40.

Miller, Lynn H. "Regional Organizations and Subordinate Systems." In *The International Politics of Regions*, edited by Louis J. Cantori and Steven L. Spiegel, 357-80. Englewood Cliffs, NJ: Prentice-Hall, 1970.

Ministerial Declaration: Free Trade Area of the Americas. Miami. "F.T.A.A. Eighth Ministerial Meeting." November 20, 2003. http://www.ftaa-alca.org/ministerials/miami/Miami_e.asp (accessed February 10, 2011).

Molineu, Harold. *U.S. Policy toward Latin America: From Regionalism to Globalism*. 2nd ed. Boulder: Westview Press, 1990.

Mommsen, Wolfgang J. *Theories of Imperialism*. New York: Random House, 1980.

Motyl, Alexander J. "Is Everything Empire? Is Empire Everything?" *Comparative Politics* 38, no. 2 (2006): 229-49.

———. "Why Empires Reemerge: Imperial Collapse and Imperial Revival in Comparative Perspective." *Comparative Politics* 31, no. 2 (1999): 127-45.

Mouritzen, Hans. *Theory and Reality of International Politics*. Aldershot, UK: Ashgate, 1998.

Munck, Ronaldo. "The Democratic Decade: Argentina since Malvinas." *Bulletin of Latin American Research* 11, no. 2 (1992): 205-16.

Murphy, Gretchen. *Hemispheric Imaginings: The Monroe Doctrine and Narratives of U.S. Empire*, New Americanists. Durham: Duke University Press, 2005.

Myers, David J., ed. *Regional Hegemons: Threat Perception and Strategic Response*. Boulder: Westview Press, 1991.

Napoleão, Aluízio. *Rio-Branco e as Relações entre o Brasil e os Estados Unidos*, Comissão Preparatória Do Centenário Do Barão Do Rio-Branco. Monografias. Rio de Janeiro: Ministério das Relações Exteriores, 1947.

New York Times. "Aid for Mexico Gives Economy Shot in the Arm." February 2, 1995.

———. "Brazil's Old Ruler Dead." December 5, 1891.

———. "Brazilian Friendliness." January 16, 1908.

———. "Dom Pedro and Brazil." December 6, 1891.

———. "Negotiators Fail to Agree on Free Trade Proposal at Americas Summit." November 6, 2005.

Norden, Deborah L., and Roberto Russell. *The United States and Argentina: Changing Relations in a Changing World*, Contemporary Inter-American Relations. New York: Routledge, 2002.

Nye, Joseph S. *Pan-Africanism and East African Integration*. Cambridge, MA: Harvard University Press, 1965.

O'Brien, Thomas F. *Making the Americas: The United States and Latin America from the Age of Revolutions to the Era of Globalization*. Albuquerque: University of New Mexico Press, 2007.

O'Keefe, Thomas Andrew. *Latin American and Caribbean Trade Agreements: Keys to a Prosperous Community of the Americas*. Leiden: Martinus Nijhoff Publishers, 2009.

O'Neill, Jim. "Building Better Global Economic Brics." In *Global Economics Paper No: 66*. London: Goldman Sachs, 2001.

Oliveira Lima, Manuel de. *O Movimento da Independencia (1821-1822)*. 6. ed. Rio de Janeiro: Topbooks, 1997.

Padelford, Norman J. "A Selected Bibliography on Regionalism and Regional Arrangements." *International Organization* 10, no. 4 (1956): 575-603.

Padros, Enrique Serra. "A Ditadura Brasileira de Segurança Nacional e a Operação 30 Horas: Intervencionismo ou Neocisplatinização do Uruguai?" *Ciências&Letras [Porto Alegre]* jan/jun, no. 37 (2005): 227-49.

Parker, Phyllis R. *Brazil and the Quiet Intervention, 1964*, Texas Pan American Series. Austin: University of Texas Press, 1979.

Pastor, Robert A. *Whirlpool: U.S. Foreign Policy toward Latin America and the Caribbean*, Princeton Studies in International History and Politics. Princeton, NJ: Princeton University Press, 1992.

Pedersen, Thomas. "Cooperative Hegemony: Power, Ideas and Institutions in Regional Integration." *Review of International Studies* 28, no. 4 (2002): 677-96.

Perez, Louis A., Jr. "Intervention, Hegemony, and Dependency: The United States in the Circum-Caribbean, 1898-1980." *The Pacific Historical Review* 51, no. 2 (1982): 165-94.

Perkins, Dexter. *The Monroe Doctrine, 1867-1907*, The Albert Shaw Lectures on Diplomatic History, 1937. Gloucester, MA: P. Smith, 1966.

Petras, James. "U.S. Offensive in Latin America: Coups, Retreats, and Radicalization." *Monthly Review* 54, no. 1 (2002): 15.

Phelan, John Leddy. "Pan-Latinism, French Intervention in Mexico (1861–7) and the Genesis of the Idea of Latin America." In *Conciencia y Autenticidad Históricas; Escritos en Homenaje a Edmundo O'Gorman, Emerito, Aetatis Anno Lx Dicata*, edited by Juan Antonio Ortega y Medina. México: UNAM, 1968.

Phillips, Nicola. "Hemispheric Integration and Subregionalism in the Americas." *International Affairs (Royal Institute of International Affairs 1944-)* 79, no. 2 (2003): 327-49.

Pittman, Howard Taylor. "Geopolitics in the ABC Countries: A Comparison." PhD diss., American University, 1981.

Poitras, Guy E. *The Ordeal of Hegemony: The United States and Latin America*. Boulder: Westview Press, 1990.

Preusse, Heinz G. "The Future of Mercosur." In *Free Trade in the Americas: Economic and Political Issues for Governments and Firms*, edited by Sidney Weintraub, Alan M. Rugman and Gavin Boyd, 127-52. Cheltenham, UK: Edward Elgar, 2004.

Reagan, Ronald, and Douglas Brinkley. *The Reagan Diaries*. 1st ed. New York: HarperCollins, 2007.

Reuters. "U.S and Brazil Sign Defense Pact, No Decision on Jets." April 12, 2010. http://www.reuters.com/article/idUSTRE63B5YV20100412 (accessed December 19, 2010).

Ricard, Serge. "The Roosevelt Corollary." *Presidential Studies Quarterly* 36, no. 1 (2006): 17-26.

Robinson, Thomas W. "Systems Theory and the Communist System." *International Studies Quarterly* 13, no. 4 (1969): 398-420.

Roett, Riordan. "Brazil Ascendant: International Relations and Geopolitics in the Late 20th Century." *Journal of International Affairs* 29, no. 2 (1975): 139.

———. "U.S. Policy toward Mercosur: From Miami to Santiago." In *Mercosur: Regional Integration, World Markets*, edited by Riordan Roett, 111-24. Boulder, CO: Lynne Rienner, 1999.

Rohter, Larry. "Argentina and the U.S. Grow Apart over a Crisis." *New York Times*, January 20, 2002.

———. *Brazil on the Rise: The Story of a Country Transformed*. 1st ed. New York: Palgrave Macmillan, 2010.

———. "Free Trade Goes South with or without U.S." *New York Times*, January 6, 1997.

———. "South American Trade Bloc under Siege." *New York Times*, March 24, 2001.

Romero, Simon. "Hemisphere Trade Talks in Miami Are Reported to Hit a Bump." *New York Times*, November 17, 2003.

Rompay, Jan van. "Brazil's Strategy Towards the FTAA." In *Free Trade for the Americas?: The United States' Push for the FTAA Agreement*, edited by Paulo Gilberto Fagundes Vizentini and Marianne Wiesebron, 120-48. London ; New York: Zed Books, 2004.

Roosevelt, Theodore. *An Autobiography*. New York: Charles Scribner's Sons, 1913.

Roosevelt, Theodore, and Alfred Henry Lewis. *A Compilation of the Messages and Speeches of Theodore Roosevelt, 1901-1905*. Vol. 2. New York: Bureau of National Literature and Art, 1906.

Rosenau, James N. "The Functioning of International Systems." *Background* 7, no. 3 (1963): 111-17.

Rugman, Alan M. "Economic Integration in North America: Implications for the Americas." In *Free Trade in the Americas: Economic and Political Issues for Governments and Firms*, edited by Sidney Weintraub, Alan M. Rugman and Gavin Boyd, 90-126. Cheltenham, UK: Edward Elgar, 2004.

Russell, Roberto, and Juan Gabriel Tokatlian. "From Antagonistic Autonomy to Relational Autonomy: A Theoretical Reflection from the Southern Cone." *Latin American Politics and Society* 45, no. 1 (2003): 1-24.

Russett, Bruce M. *International Regions and the International System: A Study in Political Ecology*. Westport, CT: Greenwood Press, 1975.

Sanchez, Alex. "Chile's Aggressive Military Arm Purchases Are Ruffling the Region, Alarming in Particular Bolivia, Peru and Argentina." *Council on Hemispheric Affairs*, August 7, 2007. http://www.coha.org/chile%E2%80%99s-aggressive-military-arm-purchases-is-ruffling-the-region-alarming-in-particular-bolivia-peru-and-argentina/ (accessed September 17, 2010).

Sater, William F. *Chile and the United States: Empires in Conflict*. Athens: University of Georgia Press, 1990.

Schilling, Paulo R. *O Expansionismo Brasileiro: A Geopolítica do General Golbery e a Diplomacia do Itamarati*. São Paulo: Global, 1981.

Schott, Jeffrey J. *Prospects for Free Trade in the Americas*. Washington, DC: Institute for International Economics, 2001.

Schoultz, Lars. *Beneath the United States: A History of U.S. Policy toward Latin America*. Cambridge, MA: Harvard University Press, 1998.

Schulz, Michael, Fredrik Söderbaum, and Joakim Öjendal, eds. *Regionalization in a Globalizing World: A Comparative Perspective on Forms, Actors, and Processes*. London: Zed Books, 2001.

Schwarcz, Lilia Moritz. *As Barbas do Imperador: D. Pedro II, Um Monarca nos Trópicos*. São Paulo, Brazil: Companhia das Letras, 1998.

Sexton, Jay. *The Monroe Doctrine: Empire and Nation in Nineteenth-Century America*. New York: Hill and Wang, 2010.

Shy, John, and Thomas W. Collier. "Revolutionary War." In *Makers of Modern Strategy: From Machiavelli to the Nuclear Age*, edited by Peter Paret, Gordon Alexander Craig and Felix Gilbert, 815-62. Princeton: Princeton University Press, 1986.

Sicker, Martin. *The Geopolitics of Security in the Americas: Hemispheric Denial from Monroe to Clinton*. Westport, CT: Praeger, 2002.

Sigler, John H. "News Flow in the North African International Subsystem." *International Studies Quarterly* 13, no. 4 (1969): 381-97.

Sigmund, Paul E. "The "Invisible Blockade" and the Overthrow of Allende." *Foreign Affairs* 52, no. 2 (1974): 322-40.

Silva, Golbery do Couto e. *Geopolítica Do Brasil*. Rio de Janeiro: Livraria J. Olympio, 1967.

Silveira, Joaquim Xavier da. *A F.E.B por um Soldado*. Rio de Janeiro: Nova Fronteira, 1989.

Simons, Marlise. "The Brazilian Connection." *The Washington Post*, January 6, 1974.

Singer, J. David. "The Level-of-Analysis Problem in International Relations." *World Politics* 14, no. 1 (1961): 77-92.

Smith, Joseph. *Brazil and the United States: Convergence and Divergence*, The United States and the Americas. Athens: University of Georgia Press, 2010.

———. *Unequal Giants: Diplomatic Relations between the United States and Brazil, 1889-1930*, Pitt Latin American Series. Pittsburgh, PA: University of Pittsburgh Press, 1991.

———. *The United States and Latin America: A History of American Diplomacy, 1776-2000*. London ; New York: Routledge, 2005.

Solingen, Etel. *Regional Orders at Century's Dawn: Global and Domestic Influences on Grand Strategy*, Princeton Studies in International History and Politics. Princeton, NJ: Princeton University Press, 1998.

Sprout, Harold Hance, Margaret Tuttle Sprout, and Princeton University. Center for International Studies. *The Ecological Perspective on Human Affairs, with Special Reference to International Politics*. Princeton, NJ: Published for the Princeton Center of International Studies by Princeton University Press, 1965.

Steel, Ronald. *Imperialists and Other Heroes: A Chronicle of the American Empire*. 1st ed. New York: Random House, 1971.

———. *Pax Americana*. New York: Viking Press, 1970.

Stepan, Alfred C. *The Military in Politics; Changing Patterns in Brazil*. Princeton, NJ: Princeton University Press, 1971.

Stephenson, Sherry M. "New Trade Strategies in the Americas." In *Economic Integration in the Americas*, edited by Joseph A. McKinney and H. Stephen Gardner, 27-45. London: Routledge, 2008.

Stewart, Watt. "Argentina and the Monroe Doctrine, 1824-1828." *The Hispanic American Historical Review* 10, no. 1 (1930): 26-32.

Stratfor. "Members' Policies Spell Mercosur's Demise." October 10, 2001 http://www.stratfor.com/memberships/3653/analysis/members_policies_spell_mercosurs_demise (accessed February 9, 2011).

Sweeney, John. "Clinton's Latin America Policy: A Legacy of Missed Opportunities." *The Heritage Foundation*, July 6, 1998 http://www.heritage.org/research/reports/1998/07/clintons-latin-america-policy (accessed February 8, 2011).

Teixeira, Carlos Gustavo Poggio. "Brazil and United States: Fading Interdependence." *Orbis* 55, no. 1 (2011): 147-62.

The Independent. "The Rise and Rise of Brazil: Faster, Stronger, Higher." September 27, 2009.

Thomas, David Y. *One Hundred Years of the Monroe Doctrine, 1823-1923*. New York: Macmillan, 1923.

Thomas, Evan. *The War Lovers: Roosevelt, Lodge, Hearst, and the Rush to Empire, 1898*. New York: Little, Brown and Co., 2010.

Thompson, William R. "The Regional Subsystem: A Conceptual Explication and a Propositional Inventory." *International Studies Quarterly* 17, no. 1 (1973): 89-117.

Tinbergen, Jan. *Shaping the World Economy; Suggestions for an International Economic Policy*. New York: Twentieth Century Fund, 1962.

Tokatlian, Juan Gabriel. "Politica Exterior Argentina De Menem a De La Rua: La Diplomacia Del Ajuste." *Escenarios Alternativos* 4, no. 9 (2000).

Tucker, Robert W., and David C. Hendrickson. *The Imperial Temptation: The New World Order and America's Purpose*. New York: Council on Foreign Relations Press, 1992.

Turner, Frederick C. "Regional Hegemony and the Case of Brazil." *International Journal* 46, no. 3 (1991): 475-509.

U.S. CIA. General Reports. "C.I.A. Activities in Chile." September 18, 2000. http://www.cia.gov/library/reports/general-reports-1/chile/index.html#1 (accessed December 1, 2010).

U.S. Congress. Senate. Select Committee to Study Governmental Operations with Respect to Intelligence Activities. "Covert Action in Chile, 1963-1973: Staff Report of the Select Committee to Study Governmental Operations with Respect to Intelligence Activities, United States Senate." Washington: U.S. Govt. Print. Off., 1975.

U.S. National Archives and Records Administration. "Secret Department of State Memorandum from Theodore Eliot Jr. To Henry Kissinger." Department of State Subject-Numeric Files 1970-73, National Archives. November 27, 1971.

———. "Secret Department of State Telegram to U.S. Embassies in Brazil and Argentina"; Subject-Numeric Files 1970-73. August 20, 1971.

———. "Top Secret Memorandum from Henry Kissinger on a Meeting between the U.S. President and British Prime Minister Edward Heath": VIP Visits boxes 910-954, Nixon National Security Council Materials. December 20, 1971.

U.S. State Department. Foreign Relations of the United States. "Memorandum for the President's File." Washington: December 9. Volume E–10, Documents On American Republics, 1969–1972, Document 143, 1971.

——. "Memorandum from the Acting Director of Central Intelligence (Cushman) to the President's Assistant for National Security Affairs (Kissinger)." Washington: December 29. Volume E–10, Documents On American Republics, 1969–1972, Document 145, 1971.

——. "Memorandum from the Senior Department of Defense Attaché in France (Walters) to the President's Assistant for National Security Affairs (Kissinger)." Washington: Undated. Volume E–10, Documents On American Republics, 1969–1972, Document 144, 1971.

——. "National Intelligence Estimate 93–72." Washington: January 13. Volume E–10, Documents On American Republics, 1969–1972, Document 146, 1972.

U.S. State Department. Reading Room. "Secret U.S.Embassy Preliminary Analysis and Strategy Paper - Uruguay": Microfiche on Human Rights in Uruguay 1971-1983. August 25, 1971.

Vasquez, John A. "Why Do Neighbors Fight? Proximity, Interaction, or Territoriality." *Journal of Peace Research* 32, no. 3 (1995): 277-93.

Veja. "O Brasil Diz Não." September 6, 2000, 42-49.

——. "Pagina Negra: As Tenebrosas Transações do Itamarati no Chile." November 13, 1985, 91.

Villalobos, Marco Antônio. *Tiranos Tremei! Ditadura e Resistência Popular no Uruguai (1968-1985).* Porto Alegre: EDIPUCRS, 2006.

Vizentini, Paulo Gilberto Fagundes. "The FTAA and US Strategy: A Southern Point of View." In *Free Trade for the Americas?: The United States' Push for the FTAA Agreement,* edited by Paulo Gilberto Fagundes Vizentini and Marianne Wiesebron, 11-22. London: Zed Books, 2004.

Wagner, R. Harrison. "Economic Interdependence, Bargaining Power, and Political Influence." *International Organization* 42, no. 3 (1988): 461-83.

Wallace, Michael D. "Clusters of Nations in the Global System, 1865-1964: Some Preliminary Evidence." *International Studies Quarterly* 19, no. 1 (1975): 67-110.

Waltz, Kenneth N. "International Politics Is Not Foreign Policy." *Security Studies* 6, no. 1 (1996): 54 - 57.

Waltz, Kenneth Neal. *Theory of International Politics.* 1st ed. Boston, MA: McGraw-Hill, 1979.

Washington Times. "Obama: U.S. Supports Rise of Brazil's Economy." March 19, 2011.

Watson, Adam. *The Evolution of International Society: A Comparative Historical Analysis.* London: Routledge, 1992.

Weidenmier, Marc D., and Kris James Mitchener. *Empire, Public Goods, and the Roosevelt Corollary.* Cambridge, Mass: National Bureau of Economic Research, 2004.

Weintraub, Sidney. *Development and Democracy in the Southern Cone: Imperatives for U.S. Policy in South America,* Significant Issues Series V. 22, No. 1. Washington, DC: Center for Strategic and International Studies, 2000.

Weis, W. Michael. "Pan American Shift: Oswaldo Aranha and the Demise of the Brazilian-American Alliance." In *Beyond the Ideal: Pan Americanism in Inter-American Affairs,* edited by David Sheinin, 133-52. Westport, CT: Greenwood Press, 2000.

Welch, Richard E. *Imperialists vs. Anti-Imperialists: The Debate over Expansionism in the 1890's,* Primary Sources in American History. Itasca, Ill: F. E. Peacock Publishers, 1972.

Wendt, Alexander. "Anarchy Is What States Make of It: The Social Construction of Power Politics." *International Organization* 46, no. 2 (1992): 391-425.

——. *Social Theory of International Politics,* Cambridge Studies in International Relations 67. Cambridge, UK ; New York: Cambridge University Press, 1999.

Wendt, Alexander, and Daniel Friedheim. "Hierarchy under Anarchy: Informal Empire and the East German State." *International Organization* 49, no. 4 (1995): 689-721.

Wesson, Robert G. *The United States and Brazil: Limits of Influence,* Studies of Influence in International Relations. New York: Praeger, 1981.

Whitaker, Arthur Preston. *The United States and the Southern Cone: Argentina, Chile, and Uruguay*, The American Foreign Policy Library. Cambridge, MA: Harvard University Press, 1976.

―――. *The Western Hemisphere Idea: Its Rise and Decline*. Ithaca, NY: Cornell University Press, 1954.

Williams, William Appleman. *Empire as a Way of Life: An Essay on the Causes and Character of America's Present Predicament, Along with a Few Thoughts About an Alternative*. New York: Oxford University Press, 1980.

Winslow, Earle Micajah. *The Pattern of Imperialism, a Study in the Theories of Power*. New York: Columbia Univ. Press, 1948.

Yofre, Juan Bautista. *Misión Argentina en Chile, 1970-1973*. Providencia Chile: Editorial Sudamericana, 2000.

Young, George B. "Intervention under the Monroe Doctrine: The Olney Corollary." *Political Science Quarterly* 57, no. 2 (1942): 247-80.

Zajac, Andrew. "Nixon Offered Brazil Money to Undermine Allende, Records Show." *Los Angeles Times*, August 16, 2009.

Zakaria, Fareed. *The Post-American World*. 1st ed. New York: W.W. Norton, 2008.

Zartman, I. William. "Africa as a Subordinate State System in International Relations." *International Organization* 21, no. 3 (1967): 545-64.

Zirker, Daniel. "Brazilian Foreign Policy and Subimperialism During the Political Transition of the 1980s: A Review and Reapplication of Marini's Theory." *Latin American Perspectives* 21, no. 1 (1994): 115-31.

Index

About the Author

Dr. Carlos Gustavo Poggio Teixeira was born in Sao Paulo, Brazil, where he completed his bachelor's and master's degrees in international relations. His master's thesis on the neoconservative thought in foreign policy won the Franklin Delano Roosevelt American Studies Award granted by the US embassy in Brazil to studies on the United States, and it was published in Portuguese in 2010. He holds a PhD in international studies from Old Dominion University, where he studied under a scholarship supported by a joint program between the Brazilian Ministry of Education—through CAPES—and the US Department of State—through the Fulbright Program. Currently, Dr. Teixeira is professor of international relations at PUC-SP and FAAP, both in Sao Paulo.

Made in the USA
Lexington, KY
03 August 2015